MW00844411

Hybrid Cloud Infrastructure and Operations Explained

Accelerate your application migration and modernization journey on the cloud with IBM and Red Hat

Mansura Habiba

BIRMINGHAM—MUMBAI

Hybrid Cloud Infrastructure and Operations Explained

Copyright © 2022 Packt Publishing

All rights reserved. No part of this book may be reproduced, stored in a retrieval system, or transmitted in any form or by any means, without the prior written permission of the publisher, except in the case of brief quotations embedded in critical articles or reviews.

Every effort has been made in the preparation of this book to ensure the accuracy of the information presented. However, the information contained in this book is sold without warranty, either express or implied. Neither the author, nor Packt Publishing or its dealers and distributors, will be held liable for any damages caused or alleged to have been caused directly or indirectly by this book.

Packt Publishing has endeavored to provide trademark information about all of the companies and products mentioned in this book by the appropriate use of capitals. However, Packt Publishing cannot guarantee the accuracy of this information.

Group Product Manager: Rahul Nair
Publishing Product Manager: Surbhi Suman
Senior Editor: Shazeen Iqbal
Content Development Editors: Rafiaa Khan and Nihar Kapadia
Technical Editor: Nithik Cheruvakodan
Copy Editor: Safis Editing
Project Coordinator: Shagun Saini
Proofreader: Safis Editing
Indexer: Tejal Daruwale Soni
Production Designer: Ponraj Dhandapani
Senior Marketing Coordinator: Sanjana Gupta
Marketing Coordinator: Nimisha Dua

First published: August 2022
Production reference:1120822

Published by Packt Publishing Ltd.
Livery Place
35 Livery Street
Birmingham
B3 2PB, UK

978-1-80324-831-8

www.packt.com

To my mom, Nazmun Nahar Khanam, and my dad, Abdul Wadud Khan, for being the best parents I could ever ask for. I owe them everything joyful and sound in my life. Also, to my brother, Nafiul Islam Khan (Earth), for being my best friend and counselor.

– Mansura Habiba

Foreword

Hybrid cloud is one of the most complex, exciting, and impactful areas to work in, helping organizations to redefine their business, migrate applications to new platforms, modernize workloads, adopt new consumption models, and eliminate waste. Open source, Kubernetes, and OpenShift have been at the forefront of this transition, allowing developers to build once and manage anywhere.

This book is the reference I wish I had when I was starting out in application modernization and migration! It's packed with information and provides a systematic approach, starting with business understanding and requirements mapping, and then deep-diving all the way to low-level design and technical architecture. It does a fantastic job of explaining concepts, key decisions, alternatives, and the impact of every approach, and teaches you how to think like an architect!

I had the pleasure of meeting Mansura a few years ago at an innovation session hosted by the Academy of Technology, where she joined my patent team and impressed everyone with her knowledge, confidence, and expertise across the software development life cycle. I was thrilled to learn she wanted to join our team as a cloud solutions leader and use that experience to help clients adopt the cloud and design better solutions, speaking as someone who's "been there and done it" and our go-to architect for complex solutions that require a DevSecOps mindset and a strong ability to lead.

Within a few years, I was thrilled to see Mansura author several courses and certifications, file multiple patents, obtain her Ph.D., and get appointed by the IBM Academy of Technology as a result of her giveback and leadership in the technical community, and take on a new challenge as a hybrid cloud platform architect, building a new offering from scratch. Prolific doesn't even begin to describe it. To quote a colleague, "She's everywhere – if you need help, just go to Mansura!"

Happy reading!

Mihai Criveti,

CTO Cloud Native and Red Hat Solutions,

STSM & RHCA II, IBM Consulting

Contributors

About the author

Mansura Habiba is a platform architect at the Hybrid Cloud Management Center of Competency at IBM. She has been working in IT, application development, application modernization and migration, and architecture design for over 15 years.

Mansura has a Ph.D. in artificial intelligence from Maynooth University, Ireland. She is a certified solution architect for IBM Cloud and IBM Cloud Pak for Automation, a certified site reliability engineer and certified administrator for IBM Cloud Pak for Watson AIOPs, a certified professional IBM cloud developer, and a professional IBM Watson developer. Mansura can be found providing and sharing information on social media, at industry conferences, on her blog site, and on her YouTube channel.

About the reviewers

Rafflesia Khan works for IBM in Dublin as a software developer. She specializes in developing and testing full stack software applications. In addition, she is a part-time Ph.D. student at the University of Limerick, Ireland. She has a BSc and MSc in computer science and engineering from Khulna University, Bangladesh. Having a strong background in problem analysis, programming, designing, developing, debugging, and testing, she is committed, hardworking, creative, and proactive. She taught computer science at Khulna University for almost a year and participated in teaching at UL as a moderator. During the past 3 years, she has published some work and is currently engaged in ongoing research projects.

Dwarkanath Rao has over 21 years of experience as a quick learner and adopter of new technologies. He is a highly experienced and seasoned strategist, with an excellent track record in delivering highly complex large-scale enterprise infrastructure. He is a good customer-facing leader with great presentation skills. Guiding clients across Europe and Canada through hybrid cloud strategies, he collaborates with CTOs and CIOs in building trust and developing their cloud journey and strategy, focusing on cost savings and technical innovation to enhance their IT business operating models and deploying modernized application rollouts in a timely manner.

Table of Contents

2

Understanding Cloud Modernization and and Innovation Fundamentals

3

Exploring Best Practices for the Cloud Journey

Part 2: Cloud-Native Methods, Practices, and Technology

4

Developing Applications in a Cloud Native Way

5

Exploring Application Modernization Essentials

Part 3: Elements of Embedded Linux

6

Designing and Implementing Cloud Storage Services

7

Designing and Implementing Networking in Hybrid Cloud Infrastructure

8

Understanding Security in Action

9

Designing a Resilient Platform for Cloud Migration

10

Managing Operations in Hybrid Cloud Infrastructure

Appendix A – Application Modernization and Migration Checklist

Index

Other Books You May Enjoy

Preface

Hybrid Cloud Infrastructure and Operations Explained discusses the best practices for application migration and modernization using various products and technologies from IBM and Red Hat. This book starts by explaining the fundamental concepts of application migration and modernization in terms of cloud journey strategies for organizations to help them understand the underlying aspects and drivers of cloud adoption and how they can achieve the best result out of it. The book then proceeds to explain different components such as compute, storage, networking, security, and operations to establish those fundamental concepts with best practices and real-world use cases from different industries.

Who this book is for

Hybrid Cloud Infrastructure and Operations Explained is for anyone who develops applications, designs cloud platform architectures, leads application modernization and migration programs, and drives decisions for application modernization and migration programs from business and financial aspects. Familiarity with the cloud is not mandatory. If someone has just heard about the cloud and wants to explore business use cases, best practices, and methods for application modernization and migration to the cloud, this book is a perfect fit for them.

What this book covers

This book is broken into three sections. *Part 1* covers the fundamental concepts of application migration and modernization with innovation as well as best practices for cloud adoption.

Chapter 1, An Introduction to Hybrid Cloud Modernization, starts by introducing the cloud. It gives different popular strategies for cloud migration used in industries. This chapter also focuses on the fundamental concept of cloud migration along with recent trends and challenges by exploring real-life industry use cases. It also helps to explain the characteristics of a successful roadmap for an application migration program. Finally, this chapter sheds some light on different cloud concepts and our understanding of the cloud.

Chapter 2, Understanding Cloud Modernization and and Innovation Fundamentals, explains fundamental concepts for successful application modernization driven by innovation. Modernization is a complex process that requires extensive analysis of the strategies and proper planning. This chapter describes the dos and don'ts to select the right path for modernization. It also explores different cultural and mindset aspects of different stakeholders such as developers and solution architects.

Chapter 3, Exploring Best Practices for the Cloud Journey, explores best practices to overcome different challenges of cloud transformation. It also gives an overview of different IBM products and services that can help you migrate to the cloud successfully and enhance the innovativeness of modernization. This chapter establishes the basic set of functional as well as non-functional requirements that cloud adoption programs will explore to be successful.

Part 2 explores cloud-native methods, practices, and technologies. Each chapter explains different cloud-native development methodologies and technologies that can enhance the efficiency of application modernization.

Chapter 4, Developing Applications in a Cloud Native Way, dives into the world of development and explains different methodologies and practices for cloud-native development so that you can differentiate different technology for implementations of different types of applications. This chapter discusses the IBM Design Thinking and IBM Garage methodologies along with the Twelve-Factor methodology for application modernization in detail.

Chapter 5, Exploring Application Modernization Essentials, focuses on the fundamental requirements and challenges of application modernization. It also gives an overview of the end-to-end journey of application modernization, starting from planning to implementation.

Part 3 focuses exclusively on the cloud infrastructure to set up a platform in the cloud for organizations. The main goal of this section is to get you familiar with raw cloud infrastructure, storage, networks, security, resiliency, and continuous operations to take care of all these cloud computing resources to establish a successful platform for application migration and modernization using IBM and Red Hat products and technologies.

Chapter 6, Designing and Implementing Cloud Storage Services, looks in depth at the characteristics of cloud data storage to understand its requirements and design. It also presents a real-world use case scenario explaining how to develop a modern AI and data insights solution or modern big data hub solution using IBM and Red Hat products and technologies. It moves on to explain the architecture design details for data storage backup solutions for applications deployed on the cloud using real-world industry examples.

Chapter 7, Designing and Implementing Networking in Hybrid Cloud Infrastructure, looks at a real-world reference solution for modern network architecture for cloud workloads. Using a real-world use case, this chapter explains the main challenges and requirements of efficient network communication. It also explains how IBM Cloud Pak products can improve the efficiency of network operations.

Chapter 8, Understanding Security in Action, looks in depth at the implementation of security, regulations, and compliance for cloud services and resources. This chapter describes challenges, practices, and best practices for security in cloud modernization. It also gives an overview of different IBM products to design a secure platform.

Chapter 9, Designing a Resilient Platform for Cloud Migration, focuses on resiliency to implement reliability, high availability, disaster recovery, Always-On, cyber security, and other resiliency patterns for the raw infrastructure components.

Chapter 10, Managing Operations in Hybrid Cloud Infrastructure, describes the challenges, requirements, solutions, methods, and best practices of operation management. It also explains IBM reference architecture for different operation and management solutions.

Download the color images

We also provide a PDF file that has color images of the screenshots/diagrams used in this book. You can download it here: `https://packt.link/e5GGM`

Get in touch

Feedback from our readers is always welcome.

General feedback: If you have questions about any aspect of this book, mention the book title in the subject of your message and email us at `customercare@packtpub.com`.

Errata: Although we have taken every care to ensure the accuracy of our content, mistakes do happen. If you have found a mistake in this book, we would be grateful if you would report this to us. Please visit `www.packtpub.com/support/errata`, select your book, click on the Errata Submission Form link, and enter the details.

Piracy: If you come across any illegal copies of our works in any form on the Internet, we would be grateful if you would provide us with the location address or website name. Please contact us at `copyright@packt.com` with a link to the material.

If you are interested in becoming an author: If there is a topic that you have expertise in and you are interested in either writing or contributing to a book, please visit `authors.packtpub.com`.

Reviews

Please leave a review. Once you have read and used this book, why not leave a review on the site that you purchased it from? Potential readers can then see and use your unbiased opinion to make purchase decisions, we at Packt can understand what you think about our products, and our authors can see your feedback on their book. Thank you!

For more information about Packt, please visit `packt.com`.

Share Your Thoughts

Once you've read *Hybrid Cloud Infrastructure and Operations Explained*, we'd love to hear your thoughts! Scan the QR code below to go straight to the Amazon review page for this book and share your feedback.

https://packt.link/r/1803248319

Your review is important to us and the tech community and will help us make sure we're delivering excellent quality content.

Part 1: Moving to Hybrid Cloud

This first part discusses cloud adoption strategies, functional and non-functional requirements for modernization, along with impacts and fundamentals. Relevant reference solutions will be used to provide real-world use cases. The main objective of *Part 1* is to help you understand the fundamentals of application modernization and migration and get familiar with best practices to migrate to the cloud. This part of the book comprises the following chapters:

- *Chapter 1, An Introduction to Hybrid Cloud Modernization*
- *Chapter 2, Understanding Cloud Modernization and and Innovation Fundamentals*
- *Chapter 3, Exploring Best Practices for the Cloud Journey*

1
An Introduction to Hybrid Cloud Modernization

Moving from on-premises to the **cloud** is a very challenging task. Many enterprises are evaluating the process of **cloud migration**. This chapter will take a real-world scenario of an organization in the retail industry under cloud migration and look at its impact on the business. For simplicity, we will introduce the use case of **Landorous**. We will also get familiar with popular cloud migration patterns in different industries and evaluate them for Landorous to understand the best practice for a cloud migration *strategy adoption*. The Landorous case introduces cloud migration's business and technical challenges and pain points. Later in this chapter, we will evaluate a suitable roadmap for cloud migration to overcome these challenges.

In this chapter, we are going to cover the following main topics:

- An overview of the cloud migration problem
- Understanding the fundamentals of the cloud and cloud migration
- Learning about the industry patterns for cloud migration
- Developing a roadmap for successful cloud migration and modernization
- Discovering the myths in cloud migration

An overview of the cloud migration problem

This section describes the functional/business requirements for the Landorous use case, as follows:

1. We will discuss the challenges of the Landorous use case. As one of the world's largest retail companies, this organization has many on-premises-based workloads. The core pain point for Landorous is that the maintenance outage every week causes a loss of millions, affecting the company's cash flow. In addition, the maintenance outage is a painful process and time consuming. For 8 hours of maintenance outage each week, they lose approximately 1.5 million USD in revenue. The lead developer and teams need to work on weekends for the maintenance outage. Due to manual and redundant activities, several problems arise during the maintenance outage window every week. The company has outsourced some of its development work to third-party organizations, which costs a lot.

2. The business teams want to move fast and scale up. However, with the current infrastructure, this is very tough. Therefore, they have assessed that a simple web application integration to their integration platform takes 2 and a half months, excluding the functionality development work. *Figure 1.1* shows the workload of the current ecosystem:

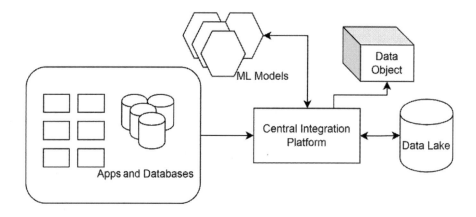

Figure 1.1 – The current workload in data centers

In addition, the core integration platform connects multiple systems that are situated either on-premises or on other public clouds, as shown in the following **system context** diagram:

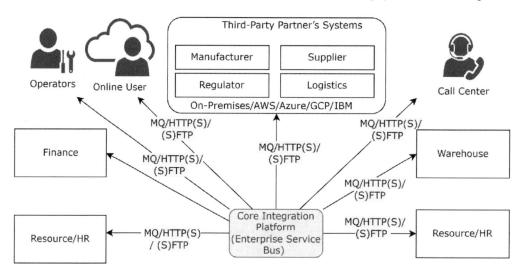

Figure 1.2 – The system context diagram

3. The company wants to create new business opportunities as well as new departments. However, the current infrastructure needs a considerable investment for additional hardware and software. They also need extra management and support for new infrastructure in their on-premises data center. In addition, they are constantly struggling to find skills, and manual management is not helping them at all.

4. Some simple workflows – for example, validating the age of a customer for alcohol or validating an e-prescription for medicine – are manual, which causes a delay in service execution. The customer has expressed their dissatisfaction with that.

5. The on-premises data warehouse requires an extreme level of governance, security, optimization, and orchestration for maintenance. All those activities are primarily manual and dependent on a database administrator group.

6. Applications have been developed over decades based on legacy technology. There is a lack of documentation and automation for deployment.

7. There is a profound link between application data and its enterprise complexities. Any simple change to the application requires an extreme level of effort and investment. Therefore, *strangling the Matrix from Hell* in monolithic applications is very challenging.

8. A legacy workload inherits complex integration models with non-standard data models, which imposes challenges. For example, let's assume that several COBOL applications have been running without support for the last year due to a lack of skills and expertise.

9. The customer wants to improve service quality as well as customer satisfaction. Therefore, they intend to use **artificial intelligence** (**AI**) to use modern technology, such as process mining, automated workflow, and business insight. However, setting up modern technology in their on-premises data center is very expensive, and the time to market is exponentially high.

As shown in *Figure 1.1*, the organization has a different kind of workload in its existing data center. The applications for the customer are too many, as shown in *Figure 1.3*:

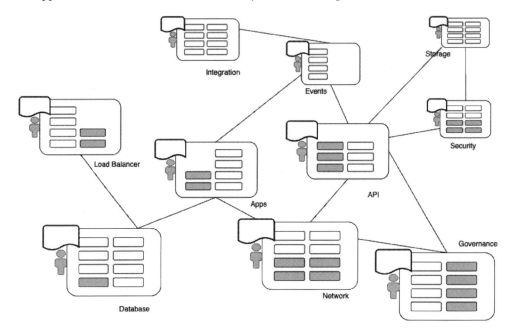

Figure 1.3 – A typical hairball infrastructure for on-premises
monolithic applications and integrated workloads

The company sets some goals for improvement, as follows:

- Decrease outages, reduce painful processes, and allow teams to move fast and scale.
- Increase cash flow with automation and reduce cost for infrastructure buildings and management.
- Validate a business case that will provide immediate and long-term net worth due to cloud transformation.

The company started a program to explore different business cases to achieve these goals, as follows:

- Add more workforce and increase skills and benefits for the existing workforce.
- Add an incentive for an additional working hour.
- Refresh technology and add new components to the existing data center.
- Cloud migration.

To help this organization migrate their workload to the cloud and get the maximum benefits from the program, we need to understand the requirements, business value proposition, current workload, main challenges, and other dependencies. We also need to define the correct roadmap for their cloud migration.

Let's now understand the basics of cloud transformation, different industry strategies, and their potential benefits, which will help us define the roadmap for the organization.

Understanding the fundamentals of the cloud and cloud migration

There are many benefits of cloud migration and modernization, such as the diversity and agility of IT operations and providing a cost-effective secured platform and a ready-to-run platform for AI innovation. As a result, major cloud providers continuously improve their offerings by adding services, securing platforms, efficiently managing the infrastructure, and providing competitive advantages in many areas.

However, it is still essential to determine the right cloud migration solution for organizations. To design the right solution, we need to understand the core concept of cloud migrations. This section will cover cloud computing, explore the different cloud models, and explain what a cloud migration is.

What is the cloud?

According to the **National Institute of Standards and Technology (NIST)**, the cloud can be defined as follows:

> *A model for enabling convenient, on-demand network access to a shared pool of configurable computing resources, such as networks, servers, storage, applications, and services, that can be rapidly provisioned and released with minimal management effort or service provider interaction.*

Therefore, a hosted *data center* is not cloud-based according to NIST. A hosted data center is a **private cloud** in the **information technology** (**IT**) industry. As a result, we will also consider the recent trends and terminology in the IT industry. Most cloud migration projects can be put into the following two categories:

- **Cloud to cloud**
- **On-premises to cloud**

In this book, we will mainly focus on *on-premises to cloud* migration projects.

Different cloud models

Cloud models can be primarily of two kinds – **delivery models** and **service models**. *Figure 1.4* shows the model classification for the cloud:

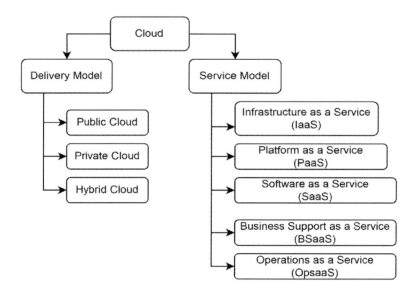

Figure 1.4 – Two kinds of cloud models

In the following sections, we will look at each of these models in detail.

Delivery model

In addition to the public cloud, there are two other delivery models, known as the **private cloud** and **hybrid cloud**, as depicted in *Figure 1.4*.

Private cloud

Different sources define the private cloud with slightly different definitions. For example, this is how *IBM Cloud Learn* defines it:

> *Private cloud is a cloud computing environment dedicated to a single customer. It combines many of the benefits of cloud computing with the security and control of on-premises IT infrastructure.*

In *Preparing for Your Migration to the Cloud* by Steve Francis, this is how it is defined:

> *Private cloud is simply a cloud that you build and operate yourself.*

The core characteristics of a private cloud are as follows:

- It is dedicated exclusively to a single tenant.

- Security hardening rules and policies regulate it.

- It can be hosted on-premises in an organization's data center or on a managed data center of the cloud provider.

- It is still able to have all the benefits of a cloud-native architecture.

Recently, among these three different delivery models, the hybrid cloud model is becoming very popular. The following section will discuss the different aspects of the hybrid cloud.

Hybrid cloud

Often, organizations cannot move all the workload to the public cloud due to migration costs, regulations, cloud service availability, and other reasons. As a result, these organizations often end up with cloud workloads and on-premises workloads in a **hybrid cloud model**. Another main reason for hybrid cloud is portability. Organizations often want to avoid cloud provider lock-in and deploy their workload so that applications and services can be easily decoupled from an underlying cloud provider workload. In addition, multiple cloud adoption is becoming a viral strategy. According to a 2017 survey by *Cloudify*, more than 51% of organizations have workloads in multiple clouds.

It is essential to select a suitable delivery model for cloud migration. *Figure 1.5* shows a decision tree for the cloud delivery model:

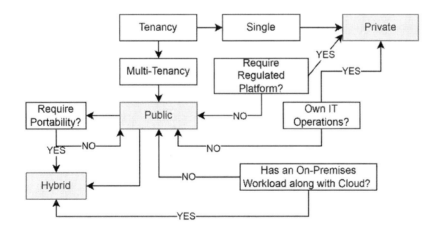

Figure 1.5 – A decision tree for the cloud delivery model selection

If migrating the workload to the cloud is not possible due to some dependency and the result of **return on investment (ROI)** analysis, hybrid cloud can be a suitable option that allows organizations to continue innovation and modernization via the cloud without interrupting the legacy workload deployed on the on-premises data center.

The next step for cloud modernization readiness is to select a service model. There are multiple types of service models used in the industry. Often, a combination of multiple service models is used for cloud modernization and migration projects to optimize the benefit. At the same time, one dedicated service model may not be the correct answer for different workloads. This section discusses the different types of service models and their benefits and limitations.

Service model

Figure 1.6 shows the primary **service models** for the cloud. However, in addition to the primary services, two services, the **business support service (BSS)** and **operation support service (OSS)**, are becoming popular. Therefore, the three service models can be described as follows:

- **Infrastructure as a service (IaaS)** provides companies with computing resources, including servers, networking, storage, and data center space, on a pay-per-use basis. The developers hide the low-level details, and they can focus on innovation.

- **Platform as a service (PaaS)** provides a cloud-based environment with computing, storage, network, and other capabilities to support the complete life cycle of implementation, deployment, and delivery of applications, without the cost and complexity of buying and managing the underlying hardware software, provisioning, and hosting.

- **Software as a service (SaaS)**, or cloud-based applications, run on distant computers "in the cloud" owned and operated by cloud providers. The user can access them from their computers through the internet and a web browser.

- **Business support as a service (BSaaS)** provides support for continuous business insights. BSaaS is an advisory service. This service plans for workload migration to the cloud and continues the business as usual.

- **Operation as a service (OpsaaS)**: Workloads on the cloud need continuous management through cloud operations, data operations, and security operations. Often, these operations are provided as a service to organizations. The cloud operation model is essential to continue operations to ensure **high availability (HA)**, business continuity, resiliency, security, and DevOps. OpsaaS provides continuous support for different cloud operations.

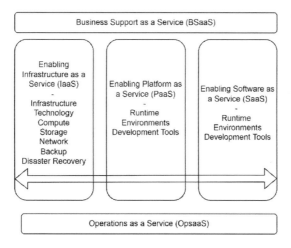

Figure 1.6 – Service models

Understanding the service model and delivery model is essential. However, the application migration and modernization project are more significant than selecting the exemplary service and delivery models. Several different drivers, such as the current workload, application, user experience, complexity of the infrastructure, and business use cases, drive the cloud migration and modernization project in multiple phases. This book will discuss the different aspects of cloud migration and modernization. Let's start by getting familiar with the definition of cloud migration.

What is cloud migration?

Cloud migration refers to when enterprises move some or all of their data center workloads and capabilities to a *cloud-based infrastructure* to enable cloud readiness. Cloud readiness is the capabilities provided by enterprises, as shown in the following diagram:

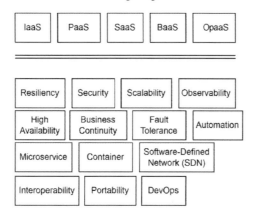

Figure 1.7 – Cloud readiness

Once we define cloud readiness, it will help us classify existing workloads and determine the cloud migration maturity model. In the following section, we will learn about different cloud migration and maturity models.

Cloud migration maturity model

The cloud migration maturity model is simply a classification of a workload to determine the priority and feasibility of a workload for the cloud migration process. It's essential to classify current or *as-is* workloads based on their characteristics and cloud computing defined by NIST.

We can classify different workloads into four categories of current or *as-is* infrastructure, based on their score of cloud readiness.

Non-cloud

Not all legacy workloads deployed on-premises can be moved to the cloud. If on-premises workloads do not show any cloud-readiness characteristics, as shown in *Figure 1.7*, they cannot be migrated to the cloud. In addition, modernizing a legacy workload can be very expensive. If there is no sufficient business value for modernizing or migrating a legacy workload, organizations may keep them in their current state. These workloads cannot be migrated to the cloud efficiently. Therefore, they need to remain on-premises or be listed for either a *Retain*, *Retire* or *Replace* migration strategy – three things we will touch on later in this chapter.

Cloud-friendly

Cloud-friendly workloads are not primarily designed with cloud-ready architecture. However, they can be changed or refactored to achieve cloud-ready architecture. Workloads that can be decoupled from the underlying compute, storage, and network are especially suitable candidates for cloud-friendly workloads. They need a significant redesign, but it is possible to measure the efficiency of the migration process, and the business impact can be clearly defined. These workloads are suitable candidates for *Re-Architect* and *Re-Innovate* migration strategies, which we will touch on later.

Cloud-ready

If on-premises workloads have a cloud-ready architecture with observability, fault tolerance, interoperability, portability, security, and scalability, they are ready for cloud migration. As a result, these workloads are suitable candidates for *Re-Host* and *Re-Factor* migration strategies.

Cloud-native

Cloud-native applications are implemented with microservice architecture to implement most of the design principles of cloud-ready characteristics. Hence, these workloads are suitable candidates for *Re-Host* and *Re-Platform* migration strategies.

Main drivers for cloud migration

The main drivers for cloud migration can be financial, business strategy, agility for IT operations, and innovation. Here are some critical technical drivers for cloud migration:

- Most applications in a legacy environment suffer from the **Matrix from Hell**, which is the challenge of decoupling applications and packaging them in a format to run on the cloud regardless of language, framework, and other dependencies. If the current applications are containerized, this problem is already solved, and moving those applications to the cloud is easier.

- Organizations have been developing workloads for a long time, and decades of application evolution with legacy application development patterns often create the Matrix from Hell, as shown in *Figure 1.8*. Many monolithic applications are interconnected in such a complex way that changing them, such as adding new features and optimizing existing features, becomes very challenging. The Matrix from Hell makes the maintenance of applications extremely difficult. Even making a simple change in the application takes lots of effort – this increases the CPU, memory, and storage consumption of the application.

- It is difficult to access data in legacy applications. Therefore, introducing modern technology for data analysis is very challenging.

- Enterprises need to significantly reduce their time to market to survive amid extreme competitiveness. Therefore, there is a need to shift management for the computing, storage, platform, and network to the service provider so that developers can focus on innovation, ultimately reducing the time to market.

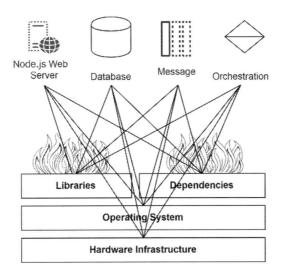

Figure 1.8 – The Matrix from Hell for a simple Node.js application

- Enterprises struggle to keep up with modern technology. This is not only due to a skills crisis but also because modern technology requires a specific platform setup. However, on the cloud, they are available as IaaS, PaaS, or SaaS. It is also straightforward to integrate with modern technology. For example, provisioning a blockchain platform on the IBM public cloud only takes a few minutes. With the IBM-managed **Red Hat OpenShift** platform, IBM takes responsibility for compute, storage, and network management and support. Therefore, developers are not burdened with maintenance, which is time consuming, and can focus on innovation.

- Operation cost is very high, and there are capacity limitations in an on-premises data center.

- Skill is limited to modern technology. Therefore, often, industries fail to scale along with demand due to a lack of skills and expertise.

- Compatibility with regulations and compliance often requires additional cost and effort.

- A constrained business process imposes additional challenges.

- Defining business uses is essential to driving a successful cloud migration project. In addition, these business use cases also help to define different **key performance indicators** (**KPIs**) to evaluate the cloud migration projects.

Before starting the journey to the cloud, we need to prepare and assess the cloud migration projects in the next section. Different industries follow different patterns for migrating a workload from on-premises to the cloud.

Learning about the industry patterns for cloud migration

Cloud migration moves workloads from a **source environment** to a **target environment**. In most cases, the source environment is an on-premises data center, and the target environment is the cloud. This section will present the nine most used cloud migration patterns, known as the **nine Rs**.

Re-Host

Enterprises use the **Re-Host** strategy to move workloads (applications, databases, and so on) from an on-premises server to a **virtual machine** (**VM**) in the cloud without making significant changes. Re-Host is an overall strategy and is also known as lift and shift. Although this strategy makes the cloud migration process faster and cheaper, it prevents enterprises from benefiting from cloud readiness and can increase management costs even more than on-premises. Furthermore, as with other patterns, Re-Host is not always suitable for every type of workload migration to the cloud. *Table 1.1* shows the benefits and limitations of a Re-Host strategy to move workloads:

Pros	Cons
A small team can migrate a significant workload quickly with minimum cost. The on-premises cost is also reduced.	As applications are moved with minimum changes, they often fail to get the advantages of cloud readiness and may cost more to run on the cloud.
As the workload is just moved to a new infrastructure, the application experience remains unchanged.	As applications are not optimized for cloud environments, troubleshooting can be complex.
Without new hardware, enterprises can scale up. It is also not required to over-provision services to deal with peak hours.	As the integration mechanism among different services is not optimized for the cloud environment, latency can increase significantly.
Cloud security services such as **identity and access control management (IAM)**, **multi-factor authentication (MFA)**, and other unified hybrid security processes increase the application's security. As a result, applications are saved from internal intruders.	Enterprises often try to mirror their on-premises infrastructure on the cloud, which can be more expensive, and at the same time, restrictions for the cloud can even make lift and shift logically impossible.
This is the easiest way to move to the cloud.	Once workloads are moved to the cloud, additional modernization of the cloud effort is essential to improve efficiency. Therefore, Re-Host is not a recommended pattern for migration.

Table 1.1 – The benefits and limitations of the Re-Host pattern

Re-Factor

This approach introduces cloud readiness to applications and databases to scale on demand and adopt cloud readiness features such as security, speed, and resilience. According to Gartner, the **Re-Factor** pattern restructures and optimizes existing code without changing its functional and non-functional behavior to remove technical debt, which later needs to be refactored. This strategy requires changing the code of existing applications, redesigning the integration between components, or replacing existing components with modern alternatives. For example, significant code needs to be changed to modernize a monolithic application to a set of microservice applications or replace a SQL database with a NoSQL database.

Figure 1.9 shows the simplified list of activities to migrate a workload from on-premises to the cloud using the Re-Factor migration pattern. Here is a list of activities to transform an as-is platform into a to-be platform:

- Containerize existing monolithic applications.

- Automate processes for data discovery, data and application dependency mapping, data movement, and synchronization.

- Replace the on-premises database with an appropriate **database as a service (DBaaS)**, based on the data characteristics.
- Configure the application.
- Establish a DevOps pipeline.

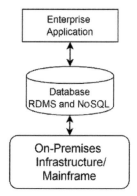
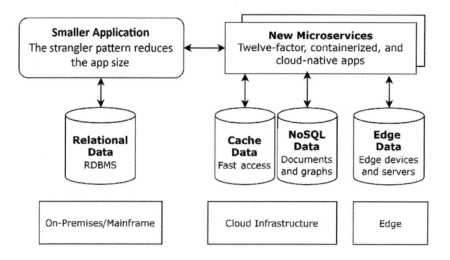

Figure 1.9 – The activities to migrate a workload using the Re-Factor pattern

The benefits and challenges of the Re-Factor migration strategy are described in *Table 1.2*:

Pros	Cons
As applications are refactored to get the optimum advantages of the cloud, the running and management of applications become significantly easier.	This pattern is comparatively more expensive than relocating base patterns, such as Re-Host and Relocate.
Redesigning the integration between components improves the application's performance, security, and other non-functional capabilities.	As applications are refactored, it is essential to perform end-to-end tests for functional and non-functional capabilities.
Licensing expenses and legal restrictions can be avoided by replacing existing components with modern alternatives.	The decommission of existing components can add costs.

Table 1.2 – The pros and cons of the Re-Factor cloud migration strategy pattern

Re-Platform

Re-Platform is the middle ground between Re-Host and Re-Factor. Instead of moving a large set of workloads, only a few are moved to the cloud to take advantage of it. So, for example, instead of using an on-premises-hosted *Db2 warehouse*, which is very difficult to manage, enterprises can use the IBM *Db2 WareHouse as a service* on the IBM public cloud. The main benefit of Re-Platform is that it provides the capabilities to use managed services to reduce the cost and effort of operations significantly. In addition, no additional skill is required for the cloud alternative, as the components are included as a managed service. This pattern maximizes the benefits of the cloud and helps to enforce standard security for the managed service. As a trade-off, this pattern is comparatively more expensive than relocate base patterns, such as Re-Host and Relocate.

Figure 1.10 shows that applications, databases such as Oracle, SQL Server, and other middleware deployed on on-premises infrastructure can be moved to the cloud using the Re-Platform migration pattern:

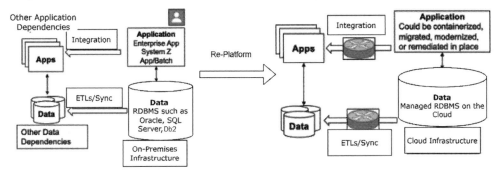

Figure 1.10 – Migrating workload from on-premises to the IBM cloud using the Re-Platform pattern

Some of the aims of Re-Platform can be described as follows:

- To simplify and automate the movement from Oracle to other RDBMS (such as Postgres) on IBM Cloud data services or Cloud Pak for Data

- To adopt best practices to optimize the target database configuration for performance, HA, resiliency, and other non-functional requirements

- To containerize applications and deploy them on PaaS over the IBM public cloud

Replace

Replace is a very early stage of cloud migration. By the end of 2020, only 26% of the worldwide workload had moved to the cloud. The remaining 74% were still in on-premises data centers. Thus, enterprises are at an early stage of their cloud journey. Every step, they are learning and reinventing themselves. Therefore, it is common for enterprises to just drop existing platforms and rebuild their workloads on a public cloud environment. The benefits and challenges of the Replace migration strategy are described in *Table 1.3*:

Pros	Cons
Applications are redesigned to get the maximum advantage of the cloud.	The cost of cloud migration is comparatively high.
This pattern helps to redesign the end-to-end solution to enable a business objective with the cloud-nativeness. Therefore, the new solution is more scalable, secure, resilient, and modern by design.	Once the new applications are deployed, legacy workloads are decommissioned; therefore, an efficient decommission process is essential.

Table 1.3 – The pros and cons of the Replace cloud migration strategy pattern

Re-Architect

Applications are rebuilt from scratch on public cloud infrastructure. Re-Architect can be explained as materially altering application code to shift it to a new application architecture, such as a PaaS on the cloud, and fully exploiting the application platform's new and better capabilities from the cloud. Re-Architect pattern development can start by breaking apart application monoliths into smaller packages or microservices surrounding a more significant containerized workload, but this usually involves more significant code rewrites and, many times, a complete rethinking of how the application should be structured. *Cloud-nativeness* is a crucial goal for new applications.

Relocate

This strategy moves the on-premises workload to the public cloud. The difference between Re-Host and **Relocate** is that Re-Host ensures some optimization of the target platform through minor configuration changes, whereas Relocate does not focus on optimization. The main goal of Relocate is to move quickly to the cloud.

Retain

Enterprises often have legacy applications with complex dependencies that require major refactoring or are no longer valid for business cases. **Retain** is a suitable strategy for such workloads where they are identified and kept in the source environment for further processing.

Retire

Enterprises adopt this strategy to decommission legacy workloads that no longer have business requirements. In most cases, if an existing workload is not compatible for containerization or refactoring, it can be a suitable candidate for the Retire pattern – for example, they migrated the physical server on-premises to a VM on the cloud.

Figure 1.11 describes the workflow of the **Retire** migration pattern. Once the migration criteria are established, based on business requirements, DevOps culture, and other dependencies, workload migration takes place in multiple stages, such as planning, workload discovery, and design. Once the high-level design of the target platform is completed, the next step is to build the landing zone for the *to-be* platform and test its operational readiness. A continuous management operation ensures that the target platform is functioning, and the performance of the target platform is continuously measured and improved over time. Until the operation on the target platform is running at full capacity, sometimes, both the old and new target platforms are used to serve requests through load-balancing capabilities. In this transition phase, when both the old and new platforms co-exist, the KPIs and metrics for the new platform are established, using the KPIs for the old platform as a reference. Now, it is time to decommission the old VM and other legacy workloads no longer in use:

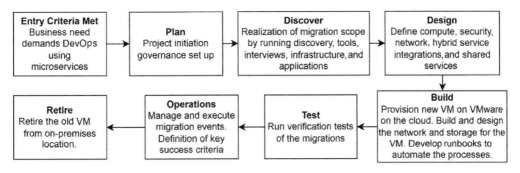

Figure 1.11 – Retiring a physical server by replacing the VM

Re-Innovate

In some cases, enterprises use the opportunity of cloud migration to re-invent themselves. For example, during the discovery phase of cloud migration, which we will discuss later, organizations might find out that AI SaaS solutions or workflow engines can replace some applications. *Figure 1.12* shows that **as-is workloads** are modernized through Re-Innovation in the **to-be** state in the cloud:

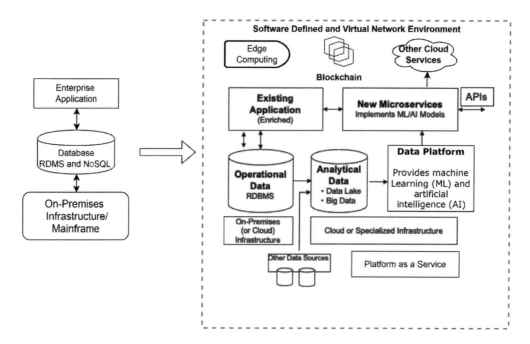

Figure 1.12 – The as-is and to-be states of Re-Innovation

Let's take the Landorous *use case* to understand the use case for different migration patterns. The migration strategy selection process is primarily driven by the cloud maturity model. Once the current workload is categorized, it can be planned for migration in multiple phases. In *Table 1.4*, we describe the cloud migration pattern selection for the Landorous *use case*:

	Workload class	Pattern	Reason
1	Applications	Retain	The Landorous project has 850+ applications deployed on 999+ VMs. The internal dependency of those applications is very complex. In addition, there is not enough documentation available. Also, there is no automated DevOps pipeline available. Applications are legacy and monolithic. The effort is too much to migrate them to the cloud without proper planning and analysis. Therefore, keeping them on-premises for now is a good decision. Once there is better visibility of the workload, they can be moved later.
2	Microservice	Re-Platform	There are 25 microservices for 2 different business units. These microservices are modern and implemented following cloud-ready architecture. Therefore, they can be easily moved to the cloud with minimum configuration changes. Moreover, they can be deployed on any managed application runtime.
3	Databases	Retire, Retain, and Replace	Databases are challenging to manage. A couple of database administrators need to manage these databases. It is better to retire on-premises databases once the data is moved to a cloud-managed DbaaS platform. However, as we planned to keep 850+ applications on-premises for the first phase, we need to consider the communication latency between those applications and a cloud-based DbaaS. Therefore, we need to categorize databases for a microservice or modern applications that can be moved to the cloud. A data warehouse, or a data lake, which can bring better results with a managed service, is also suitable for migration.
4	ML models	Re-Host (lift and shift)	These Python-written models are particular to different functionalities. However, the consumption of computing, storage, and memory is high. Therefore, they are suitable candidates for Re-Host to the cloud with minimum configuration, which will reduce the cost of computing, storage, and memory, and they can use the cloud capabilities.
5	Backend for frontend and frontend applications		There are 50 frontend applications and 221 microservice used as the backend for frontend applications. These applications are simple in design and implementation. They are already containerized. Therefore, they can be suitable workloads to lift and shift to the public cloud.
6	VM		45 VMs with 283 cores and 2.2 TB RAM are used for the core integration platform. These can be moved to the public cloud.

	Workload class	Pattern	Reason
7	Integration platform	Re-Architect	The integration platform is the central brain for the application. It is incredibly business-critical, and the maintenance outages were causing a considerable loss of revenue. Re-architecting a modern ESB platform on the cloud can solve all these problems.
8	Data lake	Re-Platform	As the data grows, data lake management is becomes very challenging. It also requires computing, storage, and memory. Without proper data orchestration, raw data in the data lake is of no use. As a result, customers cannot use it to extract business insights. Instead, a managed data lake as an SaaS can reduce the maintenance cost and, at the same time, enable HA, resiliency, scalability, security, and interoperability.
9	Manual workflow	Re-Innovate	As modern technology is easily accessible in the cloud, customers can also innovate by automating several manual workflows to improve service quality and customer satisfaction.

Table 1.4 – The migration pattern for the Landorous use case

The key to migrating a workload to the cloud is to define a complete roadmap with detailed planning for every aspect of workload migration modernization. The next task is to define an end-to-end roadmap for the cloud migration project.

Developing a roadmap for successful cloud migration and modernization

The *proper* roadmap for cloud migration makes all the difference between successful and failed cloud transformation projects. This section will discuss the roadmap in depth and show how to define the roadmap for cloud transformation projects.

The roadmap needs to answer the following seven questions step by step:

1. What is the final benefit of cloud migration?

2. What is the current state of infrastructure?

3. How do we collect information regarding the current state of infrastructure?

4. How do we transform the collected information into a migration process?

5. What are the different components (such as the delivery model, the service model, the maturity model, resources, and budget) of the cloud migration process?

6. How do we execute the cloud migration process?

7. What have we learned from the cloud migration process?

The answer to these questions is understood through the different stages of the cloud migration process, as shown in the following diagram:

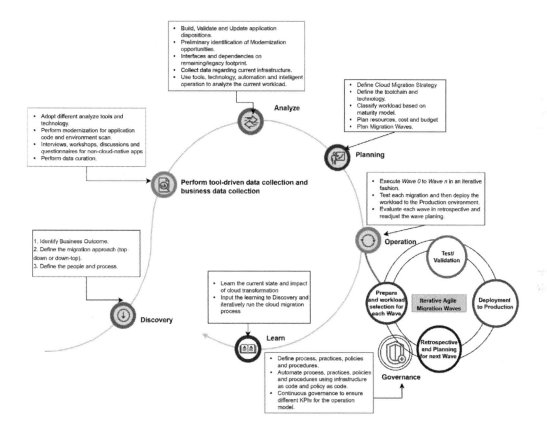

Figure 1.13 – The different stages of the cloud migration roadmap

The different stages of the cloud migration roadmap are described in the following sections.

Discovery

The main goal of the **Discovery** stage is to identify the business goals and understand the current state of the workload. Sometimes, the business goal is financial or strategic. In addition, it is also necessary to determine the metrics to measure the success against the goal once the migration process reaches the operations stage.

Once the goal is identified, the next task is to determine the cloud migration approach for decision-making and data collection. There are two main approaches, referred to as top-down or down-top, for information-gathering and decision-making. In the top-down method, decisions are made by the **chief technical officer** (**CTO**) and other C-level executives. On the other hand, in the bottom-up approach, the individuals who own certain business functionalities that cloud services can implement make the decisions. The best-case scenario recommends that even in a top-down approach, the CIO collects information from individual business units and incorporates those decisions in their own decision-making. The next task for the discovery phase is to understand the current infrastructure. The following two stages, **data collection** and **analyze**, help fully understand the current footprint of the existing workload. First, however, the discovery phase initiates the process of identifying the candidate for migration, based on the following characteristics:

- Architecture
- Security
- The cloud migration maturity model
- Performance
- Scalability
- Strategic importance
- Plans
- The agility and diversity of IT operations

Data collection

At this stage, the necessary tools and methods are organized to collect information regarding the current state of the workload and the feasibility of achieving the business goal identified at the discovery stage. The platform, data, network tools, and technologies help collect data regarding the eight characteristics identified at the discovery stage. All functional and non-functional requirements for security, resiliency, HA, and so on are identified at this stage, along with the inventory information about the current state of the workload. All data is collected to answer the following questions:

- What workloads can move to the cloud?
- Where should workloads land on the target – private, public, PaaS, or CaaS?

- What level of cloud enablement and modernization is required to move the workloads?
- Where to start – identify the priorities for the overall collection period.

Analyze

Data from the data collection phase is analyzed to understand the current state. The findings at this stage are also used as input for the next *planning phase*. Another important task at this stage is identifying the metrics for measuring success. At this stage, workloads are classified and suitable candidates or opportunities are identified. The main goal of the data collection and analysis stage of cloud migration is to identify the feasibility of cloud migration. The deliverables of the analyze stage are as follows:

- **Feasibility analysis**: Identify all the essential data collected during data collection regarding the inventory of the current workload state, and all the business requirements and business use cases during the discovery phase to analyze the feasibility of cloud migration.
- **Dependency analysis**: Identify all the dependencies, risk factors, and possible mitigation plans.
- **Workload classification**: Categorize the current workloads into different classes. It is also essential to determine the priorities of a different kind of workload migration.
- **KPI identification**: Identify all the KPIs to evaluate the cloud migration and optimize the cloud resources, and evaluate all the workload and target platforms on the cloud.
- **Governance standardization**: Identify a standard method for processes, practices, policies, and procedures for the end-to-end project during the analysis of the cloud migration project.

Planning

Now that we understand the current platform, we need to plan for the cloud migration process. At this stage, the delivery model, service model, deployment model, maturity model, resource plan, and budget are planned and evaluated. Tools such as Cloud Advisor can prepare a perspective on modernization, combining tooling output and account team insights. These evaluations, as the outcome of Cloud Advisor, are used to review and align modernization outcomes with different evaluation metrics. In addition, the preparation of high-level business cases can provide measurement constraints for success evaluation. The main deliverables of the planning stage are as follows:

- Design a runbook for test planning for each workload deployment.
- Design a KPI evaluation plan.
- Plan a business use case evaluation.
- Plan resource optimization.
- Plan cost optimization.
- All risk factors and mitigation plans for different identified risks.

Operation

Once everything is planned and we have a descriptive view of the current platform, we start the cloud migration process. The cloud migration process must be agile and iterative. Therefore, multiple waves of the operation stage are executed iteratively. Each wave consists of six stages – planning, implementation, testing/validation, deployment to production, retrospective evaluation, and learning. Automation is the key to successful smooth operations for the cloud migration project. Cloud migration itself is a complex project. Manual operation is not suitable for such a complex project. Therefore, implementing automation for operations is the fundamental requirement for the success of cloud migration projects.

Governance

An overall governance method ensures standard processes, policies, practices, and procedures to optimize cloud resources. The core objective of governance is to establish a precise and structured definition for change, policy, resource, incident, and security management. In addition to the resources and workload governance, it is also essential to establish cultural and collaboration practices and methodologies to ensure overall success.

Learn

It is essential to evaluate the roadmap of the cloud migration process continuously. Then, based on the evaluation metrics for success, the roadmap of the cloud migration process is updated. The **Learn** stage is responsible for running the evaluation of the roadmap of the cloud migration process and providing input to any other stage, such as the *discovery* and *planning* of the roadmap. At this stage, one of the essential activities is to optimize the target platform on the cloud.

Cloud migration is a complex problem, and it requires a substantial amount of effort and budget. Therefore, cloud migration needs to be well defined, using best practices and suitable migration patterns. At the same time, it is also essential to be aware of different misconceptions regarding cloud migration. Therefore, the following section will discuss some common misconceptions about cloud migration.

Discovering the myths in cloud migration

Cloud migration moves a current workload, including compute, storage, data, services, system integrations, and configuration, from *on-premises to the cloud*. The core goal of this process is to achieve particular business objectives. These business objectives are measurable from the perspectives of efficiency and effectiveness. Therefore, it is essential to plan this process with suitable assessment and metrics, design principles, strategy patterns, and best practices, and the right people, tools, and technologies.

In addition, we also need to identify the priority, risk, and relationship between the business goal and migration strategy. Finally, we need to focus on data and the results of the migration process. However, often organizations get distracted by noise and myths. This section will clarify certain myths and unfair practices about the cloud migration process. These will be presented as quotations in each subsection, followed by an explanation of the myth. This section aims to help you understand what *not to do* in a cloud migration process.

Myth – re-hosting a workload without preparing for the cloud

As we all know, the most common challenge of on-premises is that it is difficult to scale up and down with a change in demand. The cloud consistently demonstrates excellent performance for scalability. However, just re-hosting workloads does not ensure scalability. The **Re-Architect** pattern or cloud modernization are essential to ensure scalability. In most cases, applications are modernized through containerization and integrating cloud readiness by *design*. However, deploying an application on a container platform is not enough for scalability. We need to design the network infrastructure and configuration for the container platform to achieve the goal.

To avoid this problem, a cloud maturity model is beneficial. A cloud maturity model defines workload classification and determines which workloads need to be redesigned to make them cloud-ready.

Myth – relocating a workload without a cloud-native design

Relocating workloads to the cloud ensures HA by design. Enterprise applications demand HA for each cloud service to keep up with high demand levels. However, this is not necessarily true. A cloud provider will provide a certain level of service as defined in its **service-level agreement** (**SLA**). However, most of the time, it does not ensure business continuity. Therefore, enterprises need to ensure that business continuity and disaster recovery are in the plan, and modernization or Re-Architect are mandatory patterns for a *business-critical* or *production* workload.

Myth – limited knowledge about cloud computing

A public cloud is not secure.

Security combines technology, tools, processes, practices, and cultures. In addition, appropriate implementation of regulation and compliance to avoid risks is essential in the cloud. Security can be ensured if it is the *heart of development*. Along with designing a secured infrastructure, developers carry a massive responsibility to secure an application. Although industries are still heading toward hybrid cloud solutions for their workloads, the cloud adoption by different industries, such as the financial and healthcare sectors, is also increasing. Therefore, the public cloud cannot blamed entirely for security issues when security is a shared responsibility including integrated processes, rightsizing, tools, methods, and practices.

Myth – cloud migration without an objective

Cloud migration is a technical strategy rather than a business strategy.

Cloud deployment directly impacts the revenue and business outcome for organizations. Therefore, it is essential to have a business objective for cloud migration. For any cloud migration project, there should be a proper business case analysis that will drive the migration project from the financial and technical points of view. As cloud migration projects are usually expensive, without the proper business case, there are chances the project might fail. The business case also helps to take correct technical strategy and decisions for the migration project and cloud platform. If an organization simply tries replacing an on-premises data center with the cloud as their platform of choice without any solid business case, it might end up as a waste of money and effort in the end. So we need to keep in mind that cloud migration should be driven by the business strategy, which could be to reduce the time to market, or allow for massive scaling up in case of increased business popularity.

Myth – limited or no assessment for cloud migration planning

We have a simple Excel sheet, which is enough for our workload analysis for cloud migration.

We need to remember that cloud migration is only beneficial if it is done right. Therefore, it is essential to plan the cloud journey properly with details.

Myth – inefficient assessment for cloud migration

One size can fit all.

The recent trend among enterprises is to choose a single cloud as their strategic cloud and put everything in that same cloud. The outcome is already visible – often, this is not the right decision. In addition to that, no single cloud migration pattern is suitable for every type of workload. Migration patterns vary for different technology/applications.

The landscape and business goals of the transformation need to be defined clearly for a successful cloud migration project. Often, enterprises prefer to use Re-Host as their only cloud migration pattern instead of Re-Architect. However, this is not always true. A proper analysis is essential to identify the correct cloud migration pattern for different workloads. In reality, 84% of digital transformation projects fail due to siloed data and unreliable integration approaches.

Myth – cloud migration versus cloud modernization

Move first, then innovate.

Monolithic legacy applications only focus on business logic and functionality. For example, developers often use files at a specific location to store the configuration. The main focus for developers is to implement the functionalities; unit tests, integration tests, and regression tests focus on business logic only. The data, integration, management, and DevOps are often a secondary focus for developers. Therefore, moving applications as is usually makes the management more expensive and cumbersome. A more holistic focus on configuration, management, DevOps, data, and integration can modernize an application and make it suitable for cloud migration.

Summary

This chapter covered the fundamentals of workload migration to the cloud. Then, we discussed different industry patterns and strategies for cloud migration and their value to organizations. Selecting suitable patterns and strategies for cloud migration can maximize the benefits of workload migration to the cloud. This section explained the characteristics of different migration patterns, enabling organizations to choose the most suitable patterns and strategies for cloud migration based on workload classification. Then, we explained a common scenario for organizations and the roadmap for cloud migration. Finally, we discussed the different stages of a well-defined end-to-end roadmap for cloud migration, along with some myths about cloud migration.

This chapter focused on the fundamentals of cloud migration. Workload migration alone cannot bring the maximum benefits for an organization; workload modernization and innovation are also required.

In the next chapter, we will discuss the fundamentals of modernization.

2

Understanding Cloud Modernization and and Innovation Fundamentals

Organizations step into **cloud modernization** with multiple objectives. Modernization enables an organization to reduce time to market and expedite innovation, which is the ultimate strength for organizations that are competing with others. This chapter will discuss the fundamental concepts, common themes, and challenges of modernization. We will explore the mindset and agenda of different stakeholders of cloud modernization. We will also explain the features that are usually required to prepare for cloud modernization *readiness report*.

In this chapter, we are going to cover the following main topics:

- Understanding the fundamentals of modernization
- Analyzing modernization preparation reports
- Assessing the modernization maturity level
- Hybrid and multi-cloud
- Understanding a business's mindset for cloud adoption
- Understanding a solution architect's mindset for cloud adoption
- Getting familiar with a developer's mindset for cloud adoption

Let's start with the fundamental concept of modernization.

Understanding the fundamentals of modernization

The modernization concept is a fundamental requirement for modern technology. Therefore, organizations that are part of the global technology ecosystem must adopt modernization. Modernization refers to infrastructure modernization, application modernization, cultural modernization, practice modernization, and operation modernization to ensure high performance and excellent customer experience. In this section, we will discuss the fundamentals of cloud modernization.

What is application modernization?

Application modernization focuses on application behavior and integration among different applications on top of a modern infrastructure. Application modernization aims to achieve high velocity, availability, scalability, resiliency, and security for mission-critical applications. All modern platforms must have secure, resilient, and cloud-native application architecture, deployment topology, operation model, performance end-user user experience, and DevOps and **Site Reliability Engineering** (**SRE**) practices to achieve these goals. The process of evolving different application ecosystem components is what we call application modernization.

Figure 2.1 shows the goal, activity, pattern, and target state of cloud modernization and other core application modernization components. The primary goals of modernization are to apply innovation, reduce cost, and transform a workload from a legacy platform to a new modern platform through a well-organized cloud migration process. There are different modernization processes, as described in *Figure 2.1*. Containerization is crucial for successful cloud modernization. Modernization uses different technological advantages, such as **Database as a Service** (**DBaaS**), microservices, and event-driven architecture, for applications and services. Modernization is also influenced by different practices, such as DevSecOps and SRE:

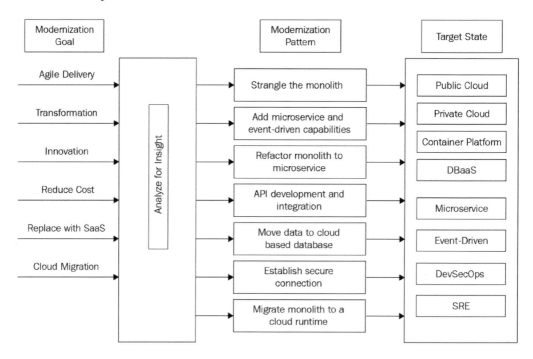

Figure 2.1 – Cloud modernization in a nutshell

Application modernization is often a complex project and requires proper planning and practices. Therefore, it is essential to be familiar with application modernization challenges. In the next section, we describe the significant challenges of application modernization.

The challenges of application modernization

Some of the core challenges of application modernization are as follows:

- Dependency on legacy applications
- Cultural adoption across different units
- A lack of necessary skills

We will look at each of these in detail.

Dependency on legacy applications

Organizations have developed hundreds of applications following legacy methodology for decades. Even though the new applications are microservices, they still interact with **legacy applications** and depend on them. Therefore, it is not easy to improve the end-to-end performance of the applications. Legacy monolithic applications often have many dependencies and interconnected components. The component diagram often looks like a very complex circuit, and it is challenging. Untangling the connections between multiple components is challenging. It is not possible to lift and shift to enable application modernization. A combination of the different migration patterns discussed in *Chapter 1, An Introduction to Hybrid Cloud Modernization*, often needs to be implemented to enable application modernization for such a complex application estate. This high-dimensional dependency of applications is also known as the **Matrix of Hell** problem. Different migration patterns, such as **Re-Platform** and **Re-Architecture**, can help containerize the monolithic application, using microservice and event-driven application architecture. Modernization is much more than just Re-Architecture applications. We will discuss the modernization process in the next chapter.

Culture adoption across different units

Change in existing culture and sentiment toward new technology adoption is critical for application modernization. If executives, business, IT support, application development, and infrastructure management units of organizations are not comfortable with changing people, processes, and practices, application modernization cannot achieve the highest performance.

A lack of necessary skills

Delivering modernization is complex, and it requires a broad spectrum of skills in a cloud platform, infrastructure, cloud services, latency, and other cloud-native characteristics. The necessary skills for cloud operation are often not available in the marketplace. Therefore, we need continuous prioritization and planning to identify a suitable component to deliver modernization. If we cannot design a landing zone that eventually becomes the configured cloud infrastructure with standard settings, policies, best practices, and guidelines for infrastructure, security, storage, and networking, it will be a failure in multiple cases. A proper combination of skilled people, processes, tools, and practices is essential for successful modernization. Modernization is a very complex and often expensive project. Therefore, planning and prioritizing to identify the most effective workload or application to modernize based on business value and **Return on Investment** (**ROI**) are essential. Continuous project assessment ensures the correct prioritization of actions to deliver modernization.

It is essential to identify the drivers to optimize modernization and ensure continuous assessment. Therefore, in the next section, we will discuss some of the significant drivers for modernization.

Drivers for application modernization

There are three different drivers for application modernization, as follows:

- **Business**
- **Customers**
- **Technology**

Table 2.1 describes the three drivers for application and workload modernization within the cloud:

Driver	Aspects
Business	<ul><li>Business priorities can be the driver for cloud modernization to reduce data center costs or any other business use cases.</li><li>Different revenue drivers optimize the ROI and reduce cost.</li><li>Innovation to adopt new technology, as well as reducing time to market, can also drive the cloud modernization journey.</li></ul>
Customer	<ul><li>Better customer experience.</li><li>Improve customer centricity with modern and feasible self-service capabilities.</li><li>Enable trust in data processing.</li></ul>

Driver	Aspects
Technology	• Overcome limited application knowledge through the modernization of the discovery model. • Overcome skilled resource limitations through the adoption of out-of-the-box services. • Reduce time-to-market challenges. • Enable faster adoption of modern technologies. • Constrained business processes. • Reduce operational costs and capacity limitations. • Increase the feasibility of accessing data from multiple sources. • Use new technology, such as IoT, blockchain, and containerization. • Use modern operations, such as **Infrastructure as Code (IAC)** and policy as code.
Culture	• Use new practices, such as DevOps, SRE, and platform engineering. • Use zero trust for security and compliance.

Table 2.1 – Drivers for modernization

Different drivers push us to adopt application modernization, and there are different approaches to adopting it. Therefore, it is essential to determine the right approach for modernization, based on business requirements, teams, culture, and tools.

Modernization approach

Application modernization needs to go through multiple steps. First, successful modernization requires proper and extensive preparation through discovery and analysis to identify suitable candidate applications for migration. Second, the nature and architecture of the selected applications control the features and architectures of the landing zones. Third, the landing zone provides the underlying baseline for modernization. Fourth, modernization continuously evolves applications, platforms, security, and practices in the target landing zone. Finally, a set of KPIs and metrics is needed to test and validate the success of modernization. These KPIs ensure the operational readiness of the platform to run production workloads. *Figure 2.2* describes the steps of application modernization:

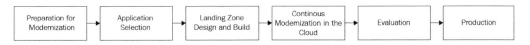

Figure 2.2 – A modernization approach

The main activities of modernization are as follows:

1. Prepare for modernization:

   - Identify the business objectives and priorities for modernization.
   - Prepare the timeframe and business value evaluation.
   - Run tools to analyze the current estate of applications. IBM Transformation Advisor is one of the prominent tools for application insight analysis.
   - Align project teams on critical objectives/use cases.

2. Application selection:

   - Categorize applications from technical and business value perspectives. Identify legacy, composite, monolithic, and cloud-native applications.
   - Select the representative application(s) to prove the approach.
   - Determine the modernization pattern for different types of applications.
   - Identify **Non-Functional Requirements (NFRs)** for the application.
   - Select the *public*, *private*, or *hybrid cloud* as the target platform.
   - Install or provision cloud services (**Infrastructure as a Service (IaaS)**, **Platform as a Service (PaaS)**, and **Software as a Service (SaaS)**).

3. Discovery and requirement analysis:

   - Understand the business case and budget for cloud modernization program
   - Analyze functional and non-functional requirement

4. Build and design the landing zone:

   - Reflect the high-level design for the landing zone.
   - Automate the provision of the landing zone and repeat that in the different target environments.
   - Automate continuous evaluation to build a thriving landing zone for migration.

5. Enforce continuous modernization in the cloud by following practices:

   - Create a roadmap and continue modernization incrementally.
   - Use KPIs, business value, and the maturity model to prioritize and deliver modernization efficiently.
   - Innovate while minimizing the complexity.
   - Minimize risk and expense while maximizing business value.

6. Evaluate the following artifacts:

   - Automate unit tests to validate that the applications are running with the target KPIs.

   - Ensure health checking for the applications using liveness and readiness testing.

   - Enforce continuous performance and scale tests and tuning to ensure the applications' scalability, resiliency, and reliability.

   - Ensure high availability using continuous tests and tuning.

7. Deploy workload to production with the following practices:

   - Run application(s) that prove technical viability.

   - Define a resilient scalability pattern for applications and other workloads on cloud.

   - Frame the business value model for modernization.

8. Optimize the cloud infrastructure and platform

9. Manage the capacity of the platform to ensure the cloud service usage is optimized.

Modernization ensures that applications, data, platforms, and infrastructure are designed, built, and managed to maximize business value, increase innovation, and prepare for future needs. Modernization focuses on improving business value by reducing the time to market, increasing innovation speed, and improving the engagement experience.

This section discussed the fundamentals of application modernization and cloud infrastructure modernization at full length. Some of the key design principles for modern infrastructure are as follows:

- The "rewrite everything" or "migrate everything" approach fails as a single pattern cannot fit each cloud-native service or application. It is essential to determine the proper modernization and migration dispositions, based on business value, technology fit, and time to market.

- Application modernization is more than modernizing the application layer, therefore, platform architecture should consider following design patterns:

  - Decentralized and containerized integration

  - Message and event-based patterns

  - API enablement of applications and data access

  - Eventual consistency

  - New transaction patterns

  - Cloud-native NoSQL databases

- Modernizing the way applications are developed and maintained helps drive additional business value.

- Enforce managed security services with regular security operations.

- Modernization techniques must scale to address an entire application estate – potentially thousands of apps. Therefore, executing at scale is crucial to yielding business value.

- Collaboration among different teams: The right mindset among different technical teams is essential.

In the next section, we will focus on the preparation step of modernization. First, we will discuss the current application and platform state analysis to determine the next step for modernization and prepare accordingly.

Analyzing modernization preparation reports

For a successful migration, it is essential to prepare for the journey to cloud modernization effectively. Therefore, before planning the business objectives, it is essential to review some case studies and initiate some research. *Table 2.2* shows the research and case study analysis required for successful modernization:

#	Topic	Content
1	Case study analysis reports	<ul><li>Business objectives and an industry overview for a similar organization</li><li>Product or technology scope</li><li>Business value and result</li></ul>
2	Analysis reports	<ul><li>Details of the cloud migration discovery tool utilized and the reason for utilizing this specific tool</li><li>A cloud migration analysis report as evidence of the successful use of the proposed discovery tool(s)</li><li>A list of information typically contained in a cloud migration analysis report</li></ul>
4	A cloud migration strategy	A cloud migration strategy document, including the elements expected in a migration strategy

#	Topic	Content
5	Migration planning	• End-to-end planning for migration • A cloud migration plan previously compiled for any similar organizations • An additional report with evidence of different risks, such as dependencies, incompatibilities, security architectures, connectivity, network settings, data transfer speeds, and mitigation
6	Cloud optimization	• Optimization tools utilized during a cloud migration project. • Details of any optimization activities performed on legacy or single-instance applications or software to enable or facilitate cloud hosting of such applications as part of cloud migration. • Detail the effectiveness of the optimization activities by providing the results.
7	Resiliency	• Detail a disaster recovery proposal or plan, including load-balancing strategies or policies, compiled as part of cloud migration. • Detail the considerations considered when drafting a disaster recovery plan. • Detail practices and topologies for the backup and restoration of workloads.
8	A deployment model for application and data	• Either centralized or decentralized deployment models. • Detailed planning for transactional data transfers and complete data mapping (from source to target). • A test plan for a deployment model. Design and implementation of a runbook for automated migration scripts. • Complete data mapping (source to target). • Detail data format templates.

Table 2.2 – Preplanning case study analysis reports

A comprehensive report on the analysis of the current state of the applications highlights the primary drivers, both technical and financial. *Table 2.2* shows a sample checklist for planning for the architecture design of resilient systems. The main goal of the assessment is to determine the maturity level of the modernization process for the legacy platform. Therefore, the next section of this chapter focuses on the determination techniques for the modernization maturity level for the organization.

Assessing the modernization maturity level

The modernization maturity level helps you to understand the current state of the applications and foresee the risks, assumptions, issues, and dependencies of the modernization process. It helps to plan the next step for the modernization program efficiently. The higher the maturity level is for any organization, the lower the required effort and budget for modernization. *Table 2.3* shows the **modernization maturity model**. The maturity model focuses on the maturity level of the current platform, applications, data, and day-two operations. An organization needs to scope different components in *Table 2.3* based on the current maturity level. An organization can be at a different level for different components. For example, they can currently be on level 3 in terms of the platform, but their applications are containerized, so they are on level 5 for applications. The final scorecard is driving input for the modernization planning of the organization:

Level	Platform	Application	Data	Operation
1	All workloads are hosted in a data center.	Monolithic applications usually have thousands of dependencies. The legacy application is often not managed over the years.	Data is saved in a fixed location with a hardcoded path.	Regular outage windows for 6–8 hours with manual operations.
2	Applications and middleware are dependent on the underlying hardware of the data center.	Dependencies are identified. Legacy applications are untangled.	Data is saved in a database with strong consistency and the **Atomicity, Consistency, Isolation, and Durability** (ACID) principles.	Regular outage windows for 6–8 hours with manual and automated operations.
3	Applications and middleware are dependent on the underlying hardware of the data center.	The stateful application is dependent on the persistence layer.	Data is saved in a database with the **Basic Availability** (**BASE**) principle, so that read and write operations are always available.	Autonomous operations but triggered manually.

Level	Platform	Application	Data	Operation
4	A different set of control planes for on-premises and a single cloud infrastructure.	Stateless applications have no dependency on the underlying persistent layer.	Data is saved in a database with the **Consistency, Availability, and Partition Resistance (CAP)** principle.	Data is encrypted at rest, replicated in multiple storages, and accessed over a secured connection.
5	A hybrid cloud platform.	Applications are containerized.	Data is stored in a distributed managed DBaaS with eventual consistency.	DevSecOps practices are adopted at all layers of development and operations.
6	A multi-cloud workload governed from a central control pane.	The integration model is based on a RESTful API and is event-driven. The 12-factor App methodology is followed across all applications.	Data has a pure and defined classification; transaction data is saved in a DBaaS with solid consistency, and other data is saved in a NoSQL DBaaS with eventual consistency.	Advanced SRE practices.

Table 2.3 – A maturity model for modernization

An organization must select a set of model platforms, applications, middleware, data, and operations for modernization. A corresponding heatmap is developed after the set of candidates is prepared. This heatmap can be transferred to the maturity model explained in *Table 2.3*. Based on the level of maturity, different target platforms can be selected. For example, applications or platforms can be migrated or modernized using a hybrid cloud platform for lower maturity levels. On the other hand, applications or platforms with higher maturity models are suitable for the **multi-cloud** platform.

The next section of this chapter discusses the characteristics of hybrid and multi-cloud platforms.

Hybrid and multi-cloud

Cloud solutions can be very complex and continuously evolving. There can be different kinds of public, private, and on-premises cloud platforms. Sometimes, a workload can be deployed on multiple cloud platforms. Based on the nature of the target workload, we can split the target platform into two different kinds, such as the hybrid cloud and the multi-cloud platform.

What is a hybrid cloud?

When distributed platforms from the public cloud, private cloud, and on-premises infrastructure are unified to create a single, robust, cost-optimal IT infrastructure for the target workload, the target workload is known as a *hybrid cloud platform*. A hybrid cloud platform can run, manage, and autoscale traditional or cloud-native workloads.

Characteristics of hybrid cloud

The core characteristics of the hybrid cloud are as follows:

- **Shared platform**: A common platform for managing and support enables an organization to enforce a standard set of policies and rules for the different workloads in their distributed hybrid cloud platform. This common platform can also enforce best practices.

- **Hybrid infrastructure capabilities**: As organizations can use the diverse infrastructure and platform capabilities on a hybrid cloud platform, they can enable granular control over resources, development, and IT operations. Organizations can use new technology and cloud capabilities for innovation and faster application modernization while continuing their business operations without interruption by using their legacy workload from on-premises infrastructure. Organizations can expedite their innovation and modernization in a hybrid cloud model by using cloud capabilities. At the same time, legacy workloads from on-premises infrastructure can continue their business processes. Hybrid cloud improves business progress by reducing product development cycles, accelerating market time, providing faster response to customer feedback, and delivering and integrating with other workloads.

- **Central governance**: It is possible to enable global cloud security and regulatory compliance rules and policies for all distributed platforms. Governance enables better security and regulations for the infrastructure.

The hybrid cloud is a ubiquitous platform for modernization applications and migration projects. Most of the time, the first phase of migration and modernization is deployed on a hybrid cloud. For example, *Figure 2.3* shows a typical hybrid cloud platform for application migration and modernization.

First, legacy traditional applications and middleware can be refactored on container platforms on-premises using the **Re-Factor**, **Re-Platform**, or **Re-Architecture** migration patterns. Later, these applications and middleware can apply **Re-Host** or **Re-Innovate pattern** on container platforms on the public or private cloud. Similarly, the legacy application can be re-hosted on a virtual machine on the public cloud. Therefore, the organization can have its workload in a hybrid platform both on-premises or on the public or private cloud:

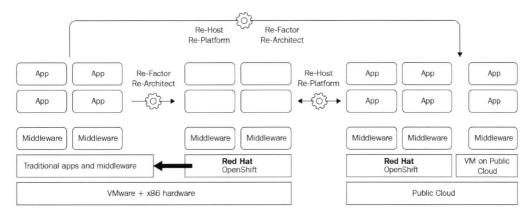

Figure 2.3 – An application migration using the hybrid cloud

Besides the hybrid cloud, multi-cloud is also getting very popular among organizations. The primary benefit of multi-cloud is that it enables an organization to use the strength of different cloud providers and design an efficient platform where they can innovate continuously to improve their business value. In the next section, we will cover the characteristics of a multi-cloud platform.

What is multi-cloud?

If an organization adopts PaaS, IaaS, or SaaS from multiple cloud service providers, such as **Amazon Web Services** (**AWS**), Google Cloud Platform, IBM Cloud, or Microsoft Azure, the distributed cloud platform is referred to as multi-cloud. These days, multi-cloud is a standard deployment model for organizations. However, a multi-cloud platform has specific characteristics that require proper planning and a roadmap for successful modernization.

The characteristics of multi-cloud

The core characteristics of multi-cloud are as follows:

- **Central governance**: As cloud services can be invoked through an API, it is possible to build central governance for all cloud services deployed on multiple platforms. It is possible to create a central visualization of events and logs using multiple monitoring tools to achieve a singular view and configure consistent response alerts. Central governance makes incident management and governance much more straightforward and flexible.

- **Consistent and common DevOps**: A standard and consistent practice for DevOps and SRE can be enforced among different organization departments that have chosen multiple cloud platforms as their target platform for their workload.

- **Central management**: A central management control plane consistently deploying applications across target environments.

- **Analytical insight using Artificial Intelligence Operations (AIOps)**: Using machine learning capabilities for event correlation, anomaly detection, fault localization, incident management, and other operations helps to modernize the overall IT service management. Similarly, the "noise" of data for metrics and telemetry can help to enrich AI-based insights for infrastructure, as well as providing standard and flexible service management and business continuity. In addition, efficiently configurable models for operations, change management, and performance management make a platform more proactive by automatically adopting corrective actions across the multi-cloud infrastructure.

- **Efficiency and optimization**: As for a best-of-breed cloud platform, services are integrated from multiple cloud providers. Therefore, a hybrid multi-cloud platform can use new technology from multiple clouds within a specific budget.

As multi-cloud provides efficiency, optimization, and faster innovation and modernization, it is trendy. *Figure 2.4* shows a multi-cloud infrastructure for a large organization. This retail organization has its DevOps, a re-hosted Active Directory on Azure, a container platform and a high-performance computing platform on IBM Cloud, Salesforce applications and SaaS on the Salesforce cloud, employee management applications and middleware on the Workday cloud, and user analysis and advertisement revenue analytics services on Google Cloud. In addition, Oracle databases are partially migrated to Oracle Cloud and their central cloud management platform on AWS. This multi-cloud solution helps them use all the new technologies and services from the different clouds:

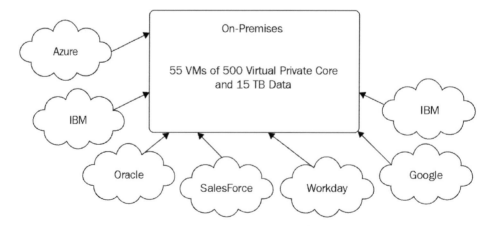

Figure 2.4 – A multi-cloud workload platform

Cloud modernization is not only a technical problem but also has commercial and cultural aspects. Different parties are engaged during cloud modernization for any organization. The overall mindset, including the culture, focus, and practices of these parties, plays a significantly important role in the success of cloud modernization.

In the next section, we will discuss the mindset of different stakeholders of the cloud modernization project.

Understanding a business's mindset for cloud adoption

Business is the main driver for any application modernization program. Therefore, a business must establish its priorities and understand the current application and workload estate. Business executives need to have a clear understanding of the application estate. Here is a list of characteristics that have a clear relationship with ROI:

- Application and data have dependencies on enterprise complexity and vice versa. Therefore, adopting modern technology and cloud-native features will help an enterprise reduce its functional complexity and define the functionality with a combination of much simpler microservice and event-driven technologies. For example, a bank has a single transaction that needs 27 minutes to complete, which is not acceptable for a good customer experience. This transaction performs a sequence of functions and services and it takes a long time, as it has some heavy operations such as governance and file processing.

- *Figure 2.5* shows a single service and its different functions in a sequence. Each function is written in the business layer and supported by the data layer in monolithic applications. Therefore, these functions are reusable in the same application but are not accessible by any other application. However, some of the functions are common for any application, such as file processing and data queries. In a microservice application pattern, these functions are exposed services and can be invoked by any application in the ecosystem with proper authentication and authorization. Microservices reduce code redundancy in different applications and can ensure a single standard for all applications. As a result, each of the operations in *Figure 2.5* can be replaced with a microservice, file processing and other heavy operations can be done as a batch job before the user request, and the result is saved in a NoSQL database. In that case, during the user request, these heavy operations can be replaced with simple user input-based queries to the database. Therefore, a 27-minute-long transaction is done in a couple of seconds. This will ultimately improve the performance and end user experience:

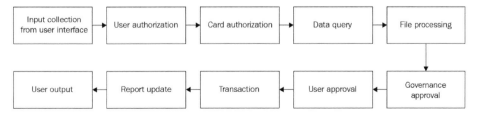

Figure 2.5 – A list of functions in sequence

- Many organizations are not compatible with the cloud, especially **Commercial off-the-Shelf (COTS)** and *as-a-service* features. COTS products are essential hardware or software that are packaged together to be used out of the box. COTS products are very popular, as they are ready to use as a service model. This is a tough challenge for cloud adoption because it impedes the faster adoption of new technology to accelerate innovation and modernization to enhance the end user experience and profitability.

- Cloud modernization does not necessarily mean abandoning an entire legacy application estate. On the contrary, cloud modernization can use legacy environments' value without business disruption. Secure and low-latency enterprise connectivity can provide reliable communication between on-premises and cloud applications. On the other hand, several migration patterns focus on using legacy environments without business disruption.

- Industries are suffering from inadequate skills in modern technologies, such as containers, microservices, DevOps, APIs, and legacy technologies such as the COBOL and Perl programming languages. Therefore, it is high time to upskill the operation and IT support people with modern technology in order to fill the skill gap in IT industries. At the same time, a new roadmap to replace legacy technologies with modern technologies needs to be established as soon as possible.

- Security has become one of the top priorities in any organization. However, complex, backdated legacy integration models with non-standard data models impose challenges and security loopholes for malicious attacks. Therefore, business executives need to establish a roadmap to ensure security by design across all applications, databases, and integrated infrastructure.

- Nowadays, a typical scenario is for an organization to have a single cloud provider policy and all its workload to stay in a single cloud provider's ecosystem, which causes the vendor lock-in problem. At the same time, not all the cloud services from the same cloud provider are suitable for each kind of application or workload the organization owns. The main challenge preventing organizations from starting a multi-cloud provider-based ecosystem is a lack of cloud management and a governance and security strategy covering multiple cloud providers. Business executives and decision-makers need to develop a strategy to overcome this hindrance, as it ultimately prevents innovation and modern technology adoption.

- Cloud service brokerage or business value evaluation of different cloud services is another missing component from the business portfolio of a cloud adoption strategy. Visibility and control to realize value from the cloud adoption strategy needs to be established and transparent at each adoption stage. This will enable executives to understand cloud adoption's ROI and business value.

- Not all applications need to exploit the capabilities of the cloud. It does not mean cloud adoption will force each item of the current estate to migrate to the cloud; instead, cloud adoption or application modernization refers to using the strength of an on-premises or private cloud and public cloud to maximize the benefits of the technology.

- Application modernization is a complex problem. Moving the workload from on-premises to the cloud does not cover 10% of the work required for application modernization. 2020's *Mainframe Modernization Business Barometer Report* stated that 74% of organizations have started a modernization program but have failed to complete it. In 2019's *Tackling the Unsexy Challenge of Mainframe Modernization*, Forrester reported that over $100 million was spent by some organizations to migrate from their mainframe systems.

- In addition, to understand the scope, complexity, and cost of application modernization, business drivers also need to know the benefits of cloud adoption and relate them to their organization's roadmap and goals.

Every cloud modernization can remedy a set of business challenges; therefore, business is the main driver for cloud modernization projects. Therefore, to achieve the desired result from a cloud modernization project, it is essential to understand the expected benefits of cloud adoption to the business.

Business benefits

The core business benefits of cloud migration are as follows:

- Integrated operations and service management can reduce incidents by 20–30%.

- Optimized DevOps enables faster time to market.

- Development delivery can increase by 40–50 user story points per squad in every iteration.

- A highly resilient and agile cloud infrastructure can save almost 30–40% of the annual cost.

- A new cloud operating model can improve testing time and performance for new environments, supporting complex user demands.

- A modern cloud-based IT estate can also improve operational continuity and overall agility.

- What used to take months can now be tested in minutes with an on-demand cloud infrastructure readily available with a pay-per-use model.

- Productivity can be improved significantly using automation levers and operational stability.

- The **Year-on-Year** (**YoY**) growth of business-impacting issues reduces significantly.

- It is simpler to reimagine user experience with user-centric models and move to a product-based delivery model.

- Dependencies on legacy systems of records and moving to systems of engagement can be reduced.

- The time to market for new enterprise-grade business capabilities increases with great speed.

- Release capacity, along with productivity and release frequency, increases to a great extent.

- Quality improvements with defect resolution time reduce over time.

- You can enforce middleware optimization in a highly scalable environment.

- You can improve business continuity.

- You can enforce highly available middleware with out-of-region disaster recovery provisions.

- You can ensure an agile, flexible check-in platform instead of a legacy check-in platform, which is no longer supported, unable to meet business requirements, and has long delivery timelines.

- You can provide an innovation platform. The platform may need quick business MVPs and the freedom to choose technologies and release them quickly.

- You can overcome data silos and accelerate analysis; manual processes for data manipulation means few skilled resources.

- You can provide better control of airline operational costs.

- You can optimize low profit margins and operating costs.

Business executives control the commercial decisions for cloud modernization. On the other hand, solution architects are responsible for making all the right architecture decisions for cloud modernization. Therefore, solution architects need to consider all known requirements and risks or limitations proactively.

Understanding a solution architect's mindset for cloud adoption

A **solution architect** needs to follow the following fundamental design principles for a successful application migration and modernization project:

- The key concept of modernization is to *build once, run anywhere consistently*, along with IaaS, PaaS, and self-service capabilities as per the application's requirements.

- A true multi-cloud strategy is where applications and workloads are deployed in multiple cloud platforms (both public and private). However, a centralized monitoring and governance platform will ensure this multi-cloud platform's security, policy, and stability.

- Modernize once and avoid recording expenses. Re-Host can temporarily reduce the cost, but applications still need to be refactored and re-innovated, which can cost more; therefore, modernization and migration are often the preferred approaches for cloud adoption.

- Innovate anywhere with anyone's technology. Solution architects should not be emotionally biased in technology selection in the case of modernization and innovation. This bias can cause poor performance and vendor lock-in. One of the essential fundamental principles to remember is that one size doesn't fit all. Technology selection should be only decided based on functional requirements and NFRs.

- Move freely and optimize for cost savings.

- Single governance and standardization should be established to reduce risk.

- High availability, scalability, and resiliency should be designed as built-in features for the cloud and application platform. The cloud only provides capabilities, but for each application estate on the cloud, these non-functional design patterns should be implemented.

- Applications deployed to multiple clusters or clouds must maintain a strict security posture.

- Security should be implemented by design, implemented, and governed continuously.

Another essential stakeholder for cloud modernization projects is the **developer**. Developers play a crucial role in the cloud modernization project's success; therefore, developers need to focus on quality, innovation, and optimization in their mindset.

Getting familiar with a developer's mindset for cloud adoption

Developers are critical stakeholders for successful application migration and modernization projects. Therefore, a developer needs to adopt the following best practices for the right cloud adoption:

- **Code quality analysis**: The target cloud solution needs to provide code quality and deployment quality analysis continuously.

- **Production-ready code deployment**: Fully automated production-ready code deployment capabilities need to be present.

- **Continuous integration and delivery**: These are core requirements for successful application migration and modernization. Each commit must be qualified by unit testing, integration testing, regression testing, code quality, dependency checking, vulnerabilities checking, and a peer review. Test-driven development can be very suitable for the best cloud migration project.

- **Strong DevOps practice**: Developers need to follow standard DevOps and SRE practices. Multiple squads need to work together in a highly collaborative environment to ensure maximum innovation for cloud resource optimization and reduce the risk of failure. Test-driven development can ensure maximum fault tolerance and quality for the implementation.

- **Automation at scale**: Use policy as code, IAC, and a maximum level of automation for different operations. The operator or developer needs to implement any policy, process, procedure, and method using IAC to ensure a central operation model can operate and govern the distributed workload regardless of the deployment location of the corresponding workload.

- **Innovation**: Refactor first and then replace the application to maximize the cloud services' advantages. Developers need to collect necessary data to understand integration and communication among different cloud services to optimize the cloud resources. In addition, the cloud provides managed services that focus on the quality and innovation of the application.

Summary

In this chapter, we discussed cloud modernization at length. We covered the fundamentals of modernization along with its different steps. We learned different approaches to executing modernization on hybrid or multi-cloud platforms. We learned about the mindsets of business decision-makers (CTO, CIO, and other CxO), solution architects, and developers, and the modernization priorities.

As we get familiar with the fundamental concepts of cloud modernization and migration, we also need to know the best practices for the cloud journey. In the next chapter, we will discuss some best practices for successful cloud adoption.

3

Exploring Best Practices for the Cloud Journey

This chapter is focused on the practices and initial assessment for the cloud journey. Cloud modernization needs time. Over time, multiple parameters for cloud modernization can change. It is a continuous process that is changing all the time. Therefore, cloud modernization and application migration can be portrayed as a journey with a defined destination. Some motivation is required to begin the journey. The journey's motivation is often different business cases, such as reducing the operation cost, time-to-market, and release frequency, among others. On the other hand, the destination of this journey is to achieve specific business value. Therefore, the end-to-end journey for cloud modernization can differ for different organizations.

A combination of standard practices, processes, policies, and procedures based on the functional and non-functional requirements can ensure the success of the cloud journey for organizations. In this chapter, we will focus on the motivation, tools, and path of the cloud journey. This will help developers and architects design cloud modernization with proper planning, processes, and practices.

In this chapter, we are going to cover the following main topics:

- Exploring fundamental practices for the cloud journey
- Planning and assessing for modernization with IBM tools
- Functional and non-functional requirements analysis
- Landing zone as a service

Exploring fundamental practices for the cloud journey

This chapter will start looking into the first steps that any organization needs to take to start the journey to the cloud. Most organizations in today's world have started their cloud journey to some extent. However, the majority of their footprints are still on-premises.

Therefore, it is essential to understand the following points:

- **Motivation**: Why cloud modernization is essential
- **Tools**: What can be migrated or modernized?
- **Path**: How to execute and deliver cloud modernization

So, we need to understand the business case to initiate the cloud journey. The correct business use case will help us to find out the answer to *why*. Once the *why* is answered, we need to look at the *what*, which mainly deals with the part of the ecosystem that can be moved to the cloud or re-innovated on the cloud.

In most cases, organizations have several components to identify which components from their IT ecosystem are suitable candidates for the cloud journey. Planning and assessment are all about answering *what* effectively. Usually, *why* guides the answer for *what*. After the candidates for the cloud journey are identified, we need to answer *how*. The answer to *how* is the solution to ensure a reliable, resilient, and available solution for the cloud journey.

Let's look at some common reasons or motivators and business cases for the cloud journey. The immediate *why* to start the cloud journey is known as the **six Cs**. Let's explore them:

- **Connectivity**: The speed and availability of connectivity mean the distance between users and data computation should be seamless and instantaneous. User experience is the driver for any business. Latency, intermittent connection, and unavailability can hamper the business significantly. Therefore, it is essential to ensure seamless and instantaneous connectivity. The cloud can bring high availability, edge intelligence, caching, nearby zones, and many other capabilities to provide seamless connections and ensure security.

- **Cost**: On-premises ownership costs (room protection, cooling, skill, and staffing) have all increased due to economic phenomena all over the world. Businesses need to reduce their costs and improve cash flow by introducing automation, reducing capital spending on infrastructure, and lowering licensing and other IT-related costs. The cloud can be an excellent place for innovation and optimization. The cloud can prevent investment in hardware, facilities and utilities, building a data center and maintaining IT teams.

- **Complexity**: Organizations need to run and evolve their business models without the distraction of doing the same for their IT environment. Ensuring high availability, resiliency, reliability, and continuity is one of the main advantages of the cloud.

- **Convenience**: The right-sizing of scale and scope of the IT environment can be done on-demand without additional overhead considerations in the cloud. Therefore, organizations can plan their budget and workload effectively on the cloud.

- **Collaboration**: The cloud enables us to overcome all technical boundaries between data, infrastructure, technology, information, customers, suppliers, and users.

- **Confidence**: In the past, security was always best kept in-house. Due to the perceived outsourcing risk and better controls and implementation of security services in the cloud, this is no longer the case. These days, the cloud is becoming secured from network, storage, compute, and operation perspective to provide end-to-end security for cloud workloads.

The *why* also varies from industry to industry. For example, for financial organizations, confidence and connectivity are primary motivators. Other industries, where user experience is the key to business success, such as the airline and automobile industries, mainly focus on connectivity and complexity for their cloud journeys. Similarly, the automobile and health industries, where innovation is happening at a higher rate, can be focused on confidence and collaboration. Therefore, the business case for different organizations drives the *why* for the cloud journey.

Once we identify the *why*, we also need to understand the *what* for the cloud. The *what* can be anything from an infrastructure or platform component to a software or service component. The core components can be one or more of the following:

- Compute

- Storage

- Network

- Middleware

- Runtime

- Data

- Application

- Operations

A couple of questions need to be asked to choose the right candidate for a cloud move. First, we need to understand which component will impact the six Cs significantly and improve the business case. For example, in the use case described in *Chapter 1, An Introduction to Hybrid Cloud Modernization*, the core **enterprise service bus** (**ESB**) state is the heart of all communication and integration. This ESB must support connectivity, complexity, collaboration, and convenience. Once we move this component to the cloud, the following pain points will be resolved:

- The ESB is not reliable and often not available. Therefore, the outage window is too long. During the outage window, the entire system is required to shut down, which downgrades the revenue significantly. The average outage per week was 12 hours before the cloud journey, and it was causing the organization a huge loss in their revenue. The cloud journey enabled connectivity and complexity. The cloud reduces latency and ensures business continuity.

- Innovation and collaboration were dependent on this component, as services from stakeholders in different public and private clouds are connected to the core ESB. It requires seamless integration without business disruption. The cloud ensures collaboration and innovation without any dependencies. Even though the average outage per week was 12 hours, it still required a huge amount of USD to manage this infrastructure. Most management operations were manual. Lack of skill and expensive skills made this component a mammoth task to maintain. After the cloud journey, the organization reduced its operation and management costs by 80%.

It is essential to understand which component can impact the six Cs most, which can be a definitive indicator for the cloud journey.

The next question to answer is *how*. The success of the cloud journey depends on *why*, *what*, and *how*. However, *how* determines the solution and operation. In the next part of this chapter, we will explore some IBM tools to determine the approach to determine the answer for *how*.

Planning and assessing for modernization with IBM tools

A suitable plan and roadmap are essential for **modernization** and **cloud adoption**. *Figure 3.1* shows the different stages of cloud adoption:

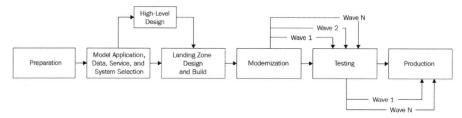

Figure 3.1 – Roadmap for modernization

Preparation

Preparation is essential for the successful migration of the workload. During this preparation stage, we need to focus on analysis. In most cases, we focus on the current inventory and requirements, which may result in a reactive target platform solution. Unlike a dynamic cloud infrastructure, a reactive target platform often lacks in growth against demand. There are cases where an organization decides to drop their cloud migration project because the vision before the migration does not match the entire cloud infrastructure. In addition, migration projects can become very complex and expensive. This situation results from wrong estimation and misunderstanding of the functional and non-functional requirements. The core activities for preparation are as follows:

- Analyze the current workload, **operating system** (**OS**) version, levels of dependency with other parts of the ecosystem, operation model, latency requirement, compliance, and regulatory requirements.

- Explore functional and non-functional requirements and measure them against the required **service-level objective (SLO)** and other **key performance indicators (KPIs)**.

- Identify several applications, databases, and infrastructure components as candidates for migration.

- Define the high-level design for the landing zone based on the identified functional and non-functional requirements for the selected candidates.

- Define a rigorous test plan that ensures the user has the required access and quality of service following migration and modernization from the target workload platform.

- Modernize the application and legacy workload automatically by using some automated refactoring methods.

Different tools and services can help you prepare for cloud migration, as shown in *Table 3.1*:

IBM Recommended Tools	Value Realized
CAST Highlight	Automatic code analysis reduces **subject matter expert (SME)** dependency and maximizes results and speed. It can rapidly analyze hundreds of applications, including vulnerabilities, dependency, resiliency, and other aspects of cloud readiness.
Application Discovery and Delivery Intelligence (ADDI)	Providing app developers with insight into mainframe code and dependencies through automated analysis.
Cloud Transformation Insights (CTI)	An AI-driven tool that provides application and infrastructure clustering recommendations.
The CAST **Application Intelligence Platform (AIP)**	Automatically performs contextual analysis of current apps, providing a basis for speeding up the modernization of apps.
Candidate Microservices Advisor (CMA)	Improves developer agility and application modernization through automated domain analysis and microservices identification.
IBM Cloud Transformation Advisor	Analyzes Java EE applications for containerization feasibility and effort.
Cloud Advisory Tool	Accelerates application disposition analysis and **return on investment (ROI)** determination.
IBM Cloud Pak for Business automation	Assists in developing application disposition recommendations.
IGNITE	Optimizes all phases of application modernization and migration by improving test case generation efficiency and test execution efficacy.

Microservices Builder (DMB)	Allows engineers to focus on business logic by offloading the need for repetitive coding through automated microservices building.
Digital Scenario Builder (DSB)	Improves time to market by automating microservices orchestration (Kafka, for example).
Mono2Micro (Java, COBOL, and .NET)	Accelerates microservices development by automating the process of application refactoring with AI.
IBM DevSecOps Commander	Allows enterprise-wide flexibility/plug-and-play of DevSecOps tools, enabling seamless integration of using the tool of choice.
Automation	Cloud Pak for Watson AIOps-driven help desk for application issues and "how-to" procedures.

Table 3.1 – Toolchain for cloud modernization and migration

IBM cloud migration service

Cloud migration services help boost the speed, performance, scalability, and security of the cloud adoption and transformation. IBM experts will help to design the best migration strategy and roadmap for a secure, repeatable, and scalable path to the cloud. The major capabilities that IBM Cloud migration service provides are as follows:

- Modernized applications deployed in the cloud with centralized management and DevOps reduce maintenance costs.

- Managed services **software-as-a-service** (**SaaS**) offerings from the cloud reduce cost and effort.

- Developers can focus on functional requirements and innovation.

IBM Garage Method for Cloud

The **IBM Garage Method** recommends a cloud-native toolkit accelerates the transformation to multi-cloud across the entire modernization life cycle through intelligent insights, automation, and integration with different cloud provider ecosystems. A combination of IBM, Red Hat, and other third-party tools is used for the different stages of modernization. These tools use advanced AI technology from IBM research to accelerate the application modernization with various architectural and microservices recommendations. These tools can also be integrated with cloud platform-native toolkits from multiple cloud platforms, such as IBM (public and private), AWS ECS, Kubernetes on EC2, and Red Hat OpenShift Container Platform.

For example, *Table 3.2* shows different tools from the IBM Garage toolkit for migration and modernization using the **Re-Host** migration pattern:

Category	Tools	Description
Strategy	**IBM Cloud Advisory Tool (CAT)**	The Cloud Advisory Tool provides a dynamic and customizable rule engine that generates a cloud adoption strategy. It gathers portfolio information and determines the disposition, cloud affinity, strategy, transformation roadmap, and total cost of ownership to remediate and migrate to the cloud using industry-specific rules and advanced analytics.
	Application Containerization Advisor	Advice on candidate applications for containerization with minimal data.
	Modernization Workflow Orchestrator	Recommendation of transformation path for an application.
	CAST Highlight	Code analysis for Java, .NET, and 50+ other technologies.
Discover	Cardinal	Discovery management.
	IBM MQ Explorer	Query and visualize IBM MQ clusters using a graph.
	CAST AIP and CAST Highlight	Code analysis for Java, .NET, and 50+ other technologies.
	Red Hat Migration Toolkit for Applications	Migrate applications from lower version of OpenShift to higher version.
	IBM Watson AIOPs	Insights from analysing ticket data from multiple domains.
	IBM ADDI and IBM **Access Risk Compliance Control** (ARC)	Mainframe code analysis.
	Candidate Microservices Advisor	Identify candidate microservices.
Recommend	CTI	Target platform recommendations and architecture for known patterns.
	IBM Cloud Transformation Advisor	Analyses on-premises workload for modernization.
	Red Hat Migration Toolkit for Applications	Provide remediation for Re-Platform to Red Hat OpenShift Container Platform.

Category	Tools	Description
Automate/ Build	E2C	DevOps-based containerization of applications.
Manage	IBM IGNITE	Cloud testing, test-driven development, and behaviour-driven development platform.
	IBM Runbook Automation	Workflow execution and management of microflows and runbooks.
	IBM Cloud Pak for Watson AIOps with ChatOps	Service automation with ChatOps and by leveraging AI capabilities.
	IBM DevOps Commander	Set up and manage DevOps instrumentation on Kubernetes platforms.

Table 3.2 – IBM and Red Hat tools for cloud modernization

Functional and non-functional requirements analysis

How is the central question here – one of the most important parts of the cloud journey is the requirements of the organizations. These requirements are mainly driven by all the actors in the cloud journey story, including the business case, applications, data, runtime, cost, and six Cs. This section takes the Landorous use case from *Chapter 1, An Introduction to Hybrid Cloud Modernization*, and describes the essential functional and non-functional requirements.

Functional requirements

Let's look at some basic functional requirements for application modernization and migration to the cloud. For a detailed understanding, we will explore the functional requirements of the Landorous use case. In the Landorous use case, the ESB and the organization's core infrastructure are moved to the cloud. *Table 3.3* shows the functional requirements of the Landorous use case in detail:

Category	Requirements
General	Fully managed platform as a landing zone for the migrated workload.
Migration	Migration of suitable workload from the data centre to target landing zones on cloud.
Modernization	Modernize applications by using insights to refactor, optimize resources and costs, and reduce complexity. Develop cloud-native apps with containers, starting with open source, standard services, the developer's tools of choice, and integrated DevOps.
Evaluation and selection of workload	The eligible workload needs to be identified and assessed for selection.
Infrastructure	Build and manage the target platform environment on the cloud.
Application	Applications need to be modernized for migration.
Operations	Build and manage the DevSecOps pipeline for the application.
Enterprise connectivity	Some workloads may remain on-premises for an extended period. Therefore, enterprise connections between cloud and on-premises locations are required. In addition, data in other clouds also needs to be communicated over secured communication channels.
DataOps	Infuse AI into all business-critical processes and workflows and operationalize AI with trust and transparency. Design tools for data management capability, for example, data federation, data catalog, data quality, and self-service analytics in multi-cloud platform can accelerate data migration process.
Automation	Increase ROI by replacing manual work with an intelligent workflow. This also improves employee productivity by automating mundane clerical tasks. Enrich content of the data analytics result with better intelligence to deliver trustworthy business insights.
Data modernization	Prioritize critical, intelligent analytics workflows for migration. Define and validate data patterns for the data migration approach. Ensure data virtualization to create a virtual normalized data model from heterogenous data in multiple databases and warehouses to support new workflows and vision. Orchestrate new operating models that will help to shift from silos to an integrated environment using real-time observability for data, workload, and operations.

Table 3.3 – Functional requirements for the Landorous project

The functional requirements control the selection process for the target platform. For example, one of the functional requirements is to build and design the data storage on the target platform. *Figure 3.2* shows the decision tree to select the target database as a service in the cloud for data storage based on the requirement for a flexible schema. Based on the decision tree, if the candidate applications require a database with a flexible schema and consistency, MongoDB is suitable as a database for document-based data:

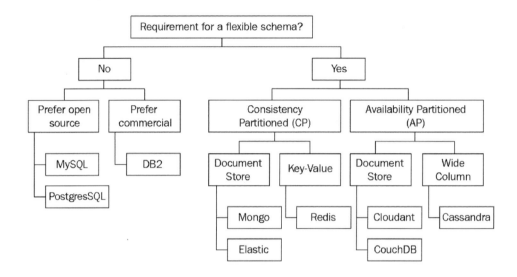

Figure 3.2 – Decision tree for the target database based on functional requirements

Similarly, functional requirements for computing can help with choosing a suitable computing platform for each set of applications that needs to be migrated or modernized on a hybrid or multi-cloud platform. For example, if the candidate applications are suitable for a container platform, they can be migrated to the container platform. Otherwise, they can be migrated to either a **virtual machine** (**VM**) or a **high-performance compute grid**. *Figure 3.3* shows the decision tree for virtualization. The key driver for the decision is whether the underlying platform supports virtualization. In the decision tree in *Figure 3.3*, different paths for virtualization on on-premises and public clouds are depicted:

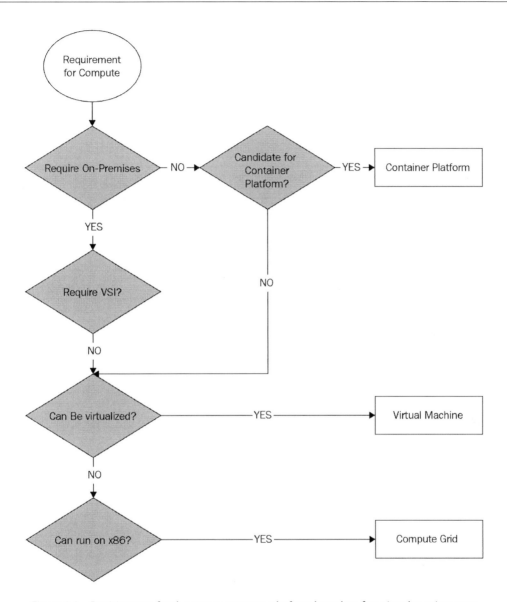

Figure 3.3 – Decision tree for the target compute platform based on functional requirements

Non-functional requirements

This section will cover some of the critical non-functional requirements for application migration and modernization. *Table 3.4* shows the non-functional requirements for application migration and modernization:

Category	Requirements
Compute	The underlying compute must provide the required performance.
Data	Design the encryption algorithm and mechanism for data encryption in motion and at rest.
Security	The proposed solution should provide security for the following: Infrastructure User and identity management and access-role management Data encryption key management Security management Authentication and authorization Activity tracking Firewall and network policy management
High availability	Design the redundancy pattern to ensure high availability: Local redundancy Zonal redundancy Regional redundancy
Monitoring and quality	Design end-to-end monitoring for applications, middleware, network, compute, and storage. All other infrastructure, platform, and middleware components must be designed. The log retention period should be clearly defined. Several days of logs that need to be backed up are known. AI-based insight and intelligent problem management processes should be designed.

Category	Requirements
Key and certificate management	Management service for the data encryption key life cycle is essential. Key service providers or customers can own data encryption keys. In addition, verified SSL certificates need to be managed for different applications. Therefore, central governance for the life cycle of keys and certificates should be available.
Backup	Workload classification, for example, the database, configuration, and VM, as well as size, determines the model and type for the backup model.
	The **Recovery Time Objective (RTO)** and **Recovery Point Objective (RPO)** for the backup should be defined.
	The type of backup model, either real-time replication or a snapshot-based backup, needs to be decided based on whether the workload is mission-critical or not. For example, if the backup requires longer RPO such as 4 hours or more, a snapshot-based backup is sufficient, but real-time replication is the preferred backup model for mission-critical data with shorter RPO requirement.
	For the snapshot-based backup model, the frequency of backup during a specific period determines the length of the RPO. For example, one full backup with six incremental backups for 24 hours can ensure an RPO for 4 hours.

Table 3.4 – Non-functional requirements

Now that we have the functional and non-functional requirements laid out, we need to design the solution for the cloud journey. First, we can focus on the **landing zone design** and **build process**. In the next part of this chapter, we will understand what a landing zone is, why we need it, what the principal characteristics of a thriving landing zone are, and what the core components of a thriving landing zone are, and we will walk through a sample of a thriving landing zone using the Landorous use case. So, let's dive in and read on.

Landing zone as a service

For application migration and modernization, the **landing zone** is a critical component. Therefore, landing zone development is key to application migration and modernization success. Once the landing zone is built, the application migration and modernization program can run as an agile project in multiple waves. For that, we need to know what the landing zone is. A landing zone can be defined as *components such as network, compute, storage, security, and operation.* These components are required to run the entire workload, such as the application, database, and software stack, on the cloud. So, we can describe the landing zone as the target platform for a migrated or new workload. The success of a well-defined landing zone depends on the design and maximum level of automation and modernization to achieve a safe, sustained, and secure platform for the landing zone. The main characteristics of the landing zone are as follows:

- A thriving landing zone must have the capabilities of a complete infrastructure, including compute, network (a firewall and load balancer, for example), storage, and security.

- It should also provide management capabilities for any component within it.

- Automation lies at the heart of the landing zone. Therefore, deploying and destroying different cloud services is essential for the landing zone.

- The landing zone should be designed so that all the components can be moved to another target platform if required.

- The landing zone can be replicated as often as required in any target platform.

- The landing zone should be constrained with minimum requirements for further customization and requirements.

- The landing zone enforce consistency in design and deployment, best practices, and configuration across multiple target platforms.

- The main principle of the landing zone is to define once and deploy as many times as possible.

- Ensure standards are maintained across all landing zones, and it is possible to enforce automation to build and manage the landing zone.

The following figure shows the different capabilities of a landing zone:

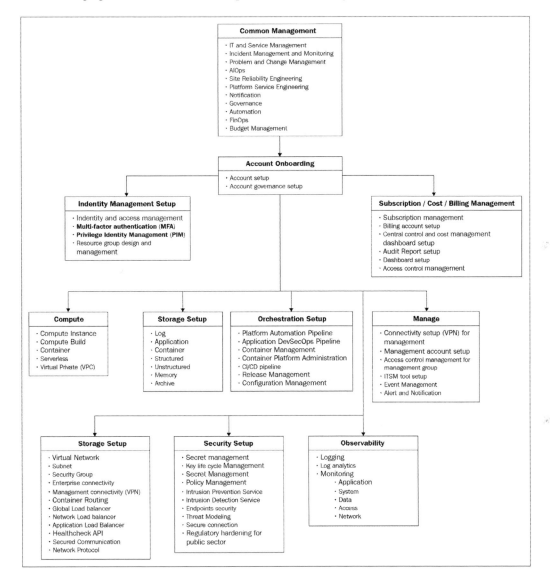

Figure 3.4 – Capabilities of the landing zone

Common management

The landing zone needs a central and **common management** platform. The processes and policies for managing the workload on either multi-cloud or hybrid cloud are generic and common. A central operation model for IT and service management is mandatory for a well-defined landing zone for the target platform. Configuration management, policy management, change management, problem management, incident management, and other IT service management should follow a standard and centralized platform. For central governance, a governing dashboard and other tools should be configured. Different components under standard management require having different capabilities.

Account onboarding

The cloud account can have multiple subscriptions and multiple accounts for any project. The core capabilities that are required for *account onboarding* are as follows:

- Capabilities to add, delete, audit, and manage governance for overall cloud account
- Capabilities to manage governance and accounts

Identity and access control management

Identity and access control management is essential for an account, users, resources, and other access. The following is a list of capabilities that are essential for identity and access control management:

- Add/remove users, roles, access groups, and identities.
- Add service ID and API key.
- Add authorization.
- Manage primary and secondary IDs to ensure only authorized personnel access the landing zone.
- Ensure RBAC rights using the principle of least privilege on all systems, subsystems, and network devices.
- Maintain audit records.
- Enable **multi-factor authentication** for the regulated cloud platform.
- Enforce a password group policy.
- Change the default policy after the installation of servers and another vendor-provided workload.

Subscription and billing management

The cloud does not have a fixed number of resources; it can grow and shrink based on requirements. Therefore, it is essential to have proper financial management of the cloud infrastructure. Here are some core capabilities for subscription and billing management for the landing zone:

- Manage different subscriptions for the same organization.
- Generate an audit report.
- Create alert and event triggering based on different events.
- Optimize the cost and bill from the different services in the cloud.

Platform design and build

Platform configuration also includes the design and provision of cloud services such as **infrastructure as a service (IaaS)**, **platform as a service (PaaS)**, and **SaaS** to build the landing zone and deploy the workload on top of the landing zone. Here are some basic capabilities required for platform design and build:

- Design high-level architecture.
- Design low-level architecture.
- Use IaC for the automated build of the landing zone.
- Use **Infrastructure as Code (IaC)** to automate target cloud platform operations
- Create and manage the IBM **Platform Runbook Automation** establishment.
- Develop AI-infused service management.
- Automate the build for repetitive tasks.
- Manage the platform.

Network setup

Another critical component of the landing zone is the **network**. The network should be secure, highly available, regulated, and protected from threats and vulnerabilities. Therefore, the network should be designed, built, and managed with sound principles and practices. Here are some best practices for the network of a secured cloud platform:

- Use software-defined infrastructure management (compute, storage, and network).
- Use GitOps.
- Practice edge management and site reliability engineering.

- Manage networking on cloud (VPC and classic) and firewall policies.

- Manage DNS, proxy, and load balancers such as **Application Load Balancer (ALB)**, **Network Load Balancer (NLB)**, and **Global Load Balancer (GLB)**.

- Manage network integrations within IBM Cloud and with client/third-party environments.

- Design, build, and manage **High Availability (HA)** and **Disaster Recovery (DR)** configurations.

- Security setup.

- Orchestration setup.

- Management setup.

Observability

Observability is the key to an efficient landing zone. Continuous monitoring and observability ensure the health and continuous service of the landing zone. Here are the essential features of observability:

- Monitor real-time disk space, memory, and processor utilization.

- Monitor container platform cluster resources.

- Monitor hardware failures through **Simple Network Management Protocol (SNMP)** trap/ **Management Information Base (MIB)** wherever feasible.

- Monitor OS services and processes.

- Monitor hypervisor availability.

- Monitor OS events as well as security events.

- Monitor high-availability cluster status and resource group status, and correct problems identified wherever applicable.

- Publish periodic reports for different KPIs based on the technical agreement with the client.

- Use the console and tools provided by the target cloud and predefined toolchain.

- Monitor the resource usage of the runtime environments of the application components (for example, JVM heap memory monitoring).

Characteristics of the landing zone

A secure and efficient landing zone must have standard configuration, procedures, policies, processes, security regulations, toolchains, pipelines, governance, deployment models, operation models, and practices across all components deployed on a multi-cloud or hybrid cloud environment. Functional and non-functional requirements for the target workload platform and the cost and budget drive the nature and technical variation of the landing zone. An example is the Landorous use case described in this book. In addition, a well-designed landing zone has other characteristics, such as the following:

- Uses new technology when it becomes ready and applies shift-left testing.

- Full automation.

- Provides complete service catalogs with maximum coverage for options to create private catalogs. These service catalogs enable self-service for provisioning different cloud services on the landing zone and the integrated capabilities defined in *Figure 3.6*.

- Uses well-defined performance indicators and usage metering to evaluate the landing zone's health and continuous monitoring.

- Enforces Code Engine and complete DevOps capabilities to improve a developer's productivity.

- Provides fine-grained *pay-as-you-go* options with comprehensive FinOps to optimize the cloud footprint.

- Provides standard control and options across multiple clouds.

- Enables continuous monitoring and AI insight-based incident management.

- Provides flexible change and configuration management from the common control plane. A landing zone requires a feasible and common way to implement design modifications and updates. There must be automatic change execution based on rules and policies to be implemented in all existing cloud accounts.

- Provides full stack (**infrastructure**, **platform**, and **application**) autoscaling capability.

- Provides *out-of-the-box* capabilities for IaaS, PaaS, and SaaS.

- Provides a fully managed service for the infrastructure, platform, database, and different software with a standard SLO and **service-level agreement** (**SLA**).

- Enables efficient deployment of any new workload using predefined cloud APIs for DevOps integration.

- Enables immediate savings by providing a commercial cloud model.

- Simplify the high-level design of the new landing zone where the process, practices, orchestration, operation, and deployment model are consistent for all workloads.

- Limits the technological footprint. A well-defined landing zone can be replicated on different cloud platforms. However, at the same time, the number of replications of the tools, processes, and procedures can increase the cost. Therefore, organizations often design a well-defined landing zone and then move similar workloads in and out of that landing zone.

Landing zone as a service

A fully managed landing zone for application migration modernization on IBM Cloud needs two major cloud accounts: the **management account** and the **target account**. This section will discuss the landing zone on IBM Cloud.

Management account

Management accounts host the central control pane for the hybrid cloud target infrastructure. Different toolchains are deployed in this account to manage the end-to-end infrastructure. *Figure 3.7* shows the management account and target account for the landing zone. Different toolchains are deployed on management accounts to manage the landing zone centrally. Some essential characteristics of a managed account are as follows:

- This account should have a similar SLA as the target workload platform.

- The operations and actions should be traceable.

- The access to the management account and the target workload platform must be authenticated and authorized.

- The tools and software used in the management account should be connected to the target workload platform over secure and seamless connections.

- The workload in the target platform can be dynamic and diverse. Therefore, the tools and services used in the management account must be configurable.

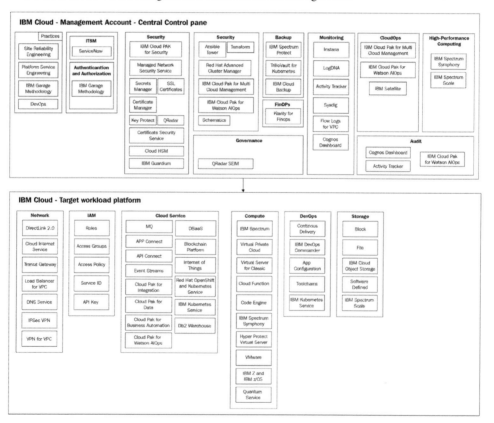

Figure 3.5 – Landing zone on IBM Cloud

Sample landing zone for the use case

The landing zone for the use case has the functional and non-functional requirements described in *Tables 3.3* and *3.4*. Based on the requirements, different components for the landing zone are shown in the following diagram:

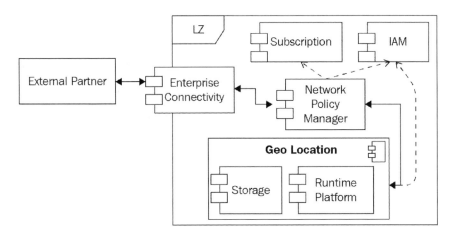

Figure 3.6 – A component model for the landing zone of the project

Based on different components shown in *Figure 3.4*, the component decisions of the landing zone are listed in *Table 3.5*. For standard functional and non-functional requirements, the associated architecture decisions are listed in the table:

Requirement	Component Decisions
Compute	RHOS on IBM Cloud.
Storage	File storage. Cloud Object Storage.
Networking	
Enterprise connectivity	IBM Cloud Direct Link 2.0.
BYOIP/edge gateway	The Customer will provide their IP address.
Global load balancing	Cloud Internet Services will provide the functionality of a global load balancer.
Network policy	Juniper firewall.
Cloud-native connectivity	OpenShift Ingress and Egress connections.

Requirement	Component Decisions
Resiliency	
Backup	IBM Cloud backup.
Disaster recovery	Active-passive between regions. Region 1 can be replicated in a passive region after the landing zone is established.
High availability	Single-region multi-zone.
Orchestration	
Automation and orchestration	Red Hat Ansible Tower.
Operation automation pipeline	GitOps.
Security	
Data: Encryption at rest	Key Protect. Hyper Protect Crypto.
Data: Encryption in motion	SSL. IPsec VPN.
Network: Firewalls/UTM, IPS/IDS	Juniper vSRX.
Network: DDoS and WAF	Cloud Internet Services.
Identity and access: Identity management	IBM Cloud IAM.
Identity and access: Privileged ID management	IBM Cloud IAM.
Security operations: Key life cycle management	IBM Key Protect.
Observability	
Monitoring	IBM Cloud Monitoring.
Logging	IBM Cloud Log Analysis.
Activity tracking	IBM Cloud Activity Tracker.

Table 3.5 – Architecture decisions for the landing zone

Figure 3.9 shows the landing zone for the ESB of the project described in *Chapter 1, An Introduction to Hybrid Cloud Modernization*. The ESB is built with **IBM Cloud Pak for Integration**. IBM Cloud Pak for Integration is deployed on the IBM-managed OpenShift cluster in two regions. Each region is an MZR region. In this use case, an OpenShift cluster is deployed in a VPC on three availability zones in each region. Applications and services from other clouds and end users from different retail stores access the ESB through an HA pair firewall. In addition, applications and services deployed in the data center communicate over a dedicated **direct link**. The persistent volume for OpenShift is built with Portworx stretched cluster deployment:

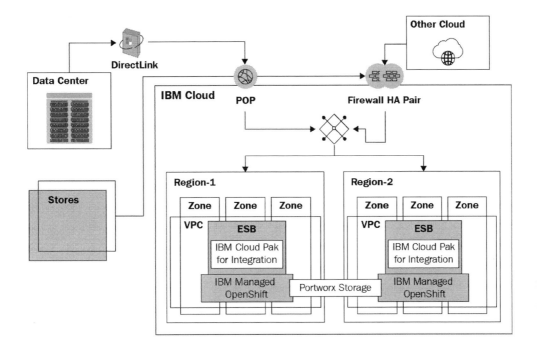

Figure 3.7 – Landing zone for the Landorous use case

The core components for the ESB state is IBM Cloud Pak for Integration and IBM Cloud Pak for Automation. Both use IBM **RedHat OpenShift and Kubernetes Service** (**ROKS**) as the runtime platform. To build the system using IBM Cloud Pak systems, initially, the landing zone needs to be developed and configured. The following is a list of the tasks that need to be carried out to set up compute, storage, network, and security for the landing zone on IBM Cloud for the architecture shown in *Figure 3.9*. These tasks include each category depicted in *Figure 3.7* for an efficient landing zone:

- Create resource groups.
- Configure availability zone.

- Build IBM Virtual Private Cloud with proper configurations for subnets, NSG rules, VPN connection (S2S).

- Provision **user-defined routing** (**UDR**) service and setup required network configuration.

- Provision **network security groups** (**NSGs**) in subnets.

- Set up Juniper firewall.

- Set up enterprise connectivity with IBM Cloud Direct Link 2.0.

- Provision and configure Cloud Internet Services as the GLBs and configure load balancer rules.

- Provision and configure application gateway.

- Set up compute:

  - Provisioning and configuration of Bare Metal servers.

  - Provisioning and configuration of hypervisors.

  - Provisioning and configuration of VMs.

  - Provisioning and configuration of container platforms.

  - Deploy monitoring agents.

  - Deploy logging agents.

  - Create autoscaling configuration.

  - Create machine sets.

  - Set up CI/CD pipeline for image curation (VM and containers).

  - Set up curated images.

  - Provision compute (VM) instances.

- Implement **role-based access control** (**RBAC**) for IBM IAM components.

- Implement Key Protect for key management.

- Implement OS image management using different tools and pipelines.

- Implement container image management in Container Registry.

- Implement security policies.

- Implement IBM Cloud tags.

- Develop OS hardening scripts.

- Develop ROKS templates for deployment automation.

- Storage setup:

- Provision storage (disks) for compute (VM) instances.

- Provision and configure storage.

- Provision IBM Cloud Object Storage instance.

- Set up custom storage infrastructure (COS, Portworx, and Gluster)

- Configure native storage infrastructure (Block, File, Object, and Endurance)

- Configure storage replication.

- Configure archive/cold storage.

- Configure storage encryption.

- Set up network:

  - Set up custom cloud-native interface.

  - Set up service mesh.

- Set up orchestration:

  - Set up Tekton CI/CD pipeline for control plane components.

  - Configure repositories.

  - Deploy control plane components.

  - Set up network connectivity to the control plane.

  - Set up monitoring, logging, and alerting.

  - Set up backup infrastructure.

  - Set up backup schedules.

  - Set up operational metrics/dashboards.

  - Set up chatbots/self-service capabilities.

  - Prepare curated image templates (VM and containers).

  - Prepare automation templates (Terraform and Ansible).

  - Set up and configure patching infrastructure (OpenSCAP, WSUS, and IBM Cloud Satellite).

  - Create AI-infused runbook automation.

  - Set up disaster recovery.

  - Set up platform testing framework.

- Observability:

  - Provision and configure cloud monitoring with IBM Log Analysis.

  - Provision and configure alerts in IBM Log Analysis.

  - Configure monitoring workbooks, dashboards.

  - Configure IBM Cloud Security Advisor.

  - Develop and configure automation scripts for startup/shutdown/pause of IBM Cloud services.

  - Configure budget alerts.

- Configure backup and retention policies in IBM Cloud Backup.

- Perform IBM DNS validation.

- Provision VMs in availability zones.

- Set up IBM Cloud functions.

- Set up IBM ROKS instances.

- Set up cloud services (for batch/other apps and APIs).

- Set up traffic gateway.

- Set up IBM DNS zones.

- Set up a **Content Delivery Network (CDN)** – one per region.

- Set up a bastion host per region.

- Set up VPN links – support only.

Summary

In this chapter, we focused on the three core topics for the cloud journey: the *why*, *what*, and *how* of organizations starting their cloud journey. These questions were answered to form the fundamental foundation for the cloud journey. In addition, we have explored different techniques to identify the answers to these three questions.

Each cloud modernization journey is driven by the *why*, which is essentially the business value achievable by cloud modernization. This chapter familiarized us with the *why* and identified some basic benefits of cloud modernization. We also learned different mechanisms to evaluate the current workload state or, in other words, *what* needs to be modernized – continuous evaluation of the *what* ensures the success of cloud modernization. We explored different tools from IBM Garage to identify and assess the right candidate for the cloud journey. Finally, we explored different techniques to answer the *how* with proper decision and planning. We explored the different IBM Cloud services, software, and technology that can help answer the question of *how* appropriately.

In the next chapter, we will focus on the execution or implementation of cloud modernization through **cloud-native development**. The success of cloud modernization depends on the practices and methods followed during the development phase.

Further reading

- CAST Highlight: Visit `https://www.castsoftware.com`, then click on **PRODUCTS** on the top bar, which will show a drop-down menu where you need to click on **CAST Highlight**.

- For IBM ADDI, visit the following link: `https://www.ibm.com/products/app-discovery-and-delivery-intelligence` and explore the details.

- For Microservice Builder, visit the following link: `https://www.ibm.com/blogs/cloud-computing/2017/06/22/continuous-delivery-microservices-builder/`.

Part 2: Cloud-Native Methods, Practices, and Technology

The second part of the book discusses the end-to-end journey for cloud adoption. Each chapter provides real-world use cases as reference solutions along with different IaaS, PaaS, and SaaS services from different public cloud providers. The main objectives of *Part 2* are to help you to develop applications to be ready for cloud deployment and to adopt the right modernization plan for application migration.

This part of the book comprises the following chapters:

- *Chapter 4, Developing Applications in a Cloud Native Way*
- *Chapter 5, Exploring Application Modernization Essentials*

4

Developing Applications in a Cloud Native Way

Cloud-native development practice is the key to cloud modernization and application migration success. Cloud-native development is a lightweight, modular, and highly automated comprehensive approach to the different activities of cloud-agnostic application development processes, such as the following:

- Developing functionality as independent services and exposing them via an API

- Ensuring the high availability and high throughput of the application

- Establishing a DevOps pipeline for the application's continuous integration and deployment

- Ensuring the testing of unit functions, integration, regression, and the performance of the application

- Ensuring clean code of a high quality

- Identifying the threat model for applications and taking the necessary steps

- Establishing the process for a disaster exercise with a disaster recovery test

- Establishing a release process for the application

This chapter will discuss cloud native development practices in detail. There are three popular cloud-native development methods:

- The Twelve-Factor method

- IBM Design Thinking

- The IBM Garage application development method

The Twelve-Factor method

First, let us get familiar with the Twelve-Factor method. Along with the twelve core factors for this methodology, we have also described some additional fundamental factors in *Table 4.1*:

#	Factors	Description
1	Code base	There should be a single master source for the code. Single-repo code can be deployed in multiple isolated environments using a DevOps pipeline and revision control. The master code base remains singlular.
2	Dependencies	A straightforward dependency management process is established. First, all DevOps pipelines across multiple applications should be integrated with a single dependency repository. Second, dependencies must be approved and authorized. Finally, they need to be upgraded periodically.
3	Configuration	Configuration must not be hardcoded in the code base; instead, it must be stored in the environments. A process for configuration management is established.
4	Backing services	Backing services are treated as attached resources.
5	Build, release, run	The deployment should hop through different stages of test, build, and deploy or release and run.
6	Processes	It is essential for cloud-native applications to be isolated services that can be run as stateless processes.
7	Port binding	Services should be exposed through specific port binding.
8	Concurrency	Applications are treated as a process, as they can be scaled out and scaled in as per requirements.
9	Development/ production parity	The platform configuration for dev, test, and production should be the same.
10	Disposability	Applications can be deployed and shut down gracefully as they are fault tolerant.
12	Logging	Logs are events triggered by applications and user interaction. Logging must follow distributed tracing concept.
13	Admin processes	Platform administration and cluster administration should be well-defined processes.
14	Observability	Monitoring end-to-end solutions is essential in a cloud-native environment as components can fail at any time. An observability solution is integrated so that notifications and other automation can start autonomously at the time of major or minor incident.
15	Optimization	Applications should have capabilities to configure and monitor expected resource utilization constraints.
16	Security by design	Applications should be developed and designed by keeping security as a central focus.

#	Factors	Description
17	Audit	Audit capabilities should be exposed.
18	Measure	Development practice should focus on measuring success and failure. The golden signals of observability, such as latency and throughput, should be measured and monitored. The error budgets for each operation and functionality should be pre-defined.
19	Blue/green test	Any different version of the same application with the same code base can be deployed on the same platform.
20	Interoperability	The application often becomes a participant in an ecosystem of services. Therefore, the interoperability between the application and the other system parts should be well defined.
21	Resiliency by design	The infrastructure, application components, database, DevOps pipeline, and all other components should be individually resilient for a highly available and resilient solution.
22	Telemetry	Telemetry is monitoring an application's performance, health, and critical metrics in complicated and highly distributed environments. Therefore, real-time monitoring and telemetry are essential for application development and deployment.

Table 4.1 – Extended Twelve-Factor methodology for cloud-native development

In the following subsections, we will describe different cloud-native application development methodology factors.

Code base

A single code base is used as the single source of truth. There are different patterns for using a single code base. In this section, we describe a relatively conservative approach. Instead of making the master the parent branch for development, a second branch is created for development. Pushing to both the development and master branch must be peer-reviewed. Any developer in the application development team can branch out from a dedicated branch for development, as shown *Figure 4.1*.

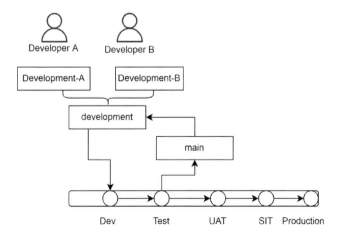

Figure 4. 1 – Single code base

Dependencies

A well-established dependency management repository acts as the central repo for all validated and authenticated dependencies should be established, which will be accessible by developers. Developers should look for the following:

- All dependencies identify, declare, and isolate any external dependencies.
- Dependencies must be consistent in all environments.
- The central repo for dependencies must be updated to avoid any conflict and backdated code.
- These dependencies must be pulled down during the build process.
- Dependencies must be explicitly declared with the associated version.
- The latest version of each dependency must be used in the application.
- Instead of packaging third-party libraries inside a microservice, it is possible to specify all dependencies in a configuration file, such as the `settings.gradle` file.

Configuration

Configuration can be a URL, link, or any other properties essential for applications. Some of the best practices that need to be followed to manage configuration are as follows:

- Configuration should be separated from application code.
- No hardcoded configuration is allowed.
- Configuration should be stored in an isolated environment separately, and only access configuration is stored in the corresponding environment. For example, configuration related to both the development and production environments should be stored in the corresponding environment branch in GitHub or a vault.
- Configuration is used at runtime rather than ingrained in the code.
- Configuration change management procedures should be defined clearly.

Backing services

Cloud-native development is focused on flexibility. Therefore, the adoption of backing services as bound resources helps applications be resilient with loose coupling between services and deployment. Backing services are all the middleware services required for the application to run, for example, databases, message queues or event streams, caching systems, notification services, monitoring services, governance systems, and so on. The critical system regarding backing services is as follows:

- Applications will only declare or provide the requirements for the backing system.
- External configuration should manage the actual application and backing system binding.

- The underlying platform or environment should control the configuration for the binding backing system to a specific application. Therefore, applications in the development environment can be configured as an instance of the MongoDB database. Similarly, applications in production can be connected to a separate instance of the MongoDB database.

- No hardcoded connection is allowed for a backing system connection to the specific instance of the corresponding system.

- The configuration for each environment should be packaged with application artifacts during the build state.

The build stage and run stage

Application deployment must run through at least the build stage and run stage during deployment and delivery. Some practices that should be followed to ensure this fifth factor are as follows:

- Each stage must be defined clearly with corresponding processes.

- There should not be any cycles among the states. States should be strictly separated from each other.

- Each state will be defined clearly. For example, the build state focuses on building everything essential to the application; therefore, no additional steps besides packaging the artifacts for the application should be defined in the build state.

- The output of the release state should have a unique ID.

Process

Applications should execute as a single, stateless process in any environment. Any process that requires a long execution time should be an external system to the application. This factor is mandatory in ensuring the resiliency of applications as containers can be killed at any time for any reason. Therefore, the states of the application should be managed within the application. So, if an application goes down, the corresponding state should not be lost.

Port binding

The host and port used to access the service should be provided by the environment, not baked into the application. Each service should be associated with a corresponding port.

Concurrency

Elasticity is mandatory for cloud-native applications. Any cloud-agnostic application should be able to be scaled up and down without any further configuration, unlike monolith applications that can only be vertically scaled by adding CPUs, RAM, and other virtual or physical resources. Nevertheless, modern containerization can make horizontal scaling even easier. Horizontal scaling results in creating multiple instances of the same process rather than a significant process.

Dev/prod parity

The lower environment should be identical to the production environment from the point of configuration and other settings. Therefore, testing and development of the product will be in a similar environment to production. The ultimate goal for an enterprise is to ensure that developers can release multiple fixes and features per day. This will only be possible if the automated DevOps pipeline can test the new changes in the lower environment with high confidence and ensure a seamless release to production.

Disposability

The Cattle vs Pets model is a critical model for cloud-native applications. A cloud-native application should be treated like cattle, where any one of the cattle could be lost or added without any emotional impact. Similarly, cloud-native application instances can be scaled in and destructed gracefully. They have no dependencies. For example, when a cloud-native application shuts down gracefully, it does not need to do any house-cleaning activities that could impact other applications or backing systems. Applications can be deployed and destructed as per requirements at any time. In addition, applications must be fault tolerant by design and implemented to enforce disposability features.

Optimization

Cloud-native applications must be optimized and disposable. If an application shutdown is disrupted due to compute exhaustion or a memory leak issue, that is unacceptable. Therefore, resource utilization should be configurable for cloud-native applications. For example, if a container requests a resource, Kubernetes only schedules it on a node that can give it that resource. Kubernetes ensures that applications are allocated the right amount of resources. Similarly, it also ensures that the correct number of resources are configured for the application in a YAML file.

Logging

Logging is essential for cloud-native development. Some cloud-native practices for logging are as follows:

- Distributed tracing: logging should be done on the microservice and component level. Lower-level logging enables the identification of services and components from the logging.

- Logs should be treated as event streams in real time.

- Proper monitoring alerts and segmentation should be created around the logging.

Administration process

This factor focuses on decoupling administrative and management activity from services or functions. Therefore, independent management capabilities are engaged for management activities such as platform updates, database migration, and microservices that can focus on business logic. This improves the traceability and debugging of applications.

Observability

Observability includes *monitoring, activity tracking,* and *logging.* Monitoring should include components and capabilities to monitor infrastructure, applications, storage, and other parts of the solution. *Table 4.2* includes the scope of observability for cloud-native application platforms:

Cloud Service Monitoring	<ul><li>Monitor cloud services</li><li>Cloud services and utilization</li><li>Cloud processes</li><li>Cloud service API access</li><li>Network controllers</li><li>Network policy and configuration</li><li>Storage controller and dashboard</li><li>Logging and activity</li></ul>
Infrastructure Monitoring	<ul><li>Monitor platform cluster resources</li><li>Monitor hardware failures through SNMP traps / MIB wherever feasible.</li><li>Monitor **operating system** (**OS**) services and processes.</li><li>Monitor hypervisor availability.</li><li>Monitor OS event logs.</li><li>Monitor high availability cluster status, resource group status, and correct problems identified wherever applicable.</li><li>Publish periodic reports for different KPIs based on the technical agreement with the client.</li><li>Leverage the console and tools provided by the target cloud and pre-defined toolchain.</li><li>Perform root cause analysis for any performance incident.</li><li>Generate reports for the availability status of different workloads.</li><li>Identify all essential alerts for platform monitoring.</li><li>Configure all essential alerts.</li><li>Participate in war room collaboration during critical situations/outages/debugging.</li><li>Collect logging and provide root cause analysis.</li><li>Set up monitoring software agents.</li><li>Diagnose transaction failure alerts/incidents and route them to the appropriate resolver group.</li></ul>

Capacity Monitoring and Management	• Provide dashboard/reports on Symphony and Scale performance and trends in order for the client to evaluate existing capacity commitments or job prioritization. • Monitor performance metrics of Symphony and Scale clusters and report any findings or tell-tale signs of future issues.
Security Health Check Monitoring	• Perform security health checks periodically.

Network Monitoring	• Monitor the security of network components:
	
	  • Security policies, network policies, and firewall policy management
	
	  • Security group management

Logging and Observability	Collect audit logs on all critical systems based on the technical agreement and client specification.
Performance Monitoring	Performance monitoring of the following components: • Monitor the resource usage of the runtime environments of the application components (for example, memory monitoring). • Manage cluster configuration for potential performance degradation and optimization.

Table 4.2 – Scope of observability

Security by design

Security by design is essential for the application development factor. Some of the essential practices for this factor are as follows:

- Code quality checking during the build phase.
- Dependency checking during the platform's build phase to guard against vulnerabilities.
- API design should also cover threat modeling.
- Vulnerability management should be integrated into the build phase in the DevOps pipeline.
- Automated security reviews for each release should be integrated with the pipeline.
- Penetration testing should be part of the application development test in the DevOps pipeline.
- Container security.

- Authorization and authentication should be used for the application as well as data access.

- Role-based access control management should be used for functions and services.

- Privileged user access groups should be used for different operations.

Blue/green test

Cloud-native applications may need to be upgraded due to patch updates or other configuration changes. In those cases, both the new and old versions of the application should be able to run independently on the same platform. For example, Kubernetes has a deployment object. Two or more different deployment `config` objects can be deployed on the platform independently.

Interoperability

Interoperability is essential for integration and API management, ensuring communication between heterogeneous systems without massive changes or development. Here are some recommended best practices to enforce the *API-first* model:

- The API should be defined and described with a clear definition, input, and output.

- Each API should be defined using a description language. The API should behave according to the description and definition.

- Each API should focus on a single business logic to avoid complexity. In addition, each API should be very clearly designed to be as effective as possible and easily mocked up.

- The focus should be on *what* rather than *how* when defining the API. So, the description should answer the following questions:

  - What is the input for the API?

  - What are the types for each input, that is, request or path?

  - What is the output for the API?

  - What is the business requirement for the API?

  - What is the protocol for the API?

Resiliency by design

Applications should be designed so they can be automatically scaled up or down. For example, Kubernetes provides horizontal scaling capabilities, which allows us to have a higher number of pods during the peak of the application's user demand and a lower number of pods during periods of lower demand.

Telemetry

Telemetry should include a description and real-time monitoring for the following:

- Domain-specific metrics specific to different teams and units of the organization.

- Health and system metrics for applications are good examples of telemetry. Therefore, each microservice should expose a health check API that can indicate the microservice's status at any time of the day.

- Health and system metrics including application start, shutdown, scaling, web request tracing, and the results of periodic health checks.

The Twelve-Factor method defines best practices for developing any modern cloud-native application. Once we are familiar with cloud-native application best practices and basic concepts, we need to establish a solid framework for application modernization. The following section discusses the IBM Design Thinking framework, which enforces the user-driven method to solve any problem with empathy and a unified approach.

IBM Design Thinking

IBM Design Thinking is described as a framework to solve problems in any domain at the speed and scale of the modern enterprise. The essential components of IBM Design Thinking practices are principles, keys, and the end-to-end loop.

Principles of IBM Design Thinking

There are three principles of the IBM Design Thinking framework:

- Users' needs are drivers for growth and metrics for success.

- Relentless innovation to improve the user experience.

- Diversity among development teams.

Users' needs are drivers for growth and metrics for success

The user's need is the focus of the product. Therefore, the number of features and the functionality released are not measured metrics for success; rather, user satisfaction and how well the user's requirements are fulfilled is the definition of success. In this framework, developers should build their user story with a definition of done, reflecting how well requirements are satisfied. In short, the metrics or language used for measuring success and "done" must be user-centered. While developing an application, the focus should remain on user requirements. Sometimes, the business case may not be connected directly to user requirements.

However, they must provide a better platform for a better user experience. Often, organizations prioritize the cost of delivery over user experience. Design thinking is not against that practice. However, there needs to be a balance between cost and user experience. Large organizations adopt different methods such as different surveys, synthetic monitoring, and continuous feedback to ensure that user experience directly impacts the application development and requirement analysis. The following practices can ensure that user needs are reflected in the application development stages:

- Enable synthetic monitoring and digital behavior monitoring.

- Enable continuous feedback from end users to validate the experience.

- Hold a Design Thinking workshop at each iteration of the development life cycle.

- Establish a review board to validate the application against the required user experience.

Relentless innovation to improve the user experience

There was a map in my room when I was a child, and I often forgot which was south and which was north. Looking at a paper map and asking passersby was my only choice to find any address in an unknown town. Now I give voice commands to my phone, which navigates me toward my destination. People's needs may not change drastically, however, the way of doing things may change. Users are looking for better and more flexible ways to execute operations. Therefore, analytics, evaluation, and user experience feedback need to be a continuous process, and the result of that evaluation and innovation must be reflected in applications. Developers need to find a way to monitor users' digital behavior and tweak applications to provide a better experience. Therefore, the following practices should be established:

- The interface, user interaction, and the interoperability of different functions, as well as applications, should be well designed.

- Each piece of code in an application must be reviewed and evaluated against the user experience level.

Diversity among development teams

Having access to the end user's experience is crucial for Design Thinking. This is assisted by having diversity among the development team members.

IBM Design Thinking keys

IBM Design Thinking has three keys:

- Hills

- Playbacks

- Sponsor users

Hills

Hills explain user requirements. Here are three hill statements:

- As a user, I want to create a personal blogging application with analytics capabilities so that I can understand my audience's demography.

- As a teacher, I want to create an assignment hub, where my students' records will be saved in a database, and the corresponding assignment will be saved in file storage so that I can score the assignment and finally share them as a mobile notification.

- As a student, I want to log in to my assignment system securely within two seconds so that I can upload my assignment files.

Each hill statement can represent an epic in the agile development method. Each hill statement emphasizes the *three w metadata*: who, what, and wow. For example, in the second hill statement, we can outline the three w metadata as follows:

- Who `<User: Entity>`: Teacher

- What `<Verb: Functionality>`: save, save; in last part (wow): score, share

- Wow `<last part, relative sentence>`: mobile notification

Playbacks

Playbacks are pre-release demos for stakeholders. Users are the critical audience of these playbacks to ensure feedback.

Sponsor users

To drive the requirements for the solution, we need to determine the correct user group to be the sponsor users. The following questions are used for this:

- Are they representative of the target user?

- Are they personally invested in the outcome?

- Are they available to collaborate?

The primary role of the sponsor users is to reduce the gap between assumptions and the natural state of progress.

Loop

The execution occurs in a loop between *observing*, *reflecting*, and *making*. If observation and reflection are not implemented, the complete analysis is meaningless; similarly, implementation and reflection on the business case without observing the user's needs and experience is a blind journey. Therefore, the implementation should be continuously reflected upon and analyzed to reduce the gap between imagination and observations of reality.

To understand IBM Design Thinking, we also need to cover some related topics:

- Empathy mapping
- Value stream mapping

Now that we are familiarized with the IBM Design Thinking framework, we need to explore how we can practice this framework in our daily application development. The IBM Garage application development method enforces Twelve-Factor and IBM Design Thinking in application modernization. The following section will explore the IBM Garage application development method.

The IBM Garage application development method

The **IBM Garage** application development method has proven to be significantly successful for enterprise application development at scale. This practice is defined based on IBM Design Thinking and extended Twelve-Factor methods. *Figure 4.3* shows the Garage loop for the development and management of enterprise applications. This practice is established based on the following goals:

- Enterprise Design Thinking at scale
- Agile for co-located and distributed teams
- DevOps for continued delivery and operations
- Digital talent and culture change
- Site reliability engineering

The core practices for IBM Garage can be divided into three categories:

- Co-create
- Co-execute
- Co-operate

The following section explores these three core practices in detail:

- **Co-create**

    - *Discover*: This stage enforces analysis and research on the current state and the target state using tools, processes, workshops, IBM Design Thinking practices, and other related activities to understand the current and target state of any given problem. The core focus of this phase is to understand the business requirement. A set of practices ensures a clear understanding and analysis of the business case. Some of the practices are as follows:

        - Frame the business opportunity within an achievable scope boundary.

        - Conduct multiple technical discovery sessions and workshops to gather data from multiple sources.

        - Identify bottlenecks by using value stream mapping.

        - Define business objectives with a clear definition of done.

        - Define organizational roles.

        - Define metrics for cost, the performance of the platform, and other resources.

        - Pay back technical debt.

        - Start with boot camp training.

        - Recognize the value of data.

        - Outline the total cost of ownership for the cloud.

        - Establish a process to assess cloud workloads regularly.

        - Translate a business problem into an AI and data science solution.

        - Mitigate risks early by adopting shift-left test practices.

        - Define the business opportunity statement with a clear goal, definition of success, and evaluation metrics.

        - Get value from technical spikes.

        - Validate the business outcomes of IT transformation.

        - Define waves and a long-term roadmap to scale transformation.

- *Envision*: A single squad of the team is given the task of designing a prototype to solve the given problem. This prototype is often described as a hypothesis. Envisioning is driven by defining a **Minimal Viable Product** (**MVP**). There are multiple MVPs in the life cycle of any project. One of the best practices is to identify at most three hill statements for each MVP and design the envisioned solution for that MVP only and iterate over and over until all the hill statements are implemented. Therefore, we can divide the activities of the envision state into two different categories, that is, MVP design and build, and beyond MVP. The following best practices are essential for a prosperous envision state in the product development life cycle:

  - MVP design and build:

    - Get started with Enterprise Design Thinking.

    - Conduct an Enterprise Design Thinking workshop to define a roadmap and an MVP.

    - Define a service portfolio.

    - Evaluate tools for DevOps and management operations.

    - Analyze affinity among different applications and components.

    - Execute a what-if analysis to understand the non-functional requirements.

    - Validate designs with sponsor users.

    - Define personas.

    - Understand users through empathy maps.

    - Solve problems through ideation and Design Thinking workshops.

    - Understand users through scenario mapping.

    - Create an MVP.

    - Conduct user research for continuous feedback.

  - Beyond the MVP:

    - Align projects by using hill statements.

    - Inception.

    - Write user stories from the hill statements.

    - Share ideas by using wireframes.

    - Use an IT maturity model.

    - Design for accessibility.

    - Design for mobile and responsive UIs to provide a better user experience.

    - Build prototypes – no one prototype is the solution for everything.

- Keep the focus on users to guide meaningful outcomes.

- The design solution for data, AI, and analytics besides applications.

- Define a data strategy.

- Normalize data at its atomic level so it can be measured.

- Understanding data needs to support AI and data science solutions.

- Run thought experiments and hypothesis-driven analysis.

- Some of the useful tools for successful envision development are Invasion and Mural.

- **Co-execute**

  - *Develop*: The application is developed with continuous feedback from different stakeholders. Other extended Twelve-Factor methodologies are followed during the development or implementation phases of the project. Some of the core practices for development with the IBM Garage method are as follows:

    - Focus on continuous testing:
      - Test-driven development.
      - Improve code through refactoring.
      - Behavior-driven development.
      - Contract-driven testing.
      - UI testing.
      - Automate tests for continuous delivery.
      - Automate continuous integration.
      - Start performance testing early.
      - Protect workload, data and applications from cross-site scripting attacks.
    - Code in one-day bits:
      - Develop code in small batches.
      - Design software iteratively.
      - Plan an iteration.
      - Manage work in a rank-ordered backlog.
      - Program in pairs.
      - Practice remote pair programming.
      - Enforce secure coding practices.

- Architecture considerations:
  - Prepare for security compliance.
  - Apply the "just enough architecture" concept to avoid unnecessary complexity.
  - Get started with architectures for infrastructure, middleware, and applications.
  - Get started with a microservices architecture.
  - Document architectures by using the C4 model.
  - Apply the Domain-Driven Design concept to the microservices architecture.
  - Implement distributed tracing in microservices-based applications.
  - Design the platform so that it can be managed using automated operations.
  - Break up monolith applications by using the Chunking strategy and the Strangler pattern.
  - Enforce threat modeling to secure the platform from intrusion and malicious activities.
- Accelerate delivery:
  - Automate continuous delivery through a delivery pipeline.
  - Remove manual steps by using automated deployment.
  - Build and deploy application or other workload using continuous delivery.
  - Automate database deployment.
  - Integrate and automate globalization.
- Data, AI, and analytics:
  - Deliver a singular data function.
  - Construct the data topology.
  - Build data storage architecture such as a data lake and a data warehouse.
  - Prepare data for AI and data science using DataOps.
- Related tools:
  - GitLab
  - Git repos and issue tracking
  - Eclipse Orion Web IDE
  - GitHub issues
  - Trello
  - Microsoft Visual Studio Code

- Bitbucket
- Unit test tools for web apps
- SpeedCurve
- Jenkins
- JIRA
- Karma
- Gradle
- Ionic
- Protractor
- IBM Cloud App ID
- Android Studio
- Angular
- Xcode
- Apache Cordova
- CocoaPods
- IBM API Connect
- Datical
- Linting tools
- IBM Cloud Tools for Swift
- Slack
- IBM Engineering Test Management
- IBM Cloud Continuous Delivery
- Delivery Pipeline
- Sauce Labs
- IBM UrbanCode Deploy
- Nexus
- Artifactory
- Tekton

- *Reason*: Enforce AI to analyze, detect, and solve different problems. Infusing AI generates different required insights and a better understanding of the solution. The fundamental practice for reasoning is as follows:

  - Integrate AI into applications, data, and processes for automation and insight.

  - Enhance and optimize existing AI and data science models.

  - Design a data topology.

  - Understand data requirements through assessments and exploration.

  - Prepare data for machine learning.

  - Evaluate and select a machine learning algorithm.

  - Test-driven development and AI machine learning.

- **Co-operate**

  - *Learn*: Multiple MVP runs iteratively with continuous learning. Some of the main subjects require continuous observation, such as the following:

    - Learn about users and their experience.

    - Enforce hypothesis-driven development and run user experiments to validate the corresponding hypothesis.

    - Envision the user experience.

    - Enforce A/B testing or blue/green testing for the platform.

    - Apply coverage analytics.

    - Detect security weaknesses by using dynamic vulnerability scanning.

    - Learn about processes for release, evaluation, and other purposes.

    - Run playbacks to gather feedback.

    - Implement analytics to improve the code quality.

    - Leverage operational analytics to identify the scope for improvement.

    - Hold a retrospective.

    - Transformation optimization.

    - Use key performance indicators to measure and guide progress.

  - *Operate*: Automation is the key to success for the seamless operation of the platform. Automation enables high availability and resiliency within an optimized budget for supporting infrastructure, middleware, data platforms, and other resources. Here are some best practices to enforce site reliability engineering and service as well as value engineering for operations:

- Ensure the app is running when users need it.
- Deploy and manage applications with container orchestration.
- Autoscale applications.
- Continuously deliver with the dark launch and feature toggles.
- Ensure application-level high availability and reversibility in the cloud.
- Build for reliability.
- Ensure operational excellence.
- Enforce the principles of modern service management.
- Test software resiliency.
- Recover fast from incidents and disasters without disruption to business operations.
- Implement a high-availability architecture.
- Automate operations.
- Change the focus of change management.
- Get started with incident analysis.
- Analyze problems by using the 5-Hows principle.
- Address the root cause of an incident while managing technical debt.
- Clarify roles and responsibilities by using a RACI matrix.
- Implement site reliability engineering.
- Operationalize application readiness.
- Communicate effectively about outages.
- Service integration and management.
- Ensure transparency by measuring service-level objectives.
- Monitor applications by using golden signals.
- Solve problems in a virtual war room.
- Enable GitOps for continuous operation.
- Automate operations tasks.
- Automate application monitoring.
- Assess the operational readiness of the application platform.
- Improve application resiliency with chaotic testing.

- Prevent system failure with the Circuit Breaker pattern.

- Capture diagnostic information by using **First Failure Data Capture (FFDC)**.

- Automate alert notifications for first responders.

- Ensure high availability and disaster recovery for on-premises applications.

- Collaborate by using ChatOps.

- Back up cloud-native apps.

- Implement health check APIs for microservices.

- Use runbooks to automate operation activities.

- Monitor IBM Cloud services deployed on the cloud.

- Limit the effect of an outage by using limited blast radius practices.

- Implement automated operations using data, AI, and analytics.

- Establish data governance.

- Deploy an AI model.

- Ensure data resilience.

Related tools recommended by IBM:

- Akamai Global Traffic Management

- PagerDuty

- IBM Engineering Workflow Management

- New Relic

- IBM Cloud Monitoring

- IBM Cloud Activity Tracker

- IBM Schematics

- IBM Cloud

- IBM Cloud Kubernetes Service

- Load Impact

- IBM Db2 products

- IBM Netcool Operations Insight

- Argo CD

Culture is at the core of all practices in the IBM Garage methodology. *Figure 4.2* shows the seven fundamental practices of the IBM Garage methodology for cloud-native application development:

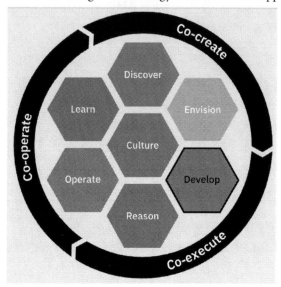

Figure 4.2 – IBM Garage methodology practices

Development teams must have certain cultural traits, as follows:

- Fail fast and learn fast.
- Have fun at work.
- Manage daily work by using Kanban.
- Run daily stand-up meetings.
- Create a clear definition of *done*.
- Plan physical spaces for excellent outcomes.
- Assemble the team to support a data-driven project.
- Empower product owners.
- Interview through pair programming.
- Hold agile ceremonies.
- Conduct workshops to align the team.
- Modernize the organization in terms of practices, tools, and cultural points of view.
- Evolve from waterfall to continuous delivery.

- Build effective squads.

- Define roles in a squad.

- Lead a squad.

- Align development and operations for success.

- Transform through a center of competency.

- Establish cloud governance.

- Establish a target operating model.

- Define critical attributes for cloud governance.

- Enact continuous improvement by using a decision-making framework.

- Get started with cloud transformation.

- Get started with remote collaboration.

- Build a Garage culture and squads.

- Collaborate through social coding.

- Pay back technical debt.

- Evaluate the design, performance, and configuration for data and applications.

IBM Garage also helps to continue the end-to-end journey for development and modernization. *Figure 4.3* shows the entire life cycle of the IBM Garage methodology:

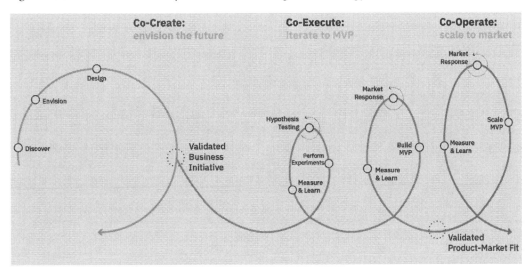

Figure 4.3 – IBM Garage at scale for enterprise

The journey starts with discovering the business requirements from user feedback, market research analysis, AI infusion, Design Thinking workshops, and other analytical activities. The hypothesis is formed based on the analysis. The hypothesis is evaluated based on user experience and business objective. Different design tools can be used to design the prototype for each hypothesis. These hypotheses must be discussed with the sponsor users and presented in front of them in multiple playbacks. It is also essential to understand the market response. **Blue/Green** or **A/B** deployment can help receive a response from different geographical markets. Based on the market response, the team needs to determine the scope for the MVP and develop the MVP. There can be multiple MVPs developed in an iterated fashion. Retrospective analysis of each MVP will help developer squads to learn and improve the product iteratively. Once the MVP is released, a continuous feedback and evaluation channel should be established to evaluate the product's value.

Summary

This chapter focused on development practices for application development and modernization. We discussed different methods for cloud-native application development. We also discussed IBM-recommended practices, methods, frameworks, and tools.

The next chapter explores the application modernization process, following the practices, methods, framework, and tools discussed.

References

- Creating cloud-native applications: Twelve-Factor applications: `https://developer.ibm.com/articles/creating-a-12-factor-application-with-open-liberty/`

- IBM Design Thinking: `https://www.ibm.com/design/thinking/page/framework`

- IBM Garage Methodology: `https://www.ibm.com/garage/method/develop/`

- Problem analysis by using the 5 Hows: `https://www.ibm.com/garage/method/practices/manage/five-hows/`

5

Exploring Application Modernization Essentials

Application modernization using cloud services and technologies is essential for organizations. Most organizations have already adopted the cloud as their strategic platform for applications and workload deployment. The digital and Agile transformation process of application modernization can create a ripple of positive benefits for organizations. An efficient and effective application modernization program will ensure effective delivery, cost efficiency, user engagement, innovation capacity, and overall growth in performance and revenue. These results can drive value for an organization's stakeholders at an unseen level. This chapter will discuss different aspects of a successful application modernization program.

We will cover the following main topics:

- Planning for application modernization
- Assessment and requirement analysis
- A reference solution for application modernization
- Use cases for application modernization

Planning for application modernization

Although applications are the core workload for modernization, modernizing infrastructure, data, processes, tools, practices, and culture for a successful application modernization program is also required. The planning process for application modernization is depicted in *Figure 5.1*:

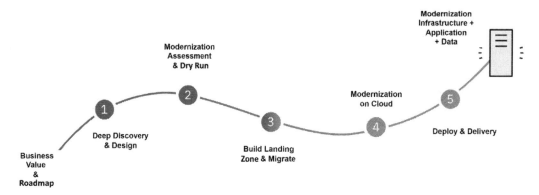

Figure 5.1 – Modernization journey

Business value and roadmap

Application modernization aims to replace the existing legacy platform with a modern platform. The core characteristics of modern application platforms are defined based on the **Business Value (BV)** and roadmap. To determine the core BV, we should consider the following:

- What applications can move to the cloud?
- Where should applications land on the target – private as well as public cloud, **Platform as a Service (PaaS)**, or **Software as a Service (SaaS)**?
- What level of cloud enablement and modernization is required to move the applications?
- Where to start – what are the quick wins and what is the overall schedule?
- How will the application be modernized?
- When will the application modernization start and end?

Different tools, such as BlueCat from IBM, can help with answering the preceding questions. Once the data relating to the previous questions is collected and analyzed, it is easy to develop the roadmap. *Table 5.1* provides an example roadmap for application modernization:

Non-Strategic Apps	Strategic Non-Differentiating Apps	Strategic Differentiating Apps	Retain and Optimize
20% rationalization and decommission	10% replace with "as a service"	60% modernization and migration	10% retain and optimize
12% consolidate to target app		12% Re-Host	
6% strategic decommission		15% Re-Architect	
2% achieve and decommission		15% Re-Platform	
		8 % Re-Innovate	

Table 5.1 – Roadmap for application modernization

Here, the organization classifies its workload into four different groups. For example, firstly, 20% of non-strategic applications are planned for decommissioning with rationalization. Next, cloud services can replace 10% of strategic applications. Finally, 60% of strategic applications are suitable candidates for modernization using one or more migration patterns. The rest of the applications can be retained for optimization first, and modernization can be done later in the cloud. *Table 5.2* shows the most remarkable data points collected from the current IT estate or landscape to identify workloads for different buckets:

Key Area	Example Data Point
Application classification	Key application attributes include identifiers, a description of core functionality, users, and connections.
Cost	The total cost of service and middleware licenses, application support, hardware, and infrastructure support needed to be estimated based on the baseline size of the target platform.
Business profiling	Criticality of the application and impact of failure/outage (financial, regulatory, operational, and reputation); strategy alignment; legal and regulatory requirements; data and security; and non-functional and **Service-Level Agreements** (**SLAs**)/black-out dates.
IT profiling	Level of technical debt in infrastructure and software versions; IT risks and issues, such as the likelihood of failure and compliance; supportability of the application, such as digital knowledge base or critical personnel dependency with limited documentation; and flexibility and potential for future growth.
Retire	Last date of cut-off or retirement of resources, read-only applications, data retention and retrieval requirements, downward growth trend or under-utilized environments and the requirement to migrate users, data, or interfaces.
Rationalization	Duplicate or redundant functions within a business area, multiple instances/versions supporting different groups of users, and availability of an existing or identified replacement application.

Table 5.2 – Core data points to analyze the current state of a workload for organizations

Deep discovery and design

Discovery is essential for modernization to understand the baseline applications, data, integration, dependencies, design, and infrastructure estate. This phase allows the organization to prioritize and plan the modernization of a legacy estate. A profound discovery of different components of the legacy estate provides a trusted knowledge base for planning and the next phase of the modernization program. The data gathered during this phase allows for better decision-making for modernization and provides the **Key Performance Indicators** (**KPIs**) and other parameters to quantify and track progress throughout the modernization life cycle from design to execution. Defining KPIs is crucial for the success of the modernization program , and this process has mammoth complexity. Therefore, only survey-based or interview-based discovery is not enough to understand the correct baseline of the current estate. This discovery stage has multiple steps.

Analysis

Automation and standard tools can generate detailed reports and identify dependencies, performance indicators, and affinities. IBM has several tools to enable this stage of modernization to be successful. IBM's Integration toolkit automatically gathers data and technology-specific tools and scripts. It discovers potential vulnerabilities, redundant tasks, affinities, and other applications. There are multiple resources, as discussed in *Chapter 4*, *Developing Applications in a Cloud Native Way*. Some examples of these tools are the **Transformation Extender** and Storage insights tools, which generate detailed analysis and reporting on collected data and reports on performance, technology debt, and affinity maps. The Transformation Repository and insights tools can plan the migration, reduce risk by understanding complexities, and accelerate *design* and *build* by automating the production of artifacts, including application questionnaires, design specifications, build sheets, and runbooks. This analysis is a continuously running event. Several IBM research assets and accelerators continuously discover current IT landscape attributes and update the analysis as the modernization program moves forward.

Data life cycle management

Once established, discovery data should be periodically refreshed to maintain currency and accuracy for migrations. The Cloud Integration and Modernization Toolkit maintains the baseline and master migration schedule, moves groups, and impacts changes in different workloads. In addition, collected data is maintained throughout the program and used to evaluate the modernization program.

Building a landing zone and migration

Some basic principles for designing a landing zone are as follows:

- The landing zone is usually built using an automated process. Therefore, the deployment of landing zones can be replicated as many times as required. This approach helps when geographic dispersion is required.

- Keep the landing zone simple and straightforward. Therefore, the operation and management process for the landing zone will be simple and effective.

- The landing zone should be extendable; therefore, even if we start with the minimum requirements, it can be extended by applying automatic provisioning of services from the designated service catalog on the platform. Similarly, the services and components can be destroyed gracefully in the case of downscaling the landing zone.

- The landing zone should ensure the required security and compliance. Different cloud services and infrastructure components must comply with the security controls defined for the landing zone.

- The landing zone design should provide the specification of the architecture. Therefore, the design can be used to build different landing zones.

- The landing zone usually consists of computing, storage, networking components, and different cloud-native services, such as firewalls, load balancing, encryption services, logging, monitoring, and **Identity and Access Management (IAM)**, to ensure that the application can be migrated to the landing zone. For example, *Figure 3.9* in *Chapter 3*, *Exploring Best Practices for the Cloud Journey*, shows the landing zone for the Landorous project.

- Functional and non-functional requirements for the solution will drive the components of the landing zone.

Modernization on the cloud

Once the landing zone is created, and workloads are moved to the cloud, it is essential to ensure that the modernization continues. After cloud adoption, organizations should focus on innovation and acceleration through cloud service adoption. Therefore, modernization on the cloud is very crucial for the success of business growth.

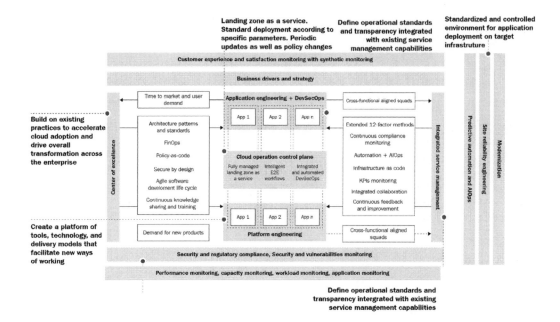

Figure 5.2 – Modernization of the cloud

Figure 5.2 shows that the end-to-end approach to modernization in the cloud focuses on some fundamental components, as follows:

- Automate the process of building a landing zone. Therefore, landing zone *build* and *management* can be provided as an automated service.

- Continuous operations should manage the complete platform. Without continuous management from a defined control plane, it is risky to maintain the desired level of KPIs and user experience.

- We should build a continuous practice to accelerate the modernization of the cloud and cloud adoption. This practice should be evaluated by time to market, demand for new products or features in applications, and user experience.

- **Platform engineering** should be an everyday activity to manage the platform's health. At the same time, automation, standard architecture patterns for platform components, **Financial Management Operations and Cultural Practice** (**FinOps**), and capacity management can improve the performance, as well as reducing the time to market.

- Security, compliance, and regulation should be part of the platform and be implemented as part of the design of the platform.

- Skill is another essential component. Developers, solution architects, operators, DevOps engineers, and security experts should continuously share knowledge in training sessions. Collaboration among squads will help them stay up to date with the ecosystem of the cloud, applications, and the demands of users.

- Enforce event-driven architecture for application and service integration.

- Modernize events and messages.

- Enforce **Artificial Intelligence Operations** (**AIOps**) for automated operations and a predictive self-healing mechanism for the infrastructure.

- Automation should be implemented as much as possible with the help of **policy as code** and **infrastructure as code**.

- Adopt **Site Reliability Engineering** (**SRE**) and platform engineering as a practice to modernize the cloud. At the same time, operations on the cloud should follow specific standards and always be controlled and configured according to the user's feedback and KPIs.

- Security controls should be implemented with continuous monitoring to avoid any violation. Policies such as *code* and *configuration policies* should be updated regularly. In addition, periodic assessments and audits, either manual or automatic, need to be in place to ensure a secured platform for the workload and applications on the cloud.

Modernize monitoring for the following:

- The health of cloud workloads, such as the continuous health monitoring of application, data, network, storage, security, policies, regulatory controls and other configurations.

- Performance management and monitoring with self-healing mechanism to maintain the desired performance for the cloud platform.

- Capacity management of the platform to ensure RightSizing, optimization of cloud waste, and budget planning.

- Synthetic monitoring of applications, UI, and activity to explore the user experience quality.

- The integrated operation and support model helps with incident management by providing automated anomaly detection, immediate notification, practical root cause analysis, and efficient incident management.

- The adoption of SRE culture is essential to continue modernization and research on modernization.

Deployment and delivery

After the code, configuration, and template are re-factored, they are deployed on the modernized platform. Applications should be deployed to production continuously and continue to deliver BV. To achieve this goal, some of the following features must be available to these applications on the modern cloud platform:

- Continuous modernization of workloads – incremental value realization

- Repetitive delivery (Agile/DevOps) to further drive incremental value

- SRE-based operational model

- Continuous improvement and feedback

- Automated SLA and other KPI monitoring to provide feedback for the next sprint

The end-to-end migration process is executed over multiple waves. Each wave focuses on customer requirements and their business strategies. The first wave of the cloud migration journey is the *design and discovery* phase, which may last from 1 to 3 weeks. During this phase, a deep analysis of the current estate of the organization is developed based on multiple IBM Garage workshops, automated tools, and processes. The core goal of this phase is to execute cloud modernization at scale with continuous innovation. Efficient and end-to-end planning is crucial for modernization. At the same time, establishing a practice for modernization is essential for success. We need to remember that cloud modernization is a continuous process for new greenfield workloads deployed on the cloud and workloads migrated from on-premises locations. The modernization program needs a motivation, which is described in detail in *Chapter 3, Exploring Best Practices for the Cloud Journey*. Once the motivation is identified, the next step is to determine the suitable workload (application, data, storage, and so on) for migration. Some metrics also need to be established to measure the success and failure of the modernization program. These metrics for drive the decisions, patterns, technology, tools, and skills required for modernization.

In the next section, we will focus on determining some critical metrics based on the fundamental requirement for any cloud modernization program.

Assessment and requirement analysis

The suitability of application modernization is measured through a mathematical formula applied to some related variables. These variables are often marked as **AppMod** variables. They can be measured individually. The idea is that they should be measured before application modernization and then either projected or measured afterward. Then, they should be calculated for the selected level of modernization: containerize, Re-Platform, Re-Factor, or externalize. Based on the organization's target, the variables will hold different values. The goal is to find what has changed for these variables over time, the **delta**. The delta will then be used in the formula.

Greg Hintermeister and Eric Herness have defined logic to determine different variables to understand the modernization strategy better. In their blog, they outline different application modernization variables, as follows:

Time Variable	Description (Development-Based)	Description (Operation-Based)
Provisioning (P)	Time to stand up environments (clusters, middleware, and pipelines, for example)	Time to stand up preproduction or production environments (clusters, middleware, and pipelines, for example)
Deployment (D)	Time to deploy new app instances in an existing environment	Time to deploy new app instances in an existing environment for production
Extensibility (E)	Time to add new function based on user needs or market changes	Not Applicable (N/A)
Scaling Speed (Ss)	N/A	Time to scale application to necessary levels to respond to demand
Resiliency (R)	N/A	Time to recover from a data center/environment outage
Maintenance (M)	N/A	Time to maintain running environments
Testing (T)	Time to test deployable units	N/A
Time to Market (Tm)	N/A	Time to deliver the new revenue-generating feature to market

Table 5.3 – Time-based application modernization variables

Application migration modernization involves cost. This cost may be due to the infrastructure, including compute, network storage and operations, labor, innovation, software and hardware licenses, and business assessment. Greg Hintermeister and Eric Herness have defined some variables to measure the cost of application modernization, as shown in the following table:

Variable	Description (Time-Based)
Infrastructure (I)	Cost of infrastructure (**Virtual Machines** (**VMs**), bare metal, and Kubernetes clusters), including what is needed for a ready reserve for future scaling needs
Labor (La)	Cost of labor per unit of measure
License (Li)	Cost of licensing for app runtime/middleware
Feature Revenue (Rf)	Revenue of a feature/unit of measure
AppMod Cost (Am)	Cost to modernize to the target level (containerize, Re-Platform, and refactor) multiplied by the cost per unit of measure

Table 5.4 – Cost-based application modernization variables

Some parameters that can compute essential matrices for cloud modernization are described in *Table 5.5*:

Parameters	Description	Computation
Time	The time saved across app life cycle stages by containerizing, repackaging, or re-factoring the application	$Vt = \Delta P + \Delta D + \Delta E + \Delta Ss + \Delta R + \Delta M + \Delta T$
Cost	The cost metrics determined from the time saved (*Vt*) and the labor costs (*La*) per unit measured	$Vc = Vt \cdot La$
Feature unit	The time saved delivering a revenue-generating feature and revenue per unit measured	$Vf = \Delta Tm \cdot Rf$ ΔTm = time saved delivering a revenue-generating feature Rf = revenue per unit
Total feature	Summation of feature units for all available features in the application	$VF = \sum_{i=0}^{f} Vf$
BV	The cost savings of less time developing (*Vc*), fewer infrastructure costs (*ΔI*), less licensing costs (*ΔIi*), plus the value of the features on the market <u>are</u> <u>increasing</u> faster (*Vf*), subtracting the investment to perform AppMod techniques (*Am*)	$Bv = Vc + Vf + \Delta I + \Delta Li - Am$

Table 5.5 – AppMod BV and other KPI calculations

In the previous section, we discussed the planning for application modernization and the cloud journey. Computing the BV for each application and selecting applications with a higher BV are the best candidate applications for application modernization. For example, we have removed the core **Enterprise Service Bus** (ESB) state and corresponding databases for the **Landorous** use case described in *Chapter 1, An Introduction to Hybrid Cloud Modernization*. To make a such an architectural decision as which component should be Retired or Re-Hosted, we can perform a small exercise to understand the **time saved** (ΔP) by simply provisioning different services after modernization, based on the comparative time for different provisioning services is shown in *Table 5.6*.

Similarly, other KPIs, as described in *Table 5.5*, are used to compute the BV for the modernization program of the ESB state mentioned in the **Landorous** use case. In this use case, additional workshops are conducted for other on-premises applications, mainframe applications, and file storage to identify the right IT landscape for the organization as the most suitable candidate for modernization. Finally, we have identified that the BV for ESB modernization is higher than other systems, and we selected ESB as the *what* or candidate for modernization:

New Cloud Service	Current (VMs)	Modernization	After Modernization
Database – provision a standalone database with a set of tables	2 weeks	**Database as a Service (DBaaS)**/ containerization	20 minutes
WebSphere	2-3 weeks	SaaS	60 seconds
MQ	2 weeks	MQ in IBM Cloud Pak for Integration with Terraform	8 minutes
Application integration	1 week	App Connect in IBM Cloud Pak for Integration with Terraform	6 minutes
API integrations	1-3 weeks	API Connect in IBM Cloud Pak for Integration with Terraform	6 minutes
Development pipeline	1-2 weeks	Deploy with IBM DevOps Commander	10 minutes
Total (before)	1,848 hours	Total (after)	51 minutes
ΔP = 1,847.09 hours			

Table 5.6 – Comparative time for service provisioning with and without modernization

In most cases, organizations move their applications and databases to the cloud and modernize them. However, the operation model remains old. Sometimes, they only forked a separate operation model for the cloud workload. As this forked operation model diversifies over time from the primary operation model, the operational model for the cloud workload and the on-premises workload becomes entirely unknown. Often, organizations forget that the complete ecosystem for the organization is a single system. The BV for the organization depends on the success of the complete ecosystem as a single system. However, when this division between the modern operation model and legacy operation model takes place, the end-to-end familiarity of the complete ecosystem gets destroyed, which introduces hundreds of complex issues and difficulties for the organization. Therefore, the global operating model for modern and legacy workloads must be interconnected and provide the same maturity level.

Modernization aims to immediately achieve a higher level of maturity for the operating model. For example, if an organization is currently at level 1, the main goal of modernization at the first stage is to move to level 2. *Table 5.7* describes different aspects that quantify the maturity level of the operation model of any organization's IT ecosystem:

Capabilities	L1	L2	L3	L4	L5
Time to market	Monthly	Bi-weekly	Weekly	Daily	Multiple times/day
Release frequency	Quarterly	Monthly	Bi-weekly	Weekly	Daily
Change frequency	Yearly	Quarterly	Monthly	Weekly	Daily
Workload containerization percentage	<10%	10-20%	20-40%	40-80%	>80%
Ratio of automation and infrastructure as code	<10%	10-20%	20-40%	40-80%	>80%
Automated DevOps and deployment(Number of commit for code commits)	<30	30-100	100-150	150-200	>200
Patch deployment ratio	<10%	10-25%	25-60%	60-90%	>90%
Number of manual security operations	>200	100-200	50-100	10-50	0-10
Resolution time	>1 month	<4 weeks	1-7 days	2-4 hours	15 minutes
Ratio of self-healing	<10%	10-20%	20-40%	40-80%	80%
Number of partners	0	1-2 (small)	1-5	5-20	>20

Table 5.7 – Maturity level for the operation model

In this section, we covered several matrices that help the modernization program with quality control and measurement.

The following section will discuss a reference solution for application modernization. In the reference solution, we will discuss the scope of the modernization project, including functional and non-functional requirements. We will also discuss the platform or *landing zone* that the applications will be migrated to and the corresponding reference architecture.

A reference solution for application modernization

We are using a monolithic application deployed on the Liberty **WebSphere Application Server (WAS)** for this reference solution. *Figure 5.3* depicts the application migration plan for this use case using the Re-Platform and Re-Host patterns. In the legacy platform, applications are not implemented following the extended Twelve-Factor App methodology. Therefore, they are not cloud-ready and cannot be migrated as is. In addition, some frameworks, such as Spring Boot, provide very comprehensive and easy-to-configure features that can expedite the re-factoring of monolithic applications to make them cloud-ready. In this case, only re-host or lift-and-shift can be used, as VM-to-VM is not sufficient for modernization.

Re-Platforming is also necessary to get the most efficient results. For a successful Re-Platform migration, applications should be Re-Architected and re-factored as part of modernization to make them cloud-ready through Re-Platforming. The first step is to discover the suitable candidate for Re-Platforming using the BV calculation described in *Table 5.5*. Then, IBM **Transformation Advisor** (**TA**) can be run for the applications running over WAS. TA can identify executable dependencies and estimate the time required to re-factor the application to move them to the cloud:

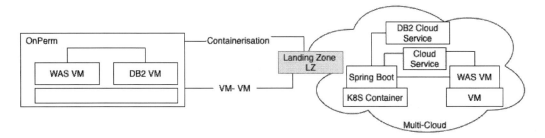

Figure 5.3 – Application migration and modernization on IBM Cloud

As existing applications are JAX-RS **Application Programming Interfaces** (**APIs**), they can be containerized with minimum effort. As a result, the landing zone for these applications is a containerized platform. However, sometimes, we cannot containerize all the applications currently deployed in the on-premises data center. They are suitable candidates for **Modernization On Cloud**. These applications can be moved to cloud first and later can be modernized using suitable patterns. For example, the part of the applications that cannot be containerized for different reasons l, can be moved to the cloud with the Re-Host pattern by creating a VM on the cloud and moving the workloads to the corresponding virtual landing zone on the cloud.

The next step is to design and build the landing zone with the necessary compute, storage, network, monitoring, security controls, and networking topology for the application to move to that landing zone. An operation model, cross-skill squad team, and continuous operation process should be established to ensure modernization on the cloud. Finally, applications should be deployed on the target platform and continue to run at scale.

We've now covered the functional and non-functional requirements for the use cases. The following section discusses the functional requirements explaining the new platform's nature, purpose, and business functionality.

Functional requirements

Let's discuss the functional requirement for this reference solution. *Table 5.8* shows the functional requirements for the reference solution:

#	Category	Details
1	Application migration assessment	Assess the current state of the applications and workload and design an efficient migration program for the applications deployed on-premises.
2	Design and build a landing zone	The system must provide an environment where data apps can be deployed.
3	Deploy at scale	Applications and other workloads need to be moved to the cloud and modernized on the cloud.
4	Platform management	Maintenance of the overall cloud platform.
5	Data migration	Data from on-premises needs to be migrated to the cloud.
6	Application management	DevOps pipeline for application delivery and integration is required.

Table 5.8 – Functional requirements

Similarly, we also need to understand the non-functional requirements for the nature and behavior of the to-be platform. Here, to-be is the new platform where the applications will be migrated.

Non-functional requirements

Non-functional requirements describe the platform's need for security, scalability, resiliency, and reliability. For different categories, the non-functional requirements are as follows:

- Application:

  - Re-factor applications following the extended 12-Factor App methodology.

  - Use cloud-native and open source services such as **IBM Cloud Kubernetes Service (IKS)**.

- Network:

  - Set up private network connectivity to access cloud services as well as the enterprise workload deployed to an on-premises platform.

  - Maintain IP addresses – **Bring Your Own IP (BYOIP)**.

  - Set up private network connectivity between applications and cloud services.

- Set up public secure network connectivity between applications and app users.

- Services are exposed over the internet.

- Geographic dispersion must be built to deploy applications globally to maintain the global demands for the application.

- Security:

  - Users must be authenticated by SSO and other authorization and authentication mechanisms.

  - Proper identity and access control mechanisms must be enabled for the platform.

  - The cloud platform must provide isolated security zones between multiple deployment environments.

  - All data at rest and in transit (app-level/**Transport Layer Security** (**TLS**) or HTTP protocols) must be encrypted with customer-provided keys.

  - The **Intrusion Prevention System** (**IPS**)/**Intrusion Detection System** (**IDS**) must be designed at all ingress/egress network transaction points of presence.

  - Vulnerability management and **Distributed Denial-of-Service** (**DDoS**) protection must be implemented.

- Resiliency:

  - The platform must provide 99.99% availability for the underlying cloud platform.

  - Primary storage data must be deployed in DBaaS, managed services, and provided backup. In addition, however, cluster configuration data needs a backup service.

  - **Disaster Recovery** (**DR**) must be designed to provide business continuation with an RTO of 4 hours and RPO of 8 hours.

  - The platform must enforce georedundancy.

- Observability:

    ▪ The platform must enable continuous monitoring of infrastructure components, the workload, the performance of the infrastructure, regulation and compliance violations, vulnerabilities, security incidents, and activity details.

    ▪ The platform must enable reporting capability for both network and infrastructure activity and transaction history.

    ▪ The platform must enable activity tracking for different changes on the cloud platform.

In the next section, we will determine different cloud services for the platform, infrastructure, and services to design a secure, highly available, and reliable platform for the migrated workload.

Solution components

To ensure functional and non-functional requirement capabilities, we need to develop a solution component mapping, as shown in *Table 5.9*:

Requirement	Component
Containers platform	Kubernetes on IBM Cloud **Virtual Private Cloud** (**VPC**). Three availability zones in two different regions.
Worker node type	VPC compute VMs.
Cluster connectivity	Private service endpoint.
Cluster isolation	Separate production and development/test clusters. For the non-production cluster, it is also recommended to create different OpenShift projects for application isolation within a cluster.
Container images registry	IBM Cloud Container Registry
VM	**Virtual Server Instance** (**VSI**) on VPC Gen 2.

Table 5.9 – Compute component mapping for application migration and modernization

Table 5.10 describes different components or services available from IBM Cloud for specific storage-related non-functional requirements:

Requirement	Component
IBM Cloud Container Registry	Cloud Object Storage (included in the IBM Cloud Container Registry service)
Persistent storage for applications	VPC Block Storage Cloud Object Storage
Primary data storage	IBM Db2 as the service for transactional data and IBM Cloudant for NoSQL PII data
Caching	Redis on IBM Cloud
Archive storage (for >30-day log retention)	Cloud Object Storage

Table 5.10 – Storage component mapping for application migration and modernization

Table 5.11 focuses on different network components, services, and a resiliency design pattern:

Requirement	Component
Enterprise connectivity	IBM Cloud Direct Link terminating to Juniper firewall to create a secure connection between cloud and on-premises data center.
Local load balancing	Private VPC load balancer (included by default in multizone OpenShift cluster) and public VPC load balancer
Global Load Balancing (**GLB**)	IBM Cloud Internet Services provides global load balancing capabilities along with DDoS detection and prevention mechanism.
Cloud-native connectivity	Private service endpoints for IBM Cloud services
Network segmentation	VPCs, subnets, **Access Control Lists** (**ACLs**), security groups, and Calico network policies
High availability	VPC multizone clusters
Backup OpenShift cluster platform	Built-in **IBM Cloud Kubernetes Service** (**IKS**) service Backup configuration and templates on GitHub A backup secret on IBM Secrets Manager IBM Spectrum Protect to back up files in VM
DR	Restoring backups

Table 5.11 – Network and resiliency component mapping

Table 5.12 describes different components or services from IBM Cloud for security non-functional requirements:

Requirement	Component
Data: Encryption	• Cluster data encryption (built-in IBM Kubernetes Service). • Encryption at rest: Cluster data encrypted with Hyper Protect Crypto Services. • Encryption in-transit: TLS encryption with IBM-provided certificates. • COS encryption at rest with Key Management System. • Encryption in transit using TLS. • VPC Block Storage has encryption at rest and in transit with customer-managed keys. • Applications use HTTPS to encrypt data in transit. • Kubernetes router is configured to use the type of TLS termination the app requires.
Data: Key life cycle management – key management	**IBM Key Protect** (**IKP**) is an integrated service with Cloudant, Event Streams, and COS on IBM Cloud for data encryption key management.
Data: Key certificate life cycle management	IBM Cloud Certificate Manager.
Identity and access: Access and role management	IBM Cloud IAM roles and Kubernetes **Role-Based Access Control** (**RBAC**) roles will enforce access controls.
Identity and access: Privileged IAM	IBM Verify provides multifactor authentication to enable multiple factors for authentication.
Infrastructure and endpoint: Endpoint protection	**IBM Managed Endpoint Protection** (**XFESS**) can be used as a service to enforce endpoint protection for infrastructure
Infrastructure and endpoint: Edge protection – IPS	Juniper on IBM Cloud.
Infrastructure and endpoint: DDoS protection	IBM Cloud Internet Services.
Infrastructure and endpoint: Edge protection	A bastion host on the VPC and VSI ensures remote access. The bastion host is used to access resources within a VPC securely. It is a virtual server instance provisioned with a public IP address and accessed via the **Secure Shell** (**SSH**) protocol. The Bastion host acts as a jump server allowing a secure connection to instances provisioned without a public IP address.
Infrastructure and endpoint: Network core protection	Security groups, ACLs, Calico, and Kubernetes network policies.
Threat detection: Vulnerability scanning and management	IBM Cloud Container Registry (with Vulnerability Advisor). Vulnerability management: X-Force RED VMS.
Threat detection and response: Threat detection	IBM X-Force Threat Management. Threat detection: X-Force Threat Management and QRadar on Cloud.

Table 5.12 – Security component mapping for application migration and modernization

Table 5.13 lists components for monitoring, logging, and observability-related non-functional requirements:

Requirement	Component
Monitoring: OpenShift cluster and cloud services	• IBM Cloud Monitoring with Sysdig can provide a unified look at cluster metrics, container security, resource usage, alerts, and custom events. • IBM Cloud Monitoring with Sysdig can aggregate metrics and monitoring of containers across OpenShift clusters and Cloud Object Storage and IBM Cloud databases within the region. • IBM Cloud Monitoring is highly available and scalable. In addition, it is integrated with IBM Cloud IAM for user access management. It can be Connected through private service endpoints. • IBM Cloud Monitoring with Sysdig ensures data availability for up to 15 months; granularity based on roll-up policy.
Logging: OpenShift cluster and apps and cloud services	• IBM Log Analysis can provide live streaming of log tailing, real-time troubleshooting, issue alerts, and log archiving. • IBM Log Analysis with LogDNA can aggregate logs across clusters and other IBM Cloud services such as Container Registry and cloud databases within the region. • IBM Log Analysis is highly available, scalable, and compliant with industry security standards and usually connected through private service endpoints. • IBM Log Analysis with LogDNA is integrated with IBM Cloud IAM for user access management. It also provides 7-30 days of log search plans using Cloud Object Storage.
Auditing/tracking	• Activity Tracker with LogDNA tracks user-initiated activities that change the state of a service in IBM Cloud. This includes how accounts are created, modified, and disabled. • Activity Tracker uses private routes between IBM Cloud services. However, the LogDNA web UI is not currently supported on the service endpoint network. • The **Health Insurance Portability and Accountability Act (HIPAA)** of 1996 enforces the availability of a 30-day event search plan. • Can archive events in Cloud Object Storage to comply with >30-day retention policies.

Table 5.13 – Observability component mapping for application migration and modernization

Reference architecture

The landing zone in *Figure 5.4* has two regions. Each of the regions has three availability zones. A highly available platform must have at least three availability zones. For each of the two regions, an OpenShift cluster is deployed. A single cluster can have multiple projects, which can enable multiple environments, such as production, non-production, **User Acceptance Testing** (**UAT**), development, and testing. Each OpenShift cluster is deployed on three availability zones. IBM Cloud Internet Services acts as the load balancer between two regions. Cloud Internet Services also protects against intrusion and DDoS. IBM Cloud internet service terminates in the IBM POP location. **IBM Log Analysis, Activity Tracker**, and **IBM Cloud Monitoring** are used for observability of the platform. **Cloud DbaaS** is used in the reference architecture to use the strength of the managed DBaaS. Most cloud databases provide managed DBaSs, including data encryption at rest, backup, and other protections against failure. Multiple cloud services and applications deployed on the OpenShift platform access these cloud services through private service endpoints:

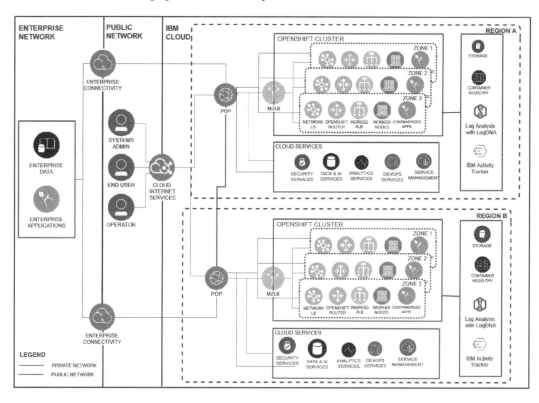

Figure 5.4 – Architecture diagram of the landing zone

Now that we discussed the reference architecture and different architecture decisions, we will discuss migration solutions for some use cases for different types of applications. The following section will discuss four different use cases to understand the difference and similarities in cloud modernization programs.

Use cases for application modernization

In this section, we will go through some application modernization use cases. Migration projects usually have multiple stages, as shown in *Figure 5.5*. First, requirement and BV analysis should generate a set of migration decisions. Migration decisions depend on the application platform, runtime, objective KPIs, and other essential dependencies. It is essential to use automated, tool-based analysis to make the most suitable migration decision using different migration patterns along with standard practice and tools. Manual and survey-based analysis alone, without any focus on business policies and values, often ends in disaster for the modernization project. These migration decisions are used as input for the next stage, where the readiness of these decisions is evaluated. For example, for application migration with the Re-Platform migration pattern, one of the migration decisions is to modernize the application and migrate it to a container platform. The readiness validation stage evaluates whether the application is eligible for modernization through Re-Platforming, where the target platform is a container platform. If the decisions can't be validated, the corresponding migration decision must be changed and revalidated:

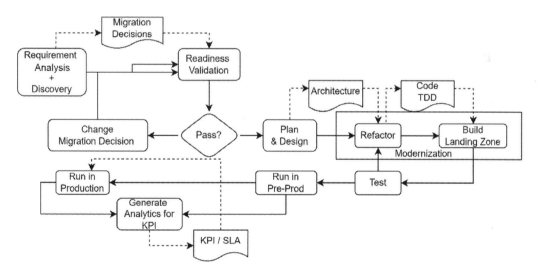

Figure 5.5 – Different stages of application migration

Migration and the new platform's design are based on different migration decisions. The artifacts generated at this stage are functional and non-functional requirements, solution architecture, architecture decisions, network design, landing zone design, and other architectures. Once the plan and design are ready, modernization kicks in. During the modernization phase, the re-factoring of application configuration and code occurs. The landing zone is built and configured based on the architecture generated at the plan and design phase. Applications are then migrated to the **test** environment. During the test phase, the modernization of the applications continues based on test results. Once the re-factored applications fulfill the acceptance criteria for the test, they are pushed into the **preproduction** environment. The preproduction environment should be as close as possible to the production environment. In the preproduction environment, analytics related to KPIs should be monitored to estimate the required **Service-Level Objective** (**SLO**) in the production environment. Based on the KPIs, the configuration production environment is configured. Finally, the applications are moved to the production environment.

The following section will discuss some migration decisions for different modernization use cases.

Migrating a legacy application to the platform

The goal for this use case is to migrate an application component to a new runtime platform. However, instead of completely Re-Architecting the applications, the organization expects to make minimal changes to code, integrations, data, and configuration to adapt to the new platform. So, first, we need to design the target state based on the current state. *Table 5.14* describes the migration target state and current state:

	Current State	**Target State**
Strategy	Time to market is too long and IT management cost is high.	Move to the public cloud to reduce the time to market and use managed IaaS, PaaS, and SaaS.
Application ecosystem	289 applications are deployed on a physical server in the data center.	Moving to the cloud with modernization is the strategy to modernize the applications.

Table 5.14 – The current and target states of the workload

Once we've identified the main requirements for the application migration use case, we need to make the primary migration decisions for this use case, as shown in *Table 5.15*:

Category	Migration Decisions	Reason
Migration pattern	Re-Factor and Re-Platform	Containerization can provide a higher BV.
Platform	Container	Use a full suite of hybrid platform services across all layers of the application.
Database	Move to a service model	Move database from Oracle to PostgreSQL on EnterpriseDB in the cloud, with little to no schema changes.
Storage	Re-factor application to become stateless	Reduce storage costs and also provide better integration and proper microservice pattern. Use the 12-Factor App methodology to achieve higher BV after modernization.
Move license	Bring your own license or use the OpEx model	Reduce TCO by over 40%. Move from CapEx to OpEx to increase BV.
Skill	Containerization Cloud service	Move database from Oracle to PostgreSQL on EnterpriseDB in the cloud, with little to no schema changes.
Tools	IBM migration tools	Use Transformation Advisor for IBM **App Connect Enterprise** (**ACE**) workloads analysis. Also use Mainframe application modernization for mainframe applications.
Cloud services	Replace VM-based middleware with cloud services	Move APIs from Apigee to API Connect. Move from open source Kafka to IBM Event Streams in the cloud. Gain high availability and auto-scaling for different services.
Method	Twelve-Factor App Methodology	Improve the application quality.
Cost	Low	Minimal changes are made to the application to containerize the frontend application.
BV	High	Reduce middleware and database licensing costs by over 60%.

Table 5.15 – Migration decisions

The end-to-end migration follows the sequence described in *Figure 5.5*. The modernization effort is minimal for this use case; therefore, no code changes are required. For example, integration configurations or deployment templates will be changed during the build phase. After testing the application on the test environment, it is deployed to production and continues to run. As the effort for modernization is low, the BV is high. However, the *discovery and requirement analysis* phase should be very thorough in making the right plan and designing an efficient solution. Using different tools for discovery can help expedite this phase with meaningful findings and migration decisions.

Modernization with the Re-Architect migration pattern

Several legacy applications are re-factored as microservices and deployed on a containerized platform for this use case. *Table 5.16* describes this use case's migration and modernization decisions:

Category	Migration Decisions	Reason
Migration pattern	Re-Factor and Re-Architect	Moving the application as-is to the cloud often causes more cost and issues, therefore to Re-Factor the legacy application and Re-Architect it for cloud deployment is the right decision.
Platform	VM and container	The underlying infrastructure can be either a VM or container. Some services can also be Re-Architected as serverless.
Business practice	Improve business-IT engagement	Reduce middleware and database licensing costs by over 60%.
Storage	Re-factor application to become stateless	Reduce storage costs and also provide better integration and proper microservice pattern. Use the 12-Factor App methodology to achieve higher BV after modernization.
Move license	Bring your own license or use the OpEx model	Reduce TCO by over 40%. Move from CapEx to OpEx to increase BV.
Skill	Containerization Cloud service	Full stack developer (Agile). Kubernetes admin. DevOps engineer. SRE.
Tools	IBM and open source migration, as well as modernization tools	Eclipse, JUnit, and Swagger. Git, Jenkins, Maven, and Liberty. Kubernetes, Elasticsearch, Prometheus, Kibana, and Fluentd.
Cloud services	Replace VM-based middleware with cloud services	Move APIs from Apigee to API Connect. Move from open source Kafka to IBM Event Streams in the cloud. Gain high availability and auto-scaling for different services.
Method	12-Factor App methodology IBM Garage Method for Cloud DevOps SRE	Improve the application quality.
Cost	The high end of medium level	Code re-factoring and service integration re-factoring are required.
BV	Medium	On average, 30% cost improvement can be achieved after the same modernization work is done with 30% less workforce.

Table 5.16 – Migration decisions

The following use cases present an example of the JBoss application, and we will use Red Hat and IBM Cloud technologies to create a reference cloud migration solution.

Modernization of the JBoss application using an extension

Sometimes, the legacy application is very complicated, and it is challenging to untangle different components without extensive effort for modernization. Moreover, as colossal effort is required, the corresponding BV may not be commercially feasible. For those use cases, instead of complicating the existing *matrix of hell*, an easy solution is to expose a critical element or new feature of the legacy application as an API or microservices for other applications to utilize. This process will also help to untangle different essential services from the complicated application integration and decommission of unessential services. While this can involve code changes in the component, it can also be accomplished through API integration. The core migration and modernization decisions are listed in *Table 5.17*:

Category	Migration Decisions	Reason
Migration pattern	Re-innovate	Introducing a microservice can improve the modernization effort and efficiency. The complicated application can be modernized without disrupting business continuity.
Platform	Container	JBoss applications are often suitable candidate for containerization as they are developed following the service concept, therefore, they can be easily often containerized using Re-Innovate to some extent.
Cost	Low	Only a single service is modernized at a time. Code from the existing application can be reused with the proper wrapper.
Tools	IBM API Connect IBM Connect OpenAPI (Swagger)	API Connect can create an API and abstract legacy interfaces. The Connect interface can access legacy mainframe components through modernized applications. All these tools can create and manage an API platform that spans multiple clouds, externalizing key interfaces between each cloud platform.
BV	High	• The BV of the legacy app is externalized to modernized/cloud-native applications. • Speed up developer consumption of on legacy components. • Prepare to use the strangler pattern on legacy workloads. • Insulate consumers from further modernization activities. • Shorten development time for new applications significantly. • Developer efficiency. • 89% less application development-related downtime. • The modernized platform is less expensive than the legacy platform.

Table 5.17 – Migration decisions

The modernized application platform for the JBoss application server and applications is depicted in *Figure 5.6*:

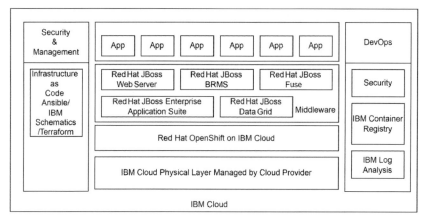

Figure 5.6 – Modern platform for the JBoss Enterprise Application

Table 5.18 describes the transition of different workloads for this use case.

Category	Workload	Transition to Cloud
Compute	On-premises physical machine	Bare metal on IBM public cloud
Application runtime	JBoss server on machine	Red Hat OpenShift on IBM Cloud
Middleware	IBM WebSphere, Oracle WebLogic, GlassFish, Apache Tomcat, and JBoss Application Server community	JBoss Enterprise Application Platform and JBoss Web Server
	Oracle Coherence	JBoss Data Grid
	Oracle Database	
Business rules and processes	Oracle BPM Suite and Oracle Business Rules	JBoss BPM Suite JBoss BRMS
Storage	Physical tape	Cloud Object Storage
Virtualization	N/A	Red Hat Enterprise Linux, Red Hat Virtualization, and Red Hat OpenShift
ESB	TIBCO, JCAPS, Sonic ESB, Mule ESB, Software AG web Methods, and Oracle ESB	Cloud services from IBM, including Event Streams, API Connect, App Connect, or Cloud Pak for Integration

Table 5.18 – Mapping for different workload transitions to the cloud

The benefits of application modernization are as follows:

- Using a PaaS for a container platform reduces the cost and effort significantly. The service provider will build and manage the underlying platform for a managed service, so developers can focus on innovation and business.

- Modernization will ensure a fast **Return on Investment** (**ROI**) and a high increase in business productivity.

- End-to-end management is out of scope for developers, and with an integrated solution for DevOps, platform management, application development, and the time to the market reduce significantly. It also results in a faster development life cycle.

- Modernization processes help to increase developer productivity.

The following section will discuss the modernization of a monolithic Java application.

Modernization of a Java application

In this section, we will discuss the features of a monolithic Java application for different business logistics and some of its key features. Let's consider we have a monolithic application storing. This application possesses the following attributes:

- This application is a core component of multiple products.

- Over time, different products have added their requirements; therefore, this application became very complicated.

- There is 78% code duplication.

- The code quality is below 30% based on the SonarQube report as there are unchecked vulnerabilities, duplication, non-standardized coding practices, and other code quality violations.

- There is too much logic in the code base; some of it conflicts with each other. Due to code duplication and bad coding patterns, these conflicts are not checked and often cause more bugs.

- Applications are deployed on WebSphere Liberty on an on-premises data center.

- As the application becomes substantial and complicated, any change can fail the entire build.

- An individual developer working on different functions can easily break the end-to-end flow; different business logic is implemented in the same file.

- There are multiple new products in the pipeline that will also use this core application to access employee records.

- The entire backend application is often bundled with different frontend applications and deployed on a server as a JAR for different products.

- The release frequency is once every 2 months as change is difficult to test. Therefore, the time to market is comparatively high.

- The maintenance window is 9 to 10 hours long on weekends.

- Release for the US and Europe happens on alternate weeks. Therefore, users in different regions can have different experiences with the same application.

As we go through these above mentioned attributes we can see that this application is way behind any sort of modern application. However, the corresponding BV is very high as it is a core component of multiple products. Therefore, it is a suitable candidate for modernization and migration. Here are some migration decisions for the solution:

Category	Decision	As Is	To Be
Migration pattern	Re-Architect	One monolithic backend application is deployed in the WebSphere Liberty app server.	One monolithic backend application is converted into the Spring Boot microservice.
New feature	Microservice	The new feature is added as a separate class in the same backend application.	All new functionalities will be developed a individual Spring Boot microservices.
Frontend application	Microservice	Existing frontend applications are deployed on the IBM Liberty profile application server as a JAR.	The frontend Angular application will be deployed as a Node.js application on the container platform.
Landing zone (compute)	Container platform (IBM Kubernetes Service)	Monolithic backend applications are deployed on an application server hosted on the machine.	Applications will be Re-Architected to become containerized. As the application was already a Java-based JAX-RS REST API, it takes minimum effort to containerize the applications.
Landing zone (storage)	Modernization with DbaaS and cloud storage	Cloud services and MemCache on the server.	Continue to use IBM Cloudant for NoSQL data, Redis for caching, IBM Cloud Object Storage for logging, bulk data, and metadata, and IBM File Storage for IKS. Use multitenancy from the managed DbaaS.
Landing zone (network)	Modernization with cloud-native service and software-defined component	Physical connectivity is established using cloud services as well as network appliances. In addition, adding a jump box can ensure seamless access.	IBM Transit Gateway for the global load balancer between multiple regions. VPC private load balancer between multiple availability zones.
Landing zone (monitoring)	Replace with cloud service	File-based logging. The DevOps engineer needs to manually collect the log and share it with the rest of the team for higher environments.	IBM Cloud Monitoring enables real-time log access by team members. This also enables alert notification and automates other incident management operations.
Landing zone (key management)	Use Cloud service	Data encryption keys were already managed by IKP. For a different tenant, different keys are generated in IKP.	
Landing zone (secret management)	Modernization with Cloud service and GitOps	Stored in files in the server.	GitOps is used to store secrets during the build and deploy phase. Certificates and other secrets are stored in IBM Certificate Manager.
DevOps pipeline	Modernization	Semi-automated, where release to higher environments is entirely manual.	• Include code quality control by adding SonarQube, FindBugs, Checkstyle, and PMD integrated with the Jenkins DevOps pipeline. *Figure 5.7* shows the build from the Jenkins pipeline. It also shows the Quality Gate setup by SonarQube. • Include vulnerabilities scanning and antivirus as part of the DevOps pipeline. • Adopted extended 12-Factor App methodology to develop new microservices and re-factor existing microservices.
Release pattern	Daily	Monthly release and bug fix. Every second week, the applications are deployed in the US region, and in the Europe region in the third week.	The integrated DevOps pipeline enables multiple releases per day to both regions. *Figure 5.8* shows a continuous delivery pipeline. Each commit goes to the smoke region automatically, which then is extended to UAT, **System Integration Testing (SIT)**, preproducton, and production. For upper environments, such as production, manual approval is still required for control. Otherwise, the **Continous Integration (CI)/Continous Deployment (CD)** pipeline is autonomous and fully automated.

Network isolation	Modernization	Deployed in different servers, and proxy servers are used for the firewall.	1. VPC on each IBM **Multizone Region** (**MZR**) for US and EU. 2. Cloud services are provisioned in individual resource groups for different environments. They are also redundant in a different region. 3. Different namespaces in IKS for different environments, such as development, smoke, SIT, UAT, preproduction, and production.
Intrusion detection and intrusion prevention	Replace with managed service	F5 firewall is used.	Juniper Firewall is used by IBM Cloud as a managed service.
Metadata processing	Re-Architect	Cron Jobs and Java processes can extract all metadata and store the result in the database.	An event-driven architecture for metadata processing is designed using IBM Event Streams.
Backup		- Managed DbaaS to provide backup and restore. - Automated backup and restore for IBM Cloudant using snapshot in a separate instance of Cloudant for Backup. - Manually back up logging in IBM Cloud Object Storage for 90 days.	Continue existing approaches. Configure IBM Cloud monitoring to back up the log for 90 days in IBM Cloud Object Storage.
Data replication	Use IBM technology	1. Create real-time replication in IBM Cloudant. 2. Create snapshot replication in IBM Cloudant. 3. Leverage cross-region storage class in IBM Cloud Object Storage. 4. File push between the primary site and data site for the log and bulk data.	1. Continue existing approaches. 2. IBM Spectrum Scale provides active file management to replicate files from the primary site to the DR site.
DR pattern	Modernization using managed services and automated provisioning of the landing zone	Active-passive in two different data centers.	Active-passive in two different regions. For example, in the EU, Germany is the primary site, and the UK is the secondary site. Each site is independent of the other.
Disaster exercise	Modernization with the semi-automated approach	Yearly test for DR. Manually switch over from primary site to secondary site and test the DR. Automated test and evaluation for DR. Before migration, this process would take 5 to 6 days. However, after modernization, the time for the DR test was 4 to 6 hours only.	
Security	Modernization	Only PII data is encrypted in IBM Cloudant. Data at rest is encrypted in IBM Cloudant and IBM Cloud Object Storage.	IBM Verify issued multifactor authentication for management and operation users. Security policies such as API key and platform keys generation are restricted.

Table 5.19 – Migration decisions for modernization of a Java application

As discussed in *Table 5.19*, setting up a code quality gate is essential for CI/CD. It speeds up the time to market, even though, initially, it is going to take some time to fix and implement *technical debt* once the gate is established and integrated into the CI/CD pipeline. *Figure 5.7* shows an example of a quality control gate using SonarQube:

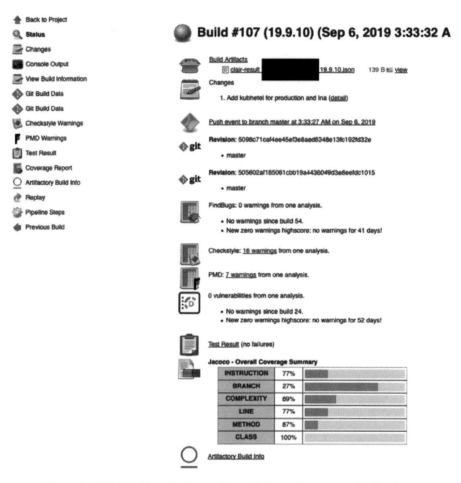

Figure 5.7 – The Jenkins pipeline and SonarQube code coverage for DevOps

Quality control for source code and deployment must be part of CD. Nowadays, it is straightforward to integrate into the Git DevOps pipeline or separate standard pipelines such as Jenkins and Travis to add vulnerability checks, code quality gates, and so on to ensure that each commit goes through specific quality control. For example, *Figure 5.8* shows a DevOps pipeline integrated with SonarQube to ensure the container image is published to the respiratory, followed by a vulnerability check and code quality gate for each commit. Therefore, if the source code is not vulnerability-free or passes the quality gate, as well as if the scanning reports any vulnerabilities for the final container image, the image push to the repository will fail.

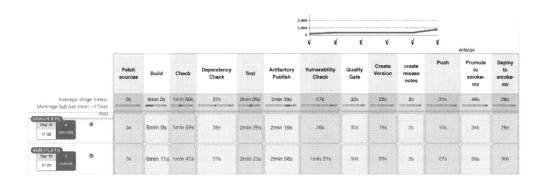

Figure 5.8 – Integrated DevOps pipeline for CI/CD

Summary

This chapter explained the basic requirements for an efficient and effective application modernization project. This chapter also discussed different stages of application modernization. For example, we got familiar with functional and non-functional requirements for application modernization and understood the assessment and evaluation of requirements to design an efficient landing zone for the target state of application migration.

We will design an effective and resilient platform in the following chapters, including storage, networking, and other cloud platform components. The next chapter will discuss the modernization of storage solutions for cloud-native workloads.

Further reading

- *Calculating Business Value of Application Modernization—A Pragmatic Approach*: https://medium.com/hybrid-cloud-engineering/calculating-business-value-of-application-modernization-a-pragmatic-approach-c45c1242fb17

- *IBM Cloud Transformation Advisor*, ibm.com, 2020 [Online]. Available at https://www.ibm.com/garage/method/practices/learn/ibm-transformation-advisorz

- *IBM Cloud Advisory Tool Virtual Demo: A CAT Walk through*, ibm.com, 2020 [Online]. Available at https://mediacenter.ibm.com/media/Cloud+Advisory+Tool+Virtual+DemoA+A+CAT+Walk+through/1_saqzokfd

Part 3: Elements of Embedded Linux

The objective of *Part 3* is to help you to understand the infrastructure of the cloud, including storage, networks, security, and resiliency. This section also emphasizes the operations that need to be carried out in order to make the best of cloud infrastructure.

This part of the book comprises the following chapters:

- *Chapter 6, Designing and Implementing Cloud Storage Services*
- *Chapter 7, Designing and Implementing Networking in Hybrid Cloud Infrastructure*
- *Chapter 8, Understanding Security in Action*
- *Chapter 9, Designing a Resilient Platform for Cloud Migration*
- *Chapter 10, Managing Operations in Hybrid Cloud Infrastructure*

6

Designing and Implementing Cloud Storage Services

Organizations are massively dependent on their business, analytics, and intelligence data. They are more pervasive when using production-level data. The consistency and continuous availability of data have become a critical mission. Some say that data is the most valuable resource for the next generation. Efficient data storage is essential for the success of modernization. An organization has different data formats, structures, sources, and relevance. A modern data storage solution must ensure complete life cycle governance for each data record regardless of the storage. Organizations bet heavily on their data and information management systems. In addition to real-time data management, resilient and secure storage, analytics, and data life cycle management are critical for organizations. Different business units of an organization often use the same data for their operations. So the same data record can have different life cycles and management procedures. As such, it is essential to establish standardization for a data storage and management system. User experience is directly dependent on data quality. Data storage needs to be appropriate for the relevance of data. In addition, the information intelligence of an organization is entirely dependent on data, so data storage should be accessible for analytics and intelligence. Backup and restore helps customers to protect their data from the following:

- Hardware or software issues resulting in data loss or data corruption

- User or administrative errors resulting in accidental data loss

- Migration, duplication, or the promotion of environments via cloning

- A natural disaster

In this chapter, we will focus on the following topics:

- Understanding the requirements of storage and database modernization
- Designing a modern data insight solution
- Modernization of a data hub platform with IBM Cloud Pak for Data
- Designing a backup solution for resilient storage and a database
- Exploring a big data analytics solution for the healthcare industry

Understanding the requirements of storage and database modernization

Often, data in legacy solutions is scattered all over in heterogeneous storage systems and data sources that are often not connected or governed. Therefore, one of the critical requirements for data and storage modernization is overcoming these issues. Simultaneously, data and storage modernization focuses on improving the quality of data. Therefore, analytics and intelligence can ensure better performance of storage and databases. We will discuss a use case from the airline industry to explore storage and database modernization, called the **Aerodactyl** use case. The core objectives of data and storage migration and modernization are as follows:

- Make data accessible with a secure and resilient storage and communication solution.
- Provide end-to-end data governance solutions to manage the life cycle of data.
- Ensure the central governance of data from heterogeneous sources. A modern data platform can act as the single point of reference for any data-related requirement.
- Ensure better data quality. A basic set of standards must be maintained for any data processing. In addition, the target data platform should be a central reservoir for all raw data.
- Improve the quality of data to produce a high-quality processed version that is a suitable candidate to apply business logic and create curated data that an entire organization can use for analytical and intelligence purposes.
- Ensure consistency of governance across datasets and data quality rules. Create standard data models that various units can leverage for their consumption requirements.
- Ensure standard data governance, including cataloging, business glossaries, data lineage, and retention policies.
- Leverage data to maximize the investment life cycle and enhance operational intelligence.

- Speed up data and analytical processing and shorten time to value to ensure that the correct data is available to the right people at the right time.

- Improve productivity and satisfaction by eliminating recreating data and allowing faster access to trusted data.

- Leverage modern solutions to replace repetitive manual activities.

- Provide an organization with a single analytical platform that supports an entire enterprise and presents a single and seamless view of trusted data from multiple sources.

- Reduce the cost of managing and maintaining data by eliminating duplicate or multiple analytical systems.

IBM Cloud provides a set of storage offerings. The following subsections discuss three different types of storage.

Block storage

Block storage is suitable for storing files using **Storage Area Network** (**SAN**) technology. This storage breaks up data into blocks and then stores those blocks as separate pieces, each with a unique identifier. Data can be spread across multiple environments in block storage.

Block storage is suitable for computing situations that require fast, efficient, and reliable data transportation.

File storage

Leveraging **Network Attached Storage** (**NAS**) technology stores the file as a directory, with trees, folders, and individual files for file storage. This storage only operates with standard file-level protocols.

NAS or a **Network Operating System** (**NOS**) manages access rights, file sharing, file locking, and other controls in file storage.

Cloud object storage

Object storage breaks data files up into pieces called objects with unique IDs stored in a single persistent key/value store, and they can also be spread out across multiple networked systems. Each object also stores metadata of the corresponding object and can be accessed using a REST API.

Container storage

A container platform requires container storage for persistent volumes. There are different kinds of container storage available. Here are some examples of container storage recommended by IBM:

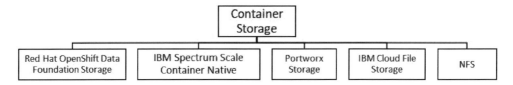

Figure 6.1 – Container storage types

In the following subsections, we will discuss five different types of container storage.

Red Hat OpenShift Data Foundation storage

Red Hat **OpenShift Data Foundation** (**ODF**) storage is OpenShift container storage. It provides a fast recovery and backup solution based on underlying storage calls and a way to isolate I/O between workloads, using a specific node or node group and storage class per workload. A **Reliable Autonomic Distributed Object Store** (**RADOS**) block device and **Persistent Volume** (**PV**) encryption ensure security at rest. The multi-cloud gateway enables caching capabilities that improve performance significantly. ODF includes 10 more functions than the former **OpenShift Container Storage** (**OCS**), enabling better RTO and RPO for backup, stretched clustering, replication, management of a storage pool, and customization of object storage daemon weight to avoid saturation on a device that also serves other workloads. For **Persistence Container Volumes** (**PCVs**), ODF is very suitable for storage. The following figure gives an overview of the stack diagram of ODF:

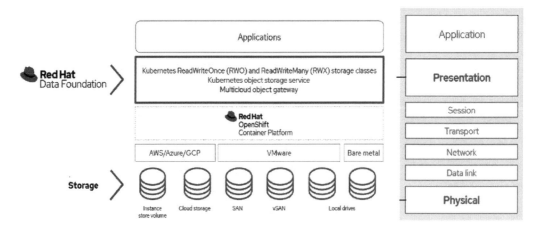

Figure 6.2 – Red Hat OpenShift Data Foundation

IBM Spectrum Scale Container Native

Figure 6.3 shows that **IBM Spectrum Scale Container Native (ISSCN)** storage leverages a clustered filesystem on IBM Spectrum Scale. ISSCN ensures concurrent access to a single filesystem or set of filesystems of a clustered filesystem from multiple nodes, either SAN-attached or network-attached. This clustered filesystem configuration ensures high performance. For the Red Hat OpenShift cluster, the clustered filesystem is mounted through the IBM Spectrum Scale CSI driver by using PCVs:

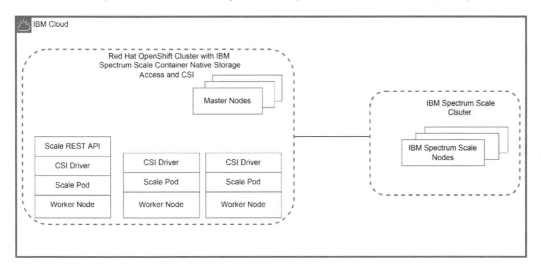

Figure 6.3 – ISSCN for Red Hat OpenShift cluster backup

IBM Cloud File Storage, NFS, or *Portworx* can also be used for PVs of containers.

In the next section, we will discuss different methods for database modernization as a service.

Database services

Modern database services should follow the **CAP** theorem, which stands for **Consistency**, **Availability**, and **Partition** tolerance. The main components of the CAP theorem are as follows:

- **Consistency** – all clients see the same data at the same time.

- **Availability** – the system continues to operate even in partial node failures.

- **Partition** – the system continues to operate despite network failures.

The main characteristics of the CAP theorem are as follows:

- The theorem states that we cannot have all three components in most cases, as there are natural trade-offs between the items.

- We can adopt the iron triangle approach of *fast, cheap, and easy – pick two* to select the correct pattern for the storage. Each side of the triangle represents one of the concepts fast, cheap, and easy. Instead of making a solution with all three characteristics, the aim is to pick any two for the best solution. Similarly, for CAP, it is *consistency*, *availability*, or *partition tolerance*, as the three sides of the triangle, and we aim to choose two of them. *Figure 6.4* shows the triangle for the CAP theorem:

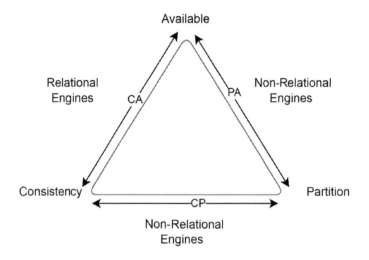

Figure 6.4 – The CAP theorem

Multiple factors drive the decision to choose database as a service. The following table discusses some of the factors:

Category	NoSQL	Relational
Volume	High volume workloads that require a large scale.	Workload volume is consistent and requires a medium to large scale.
ACID (atomicity, consistency, isolation, durability)	Workloads do not require ACID guarantees.	ACID guarantees are required.
Relationships	Data can be expressed without relationships.	Data is expressed best in a relational frame rather than in NoSQL form.

Category	NoSQL	Relational
Write safety	Needs fast writes and write safety is not critical.	Write safety is a requirement.
Data retrieval	Data retrieval is simple.	Complex queries and reports.
Geographic distribution	Data requires a wide geographic distribution.	In cases where users are centralized; therefore, data can be stored in one location.
Public clouds	The application will be deployed to shared hardware, such as with public clouds.	The application will be deployed to dedicated, large, and high-end hardware.

Table 6.1 – The decision matrix for a relational database versus a NoSQL database

Now that we are familiar with different functions and non-functional requirements for storage solutions in the cloud, we will discuss modern data insight platforms in the next section.

Designing a modern data insight solution

A modern data insight platform requires capabilities for security, redundancy, fault tolerance, data operation, automation, analytics, and visualization. Here are some of the requirements for *data platform modernization*:

- Modernize legacy data sources.
- Secure network connectivity.
- Enable continuous observability.
- Enforce user access control management.
- Develop interoperability among data collection layers with automation.
- Automate data preparation and a secure storage layer.
- Develop a data analysis layer with AI.
- Develop data infusion and a visualization layer.

Figure 6.5 details architecture decisions on the preceding eight modern data insight solution layers.

Modernize legacy data sources

Legacy data storage deployed in on-premises locations can be replaced by cloud-based data storage, providing better operations, automation, and service management. In this section, we will discuss different approaches to modernizing data storage. There are multiple steps to modernize legacy data sources, as follows:

1. Run an assessment to identify the data storage candidate based on business value.

2. Design the target state for the legacy data storage. There can be multiple types of target storage solutions. For example, instead of running badge jobs on a large amount of data stored in a local file, we can migrate that data to a managed service in the cloud or use software with automated capabilities to design more efficient solutions.

The following sections describe the design of secure and modern data storage solutions. *Figure 6.5* illustrates the significant architectural decisions for modern data storage solutions.

Secure network connectivity

Let us consider a hybrid solution where innovation and modern cloud services are deployed on IBM Cloud, but a large amount of data and legacy applications remain in the on-premises location. It is essential to build secure connectivity between applications and storage deployed in on-premises and the cloud. In the following list are some services provided by IBM Cloud to ensure secure enterprise connectivity. Deciding on the correct service depends on the volume of data transmission and the performance and latency of data communication. Therefore, direct link-based enterprise connectivity is recommended for high data volumes or when performance should be close to real time:

*   The **IBM Cloud VPN** service allows users to remotely manage all servers securely over the IBM Cloud private network (based on a **secure sockets layer virtual private network** (**SSL VPN**)).

*   An **IPsec VPN** between customer premises and IBM Cloud over the internet.

*   **Various Direct Link** connectivity options to terminate a dedicated link from the customer's premises. Currently, IBM Cloud provides two types of Direct Link:

    *   Direct Link on Classic (1.0) for classic infrastructure

    *   Direct Link 2.0

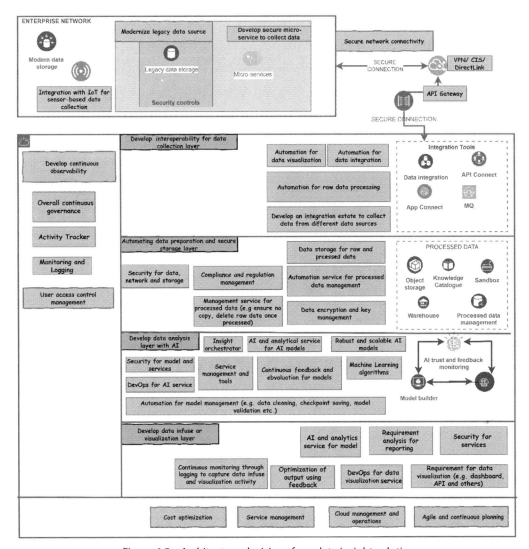

Figure 6.5 – Architecture decisions for a data insight solution

Develop continuous observability

The next activity to build a landing zone for a modern data platform is to enable continuous monitoring for performance, data consumption, data retrieval activity, a data consumption pattern, and data access activity tracking to ensure security and integrity for the data platform. The central monitoring and logging should be integrated with all components in the different layers of *Figure 6.5*. A central monitoring solution enables better operation and data insight visualization. In addition to logging and monitoring, a modern data insight solution also needs continuous activity monitoring for data access audit and security monitoring.

User access control management

Data privacy, integrity, and confidentiality should be enforced in an efficient data insight platform. **Role-based access control (RBAC)** may not be enough for a secure data platform. In addition to RBAC, attribute-based access control should be enabled. Continuous activity monitoring ensures access control management.

Develop interoperability or a data collection layer

IBM Cloud Pak for Data can work on data stored in any place, such as Snowflake, Db2 on-premises, **Relational Database Management System (RDMS)** on AWS, S3 on AWS, file storage on Azure, GCP storage, and other cloud storage. The data virtualization process enables IBM Cloud Pak for Data to connect data to other sources. In addition, there are multiple capabilities available in IBM Cloud to enable data ingestion. Most services in IBM Cloud provide automated data ingestion. Some of the services are listed in *Table 6.2*:

Ingestion automation service	Data type
IBM MQ IBM Event Streams	Sensor data and IoT
File sync IBM Spectrum Protect active file management	File (unstructured, semi-structured, and structured)
IBM API Connect IBM App Connect IBM Cloud Pak for ingestion	API ingestion

Table 6.2 – Ingestion services for different kinds of data

Automating data preparation and the secure storage layer

The storage layer has different data types – raw, processed, business knowledge, and others.

Each kind of data should be stored in secure data storage. If data such as **electronic health records (EHRs)** are stored, which require compliance and regulation management, automated monitoring and a management service should be integrated.

Data must be encrypted at rest and in transit. Data encryption keys are placed in essential management services; therefore, the keys' rotation and life cycle management are managed automatically.

Efficient services such as DataStage or Spark should be available on the platform to automatically process a large amount of data for **extract, transform, and load** (ETL) purposes.

Data quality and profiling should be automated, and policy-based data governance is essential to ensure data integrity on the platform.

Primary data, keywords, and other metadata must be managed and governed automatically.

Developing a data analysis layer with AI

AI analytics is the main component of a data insight platform, where a considerable amount of raw data can be converted to essential business knowledge or policies by using machine learning, AI analytics, and other analytics services.

Developing data infusion and a visualization layer

Finally, generated business knowledge should be expressed in a presentable way to extract information efficiently and effectively. *Figure 6.5* shows different architecture decisions required for a modern data insight platform, such as the following:

- Replace legacy data storage with modernized high-performance data storage.

- Develop a proper data ingestion layer using different technologies such as a microservices and event streams. This data ingestion layer should be able to collect data from heterogeneous data sources such as IoT devices and external systems.

- Establish secure network connectivity between applications and data storages deployed on both on-premises and the cloud with secure communication channels, such as Direct Link and a VPN. Include necessary intrusion prevention and detection mechanisms using a firewall, **Web Application Firewall** (WAF), an API gateway, and other similar components.

- Develop continuous observability with monitoring, logging, and activity tracking for security and compliance.

- Establish identity and access control management for users in the cloud and on-premises locations.

- Develop an interoperable data collection and processing layer. This collection layer must be able to leverage automation and modern techniques such as IBM API Connect, IBM App Connect Enterprise, event streams, and data virtualization.

- Secure cloud data storage and leverage AI automation for data processing. Encrypt data in motion and data at rest.

- Establish proper security operation practices for data encryption key management, identity and access control management, and certificate management.

- Manage compliance and regulation risk as well as mitigation operations.

- Build a secure data lake for processed data. After the raw data is processed using AI techniques they should be achieved after processing to reduce the cloud service cost.

- Build an AI-ready data analysis layer. Machine learning models, AI techniques, and automation are key to the success of the data analysis layer. The AI must be validated and trusted. The data analysis layer requires **Artificial Intelligence Operations (AIOps)**, **Machine Learning Operations (MLOps)**, and **Data Management Operations (DataOps)** for management.

- Develop data infusion and a visualization layer. Data should be meaningful and able to generate multiple events.

- Establish infrastructure, middleware, application, and data management practices by monitoring golden signals, site reliability engineering, release management, change management, configuration management, and so on.

In this section, we learned about the characteristics of modern data insight solutions. We used a use case to get familiar with different important architecture decisions to develop a modern data insight solution.

Modernization of a data hub platform with IBM Cloud Pak for Data

Data is an essential component for business applications. However, an on-premises **data hub** suffers from different challenges. For example, adopting new technology, including analytics and machine learning, is time-consuming and expensive. On the other hand, the cloud enables integration with new services seamlessly and in just a few clicks, reducing the time to market and enabling an organization to access insight from data. This section will discuss considerable data platform modernization on IBM Cloud. Before going into a detailed solution, let's look at the functional and non-functional requirements for a **big data hub platform**.

The first step for data hub modernization using IBM Cloud Pak for Data is to understand the functional requirements for modernization. The following subsection explores all the functional requirements for the airline industry data hub modernization use case.

Functional requirements for data hub modernization

A data hub platform modernization for the airline industry is a particular use case, as data in the airline industry exhibits some remarkable characteristics, as follows:

- **High throughput**: There are many data consumer stakeholders, such as airports, location-based services, luggage services, hotel management, transportation, and tourism. Each of these stakeholders continuously makes data access requests every second so that data request throughput is high.

- **High scalability**: Millions of users all over the geo-locations are continuously accessing data. In addition, there are holiday periods, events, and incidents that can cause an immediate change in the data request scale.

- **Dynamic**: As data is continuously accessed and modified, it is very dynamic. Caching and reliability mechanisms must be flexible and intelligent to keep pace with the data change rate.

- **Long-term and short-term dependency**: A modern data hub platform must consider both current and historical data for intelligent insight analysis. Therefore, it is essential to analyze time-based data points for effective results.

Table 6.3 shows the functional requirements of a modern data hub platform for the airline industry:

#	Category	Requirements
1		The ability to master and maintain golden copy attributes – key identifiers, locators, account linkages, ratings, classifications, and relationships.
2		The ability to support multi-level relationships and hierarchy structures – that is, creating logical groups and maintaining links in the data.
3		The ability to search for partial information based on multiple keys and the criteria defined.
4		The ability to customize matching and merging logic as needs change and evolve to identify and prevent duplicates.
5		The ability to run jobs such as inactivation, archive, purge, and a duplicate record check.
6		The ability to create and display customizable reports and dashboards based on a role (run ad hoc or scheduled).
7	Master data management	The ability to add customizable approval workflows as defined at the attribute/source/feed level.
8		The ability to configure and customize business rules at the rule/source/feed level.
9		The ability to view the audit history of an entire party life cycle since inception.
10		The ability to create alerts and notifications on specific attribute value changes.
11		The ability to support near real-time and batch processing of multiple sources of party data – feeds, messages, and so on.
12		The ability to support near real-time publishing to downstream consuming systems.
13		The ability to have error logging and to trace for TechOps teams to manage incidents.
14		The ability to have a system available and running with a defined set of SLAs.
15		The ability to manage role permissions at various levels – for example, user role type, party role type, and attribute type.

#	Category	Requirements
16	Data ingestion	The ability to handle multi-user parallel access requests for current and future demands. The solution should support multiple ingestions and integration processes via flat files, **Open Database Connectivity (ODBC)/Java Database Connectivity (JDBC)** sources, database links, messaging queues, APIs, the **File Transfer Protocol (FTP)**, and so on, with high throughput and low latency. In addition, any new standard source system/table identified by Saudi Arabian Airlines in the future should be easily configurable to ingest data at a specific frequency (for example, from batch ingestion every day to real-time ingestion) on a business requirement basis.
17	Interoperability	The ability to effectively integrate with systems and applications using any type of connectors.
18	ETL (extract, transform, and load)	The ability to provide an ETL tool where it can manipulate all types of data and perform cleaning, cleansing, and formatting efficiently. The solution must support version control for the integration code (the ETL code).
19	Data governance	The solution must be part of the unified data management platform that covers all current and future requirements for master data management, enterprise integration, platform management as a service, data quality, metadata management, big data management, and data governance.
20	Metadata management	The ability to follow metadata-driven design principles across the platform at large for all the data management and governance components.
21	Data quality	The ability to provide a data quality solution with a single data quality engine that manages all data quality needs.
22	Visualization	The ability to provide reporting and insight visualization to use data analysis results.

Table 6.3 – The functional requirements for the data platform on IBM Cloud

Architecture diagram

Figure 6.5 shows an architecture diagram for a data insight platform using IBM Cloud PAK for Data on the IBM Cloud platform. **IBM Cloud Pak for Data (CP4D)** is also available on IBM Cloud. In addition, IBM CP4D is available as a **Platform as a Service (PaaS)** on AWS and Azure. Data can be ingested using different components shown in the data ingestion layer. Similarly, data from distributed heterogeneous sources can also be connected to IBM CP4D using data virtualization. Different Watson services and IBM CP4D capabilities provide end-to-end data governance. IBM CP4D also provides data privacy and can enforce different compliance and regulation. The AutoAI and SPSS capabilities of IBM CP4D provide AI model-building capabilities with visualization, reducing model creation and training data on a distributed platform. IBM CP4D also has various capabilities for machine learning, ETL, and other analytics exercises. IBM CP4D provides an integrated data visualization service. In addition, third-party tools, such as the Cognos Analytics UI and PowerBI, can be easily integrated with IBM CP4D for data visualization:

Architecture decisions for a data platform only

Table 6.4 shows different architecture decisions for the data insight platform using IBM Cloud Pak for Data on the IBM Cloud platform. We have not covered network, security, and services in this table. Instead, we have only discussed the decisions required for a container platform, storage, data collection, data infusion, AI analytics, and data visualization:

Requirement	Component decision	Reason
Compute – container platform	Red Hat OpenShift on IBM Cloud on VPC (4.4 or later release)	IBM CP4D is developed on top of Red Hat OpenShift. IBM Cloud provides a Red Hat OpenShift managed service with high availability and resiliency.
Worker node	Bare-metal	Provides better performance
Cluster connectivity	Private endpoint only	Private endpoint is only used for regulated environments with strict network isolation requirements.
Cluster isolation	One cluster	One MZR cluster with three availability zone in two different regions.
Container images registry	OpenShift Container Registry IBM Container Registry	OpenShift on IBM Cloud clusters is set up with the internal OpenShift Container Registry to enable the automatic build, deployment, and management of apps from within the cluster. The internal OpenShift Container Registry and IBM Container Registry are used to cache images locally for faster builds and allow access to image streams from different projects. IBM Container Registry uses cross-region IBM Cloud Object storage for HA-enabled storage and includes vulnerability scanning.
Container storage	Red Hat **OpenShift Data Foundation (ODF)**	The number of data requests is high. We need a **ReadWriteMany (RWX)** claim type for Red Hat OpenShift Data Foundation. For data storage, we can configure different types of storage for different requirements – for example, block storage for a database and shared file storage for ingestion.
Storage backup	Velero and cloud object storage using ODF	Velero is an open source tool that can help us back up data in cloud object storage.

Requirement	Component decision	Reason
Data collection	Event Stream, API ingestion, data virtualization, Guardium integration, and file sync	For different types of data, different ingestion mechanisms are essential. For example, IoT and sensor data are ingested using IBM Event Streams, data in other clouds is connected using data virtualization, and so on.
Data governance	Watson Knowledge Catalog	Provides the ability for data profiling, data quality, lineage, and policy-based governance.
Master data management	Master data management IBM Match 360 with Watson	Data sources need multiple replicas as they are accessed all over the globe by the airline industry. The embedded IBM Match 360 with Watson in IBM Cloud Pak for Data resolves data records across different sources and manages the master data.
Build and train	IBM Watson Studio	Provides the ability to develop and train AI models and manage their life cycle. Runs and optimizes AI models and designs them with visual modeling. Manages business KPIs and automates optimization. AutoAI provides automatic visualization for building models.
Visualization	Cognos Analytics	Provides the ability to report and generate visualizations for insight into business knowledge.
Data operation pipeline	IBM Cloud Pak for Business Automation	Provides an intelligent workflow to design a well-established pipeline for data operations.

Table 6.4 – Architecture decisions for a data platform on IBM Cloud using IBM Cloud Pak for Data

In addition to the data operation, it is also essential to ensure protection against failure – hence why the next section explores a backup solution for resilient data storage.

Designing a backup solution for resilient storage and database

On distributed cloud platforms, data resides on software-defined distributed storage. One of the fundamental functional requirements is to ensure a resilient and secure backup solution for storage. An efficient backup solution possesses the following characteristics:

- Performed using specifically designated backup management software to strengthen the security of backed-up information.

- Different types of data can use different services or software for backup. Different types of data can also have different target storage. However, standard software and target storage can reduce the complexity of a solution.

- A detailed activity log containing the backed-up data, the date and time of the backup, the backup media used, and its physical location. This can be used for audit and validation. The log also provides control points in live processes of continuous backup. For example, using the timestamp in the log as an identifier enables you to find out the age of the backup data, which may help validate the **Retention Time Objective** (**RTO**) or RPO.

- Several backup test cases also need to be prepared to verify that the restoration process of data has been completed successfully (for example, testing the file restoration process).

- Each data storage in the primary solution should have a corresponding label in the backup solution.

The functional requirements for a backup and restore solution

The core requirements for a modern backup solution are as follows:

Category	Requirement
Size	The amount of data for the backup solution needs to determine. Often, the amount of data is a growing variable. Therefore, an efficient backup solution must incorporate the growth nature of data storage.
Type	There are different types of data based on the business requirement for that data, such as raw, processed, cache, and business analytics. Similarly, data can be of different types based on the format – that is, schema-based, non-schema-based, file-based, and others. Different types of data require different types of storage solutions and backup solutions. It is often a best practice to design a standard backup solution for different categories of data. However, sometimes it makes sense to design different backup solutions for different data types. Data for backup can be as follows: • Application data – that is, persistent volumes must be backed up. • Director-related files and structures such as `/etc./origin/leading` directory stores that have important files. • The configuration, the API, controllers, services, other tools and software, Twistlock, Aqua Sec, and NeuVector. • CI/CD tools installed in the environment need to be backed up, including software and configuration data. • Certificates generated by the installation. • All cloud provider-related configuration – keys and other authentication files. Configuration files are stored in the `/etc/sysconfig` directory. Because the masters are also un-schedulable nodes, back up the entire `/etc/origin` directory (etcd) and configs. Along with production-level data, non-production data also needs to be backed up to ensure a resilient non-production and development environment.
Geographical region	Storage solutions should be geographically distributed in a multi-region or even a multi-zone. This is a trade-off that needs to be made while designing a backup solution. The topology for a backup solution can be one of the following: • Single-zone snapshot-based – Here, the backup of the data also resides in the same zone where the primary data is stored. • Multi-zone – The backup data storage resides in a different zone but the same region as the primary data. This provides resiliency against geographical zonal failure. However, this backup solution can be more expensive than the same zonal solution. • Multi-zone and multi-region – The backup data storage resides in a different zone of another region. This provides resiliency against regional geographical failure. However, this backup solution can be more expensive than the other two topologies of the backup solution.

Category	Requirement
RTO and RPO	To define an efficient backup solution, an organization needs to determine the retention time and objectives. The RTO is the maximum tolerable downtime a business can allow. The RTO is defined as how long it will take for a system to get back online by restoring the backed-up data. For example, if a system takes 1 hour to get back online and be operational after a disruption, the RTO is 1 hour. Restoration of data should not take more than 1 hour.
	On the other hand, the RPO is the amount of data lost or that needs to be re-entered after an outage. The RPO determines how up to date the backed-up data is. For example, if a system does a backup once a day, the RPO will be 24 hours.
Backup pattern	Based on the RTO and RPO requirements, a backup solution can be either one of the following: • A fixed number of snapshots – The snapshot frequency must also be defined based on the RTO and RPO requirements. • Real-time storage replication – This backup solution is very efficient when the RTO and RPO are small. This type of solution can be expensive in comparison to a snapshot-based solution.
Self-service	To ensure faster and continuous deployment and shorter time to market, modern solutions require self-service for developers and operators. For example, some organizations may require on-demand backup for data. A well-defined interface must be exposed to the operator users of the organization to initiate on-demand backup for data by themselves. This platform should enforce a self-service portal with detailed and easy steps for any service.
Tenancy	A large organization often has multiple business units. Different units can have different data storage, which may require a different type of backup solution. Based on the tenancy, a backup solution can be either one of the following: • Single-tenant • Multi-tenant The built-in tenancy model allows organizations to reflect the organizational structure and any distribution model.
Data latency	Data must be up to date even when it is backed up. Therefore, the backup solution needs frequent or continuous integration with data sources to update data to the latest version. In addition, backup solutions need to have continuous data ingestion or replication mechanisms, which eventually provide consistency and resiliency for the target data.
Security	Security is essential for the backup solution. Some of the requirements for the backup solution are as follows: • Data should be encrypted at rest. • Centralized data access governance with identity and access control management should be established.

Category	Requirement
DataOps	The requirement for data can be dynamic. Relevant or production-level data can change its nature due to any change in a business requirement. End-to-end life cycle management and governance of the backup solution are also essential. AI-based insight and AIOps for data can improve data operation quality significantly.
Automation	DataOps and other operations for the backup should be automated and configurable. Each backup should take a small amount of time with minimum disruption. Maximum automation needs to be integrated with the operations to reduce disruption during the backup process.
Backup performance	One primary non-functional requirement for the backup solution is to ensure that the backup duration is very small and the operations can be executed fast within a short time. The throughput and latency of backup data storage should be defined to meet the requirement of a fast and efficient backup solution.
Restoration	Along with backup, a restoration operation should also be automated, fast, and efficient. In addition, during the restoration phase, data corruption should be avoided to ensure the consistency and integrity of the data.
Type of snapshot backup	There are different backup policies for snapshot backups, which determine the number of full backups and incremental or delta backups to be made. Here are different kinds of snapshot backup based on the backup frequency: Full backup – Everything is backed up on a regular schedule, regardless of whether anything has changed. The archive bit is reset upon each backup. Incremental backup – All data modified since the last backup must be backed up. The archive bit is reset. Differential backup – All data modified since the last full backup is backed up. The archive bit is not reset.
Backup governance and policy	Along with backup frequency, RTO, and RPO, it is also essential to distinguish between the different business requirements for backup, such as operational data protection, an audit, or regulatory purposes. Therefore, the backup policy should be defined based on those requirements.
Backup topology	Based on the backup type, data can be backed up in the following ways: • Cold – data is backed up and archived • Warm – data is backed up, and periodic updates are done to the whole backup by running incremental backups. • Active – either real-time replication, incremental, or regularly full backups is taken.
Caching	Data caching should be eventually consistent. A managed DBaaS reduces the organization's operations as the cloud service providers provide the service as a managed service. These managed DBaaSs are easy to integrate and manage.
Event message	Message data should be replicated in multiple regions available in the solution. Furthermore, the replication should be in real time.

Table 6.5 – The requirements for the backup and restore solution

All the requirements described in *Table 6.5* are often described as backup policies, and organizations must determine their policies during the assessment and design phase of the solution. *Table 6.6* describes a standard backup policy template for organizations:

Policy	Description
Backup application	Name of the backup application being used
Backup data	Name of the backup data
Target backup storage	Details of the backup storage
The total amount of data being backed up	The total storage capacity utilized or the size of a single full backup
Backup geographical topology	The details of a selected geographical topology
Backup topology	The details of a selected topology
Daily	Incremental, differential, full, and so on
Weekly/monthly/yearly	Full every week/month/year
Daily incremental	The number of days to retain incremental backup
Daily full	The number of days to retain full backup
Weekly full	The number of weeks to retain weekly full backup
Monthly full	The number of months to retain monthly full backup
Quarterly full	The number of years to retain quarterly full backup
Yearly full	The number of years to retain yearly full backup
Disaster recovery policy	Yes/no – whether disaster recovery for the backup data is a requirement or not
Migration	If the organization is required to migrate existing backed-up data to the cloud

Table 6.6 – A standard backup policy template

Table 6.7 shows an example of a backup policy for a containerized application deployed on IBM Cloud Kubernetes Service on IBM Cloud:

Policy	Description
Backup application	IBM Spectrum Protect Plus
Backup data	Usually, there are different kinds of data, and each category may need a different set of backup policies. Therefore, running a data discovery or classification program is essential to identify different data types and their corresponding backup policies. Here is a set of data: • Application configuration of Kubernetes • Application log and configuration • Application properties • Data from a containerized PostgreSQL database
Target backup storage	IBM Cloud Object Storage
The total amount of data being backed up	Native data – ~50 TB
Backup geographical topology	Multi-zone
Backup topology	Active
Daily	Incremental for an application and full for a database
Weekly	Full
Daily incremental	15 days
Daily full	15 days
Weekly full	4 weeks
Monthly full	3 months
Quarterly full	1 year
Yearly full	5 years
DR policy	Yes
Migration	Yes

Table 6.7 – A standard backup policy

After identifying the requirement, it is also essential to establish some best practices to design an efficient backup solution. Some of the best practices are as follows:

- Design a backup solution to back up data using an appropriate tool for different storage types, such as **IBM Spectrum Protect Plus** or cloud-native aware tools.

- When the applications store and consume data on disks or in files, it is essential to take regular backups or snapshots of that data. Use *cloud-native* snapshot technologies.

- IBM Spectrum Protect Plus or similar can back up persistent volumes and additional cluster resources and configurations.

The next section of this chapter discusses a reference data analytics solution.

Exploring a big data analytics solution for the healthcare industry

We have taken the **Landorous** use case mentioned in the first chapter for this section. The backup solution for healthcare use cases has several requirements, as described in *Table 6.8*:

Category	Requirements
Backup	All identified system data should be automatically backed up regularly.
Data classification	For the solution's efficiency, different data storage requires different backup solutions. Therefore, data is categorized into different tiers and classes.
Standard and best practices	Every application and data storage should have a backup schedule, procedure, and policy document that matches the application availability, criticality, importance, and incident management standard.
Test and evaluation	There should be formal documented procedures for performing backups, which cover the following: • The types of information and software to be backed up. • The accuracy and completeness of backup records. • The restoration procedure • The backup test procedure, including an automated restoration to check backup consistency and backup validation. • Backups should be tested quarterly to verify reliability, confidentiality, consistency, and integrity. A corresponding restoration test will also be run to ensure that the backup is appropriately working.
Backup cycles	Backup cycles are based on tier classification.
Protection	Protection of backups in the case of incident and disaster is mandatory in cloud storage.

Category	Requirements
Regulation and compliance	Backup arrangements should consider legal, regulatory, and contractual requirements, including handling sensitive information, document retention, customer information, and data retention requirements.
Backup storage	Backup arrangements should enable operating systems, application software, system software associated with technical infrastructure (computer equipment, virtual systems, network equipment, and critical infrastructure), and business information to be restored within a critical timescale (for example, the timescale beyond which a loss of service would be unacceptable to the organization) by using one or more of the following: • Online storage (which often involves backing up information to **Direct-Attached Storage (DAS)**, a **Storage Area Network (SAN)**, or **Network-Attached Storage (NAS)**) that typically provides access to backups of information almost instantaneously. • Near-line storage (which often involves backing up information to an automated tape library), which enables the restoration of information within minutes. • Offline storage often involves IT colleagues who perform backup and restore activities manually, resulting in longer restoration times.
Security	• Backups should be subject to an equivalent level of protection as live information. • Restoration locations used for recovery purposes should have the same security measures as the original data source. • All backup data containing confidential or internal information, including customer or personal data and health data, should be encrypted in line with the encryption standard.
Governance	All testing/restoration of backups should be recorded in a central repository and documented consistently to ensure that these tests can be tracked and audited. In addition, central governance of the backup life cycle should be defined.
Frequency	• Backups of essential information and software (for example, business information, systems information, and application information) should be performed frequently and in line with the period specified by the criticality assignment in the asset management register. • The RTO and RPO will determine regularly backups. An on-demand backup may also be required.
Monitoring and reporting	Monitoring and reporting tools should exist to measure the performance of backups using KPIs regularly and notify of any backup failures or errors.
Testing	• Testing should be aligned with application/system criticality and backup usability. • An organization should use a sample of backup information to restore selected information system functions as part of contingency plan testing.

Category	Requirements
Compliance	Backup retention periods should be aligned with an organization's data retention policy to ensure that all applicable regulatory frameworks, such as the **General Data Protection Regulation** (**GDPR**), are considered.
Life cycle	Industry best practices should appropriately dispose of backups. The retention period for essential business information should be determined, considering any requirement for archive copies to be permanently retained. Deleting a backup should require at least two organization colleagues, one of which should be the backup owner.
Protection and disaster recovery for backups	Backups should be protected from loss, damage, and unauthorized access, depending on the criticality of the service, by doing the following: • Storing backup media (for example, DVDs, magnetic tapes, and computer disks) to manufacturer specifications. • Locating removable media in a locked, fireproof computer media safe on-site to enable important information to be restored quickly. • Keeping copies in secure facilities off-site or in different zones to enable systems or networks to be restored using alternative facilities in the event of a disaster. • Restricting access to a limited number of authorized individuals (for example, using access control software, physical locks, and keys).
Secure backups	• Confidentiality, integrity, and the availability of backup information at storage locations and in transit should be protected. • Media backups should be stored in a secure location, preferably an off-site facility, such as an alternate backup site or a commercial storage facility. The location's security should be reviewed at least annually. • In situations where confidentiality is essential, backups should be protected by encryption according to the encryption standard. • Backup media holding data that is classified as public should also be encrypted and transferred to backup media to prevent unauthorized interception and stored on media to prevent unauthorized access.
Incident management	• Data backup processes should follow an incident response standard. • All emergency restorations of backups should follow the current incident response standard.

Table 6.8 – The functional requirements for the backup solution

What needs to be backed up

There are different types of data and files for this use case. The list of workloads that need to have an associated backup solution is as follows:

- All configuration and log files in the container platform.

- All Postgres instances on the respective container platform.

- All files located on the respective systems/servers.

- All virtual machine instances on the respective systems/clusters.

- All filesystem backups of the AIX, Linux, and Wintel servers on the OS level.

The backup solution for the containerized platform

In this solution, open source **Velero** tools are used to back up all configuration and log files in the container platform and all Postgres instances on the respective container platform. In a single-region **multi-zone region** (**MZR**), Velero runs consensus among the nodes to determine the leader zone. Once the leader is selected, the delta amount of data from other followers is copied to the leader. The backup controller then copies the data from either the `etcd` or the containerized PostgreSQL from the leader availability zone to the corresponding bucket in IBM Cloud Object Storage. *Figure 6.5* shows the backup solution for the containerized platform. Velero also provides agents for restoration, which can restore data to `etcd` or the target PostgreSQL database:

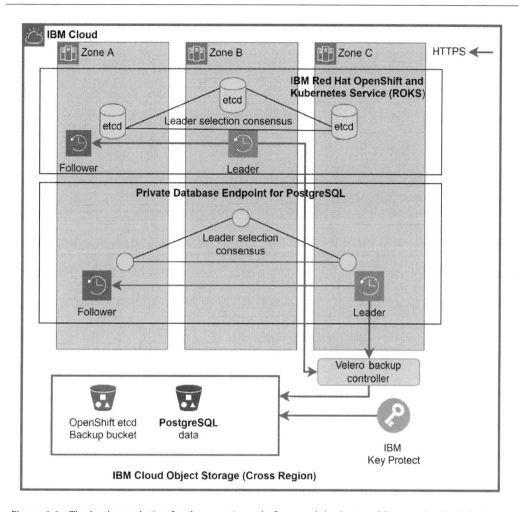

Figure 6.6 – The backup solution for the container platform and the PostgreSQL containerized database

The backup solution for all VM instances with IBM Spectrum Protect Plus

IBM Spectrum Protect Plus provides near-instant recovery, replication, reuse, and retention in hybrid cloud environments. IBM Spectrum Protect Plus can be deployed on any hybrid cloud platform.

IBM Spectrum Protect is used for enterprise workload backups. *Figure 6.7* shows the IBM reference architecture for *backup* and *restoration* using IBM Spectrum Protect for a VMware workload on IBM Cloud. **Spectrum Protect Plus** provides a GUI to configure backup policies for frequency, recovery time, and point objectives. Individual VMs and file versions can be restored using rapid recovery. In addition, IBM Spectrum Protect Plus provides data governance and scalability for long-term backup storage on top of the core capabilities of IBM Spectrum Protect:

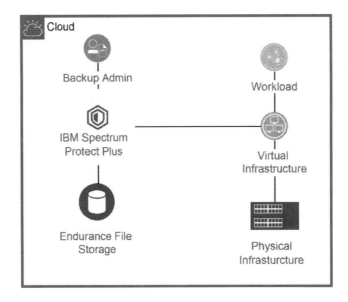

Figure 6.7 – IBM reference architecture backup and restoration using IBM
Spectrum Protect for a VMware workload on IBM Cloud

The backup solution for all files with IBM Spectrum Scale

As cloud workloads are distributed globally, sometimes the distance can reduce performance and latency. There are cases where migration projects failed terribly, and the entire workload was rolled back to on-premises. For example, in the **Aerodactyl** project, after migrating specific jobs to the cloud, they started to run slower than on-premises because the cloud data centers were four times further from the legacy data centers. **IBM Spectrum Scale** enables **AFM-based Asynchronous Disaster Recovery** (**AFM DR**). To mirror flat files and databases with sites spanning more than 1,200 miles, IBM Spectrum Scale uses **Active File Management** (**AFM**) technology, which enables IBM Spectrum Scale to replicate files asynchronously across data centers automatically. It also provides built-in automation, security, and monitoring. For the Aerodactyl project, we created two separate scale clusters in two data centers and connected the two clusters using AFM DR. In AFM DR, one site is marked as the primary site, and the other is marked as the secondary site.

Spectrum Scale copies data from the primary site to the secondary site asynchronously. First, Spectrum Scale performs an initial copy, and once that is finished, it starts incremental copying of changes in data from the primary site to the secondary site asynchronously. During disaster recovery, the secondary site can be marked as primary and continues business as usual. Both the primary and secondary sites can reverse their roles. Spectrum provides a real-time monitoring dashboard to understand resource utilization and system performance. The primary function of IBM Spectrum Scale is to provide flat file and database management. However, we used Spectrum Scale for the **Aerodactyl** project for logs and configuration, some Python jobs, and many static data files.

Summary

Storage is crucial for a practical application modernization program. Storage should be highly available, resilient, and protected against fault, disaster, cyberattacks, and other losses. This chapter explained the best practices for modern storage design through some reference solutions and use cases. We also explored IBM's offerings as well as recommendations for storage offerings.

In the next chapter, we will explore networking, another critical and essential component of modern cloud solutions. We will look at multiple use cases and reference solutions to explore the best practices for networking design.

Further reading

- *IBM Spectrum Protect Plus*: https://www.ibm.com/products/ibm-spectrum-protect-plus

- *IBM Cloud Foundation Skills Series – Block Storage Deeper Dive*: https://www.youtube.com/watch%3Fv=PBYGdk3KDz4&list=PLmesOgYt3nKCfsXqx-A5k1bP7t146U4rz&index=32

- *IBM Cloud Foundation Skills Series – File Storage Deeper Dive*: https://www.youtube.com/watch%3Fv=ZHSrUZf2e10&list=PLmesOgYt3nKCfsXqx-A5k1bP7t146U4rz&index=30

- *IBM Cloud Foundation Skills Series – Getting Started with Cloud Object Storage*: https://www.youtube.com/watch%3Fv=VEoj69V6Rfg&list=PLmesOgYt3nKCfsXqx-A5k1bP7t146U4rz&index=35

- Getting started with Block Storage. Available at: https://cloud.ibm.com/docs/BlockStorage%3Ftopic=BlockStorage-getting-started

- Getting started with File Storage. Available at: https://cloud.ibm.com/docs/FileStorage%3Ftopic=FileStorage-getting-started

- Getting started with IBM Cloud Object Storage. Available at: `https://cloud.ibm.com/docs/cloud-object-storage%3Ftopic=cloud-object-storage-getting-started`

- Red Hat® OpenShift® Data Foundation. Available at: `https://www.ibm.com/docs/en/cloud-paks/cloud-pak-watson-aiops/3.1.1?topic=requirements-storage-considerations#odf`

- IBM Spectrum Scale Container Native. Available at: `https://www.ibm.com/docs/en/scalecontainernative?topic=o-introduction`

- Portworx storage. Available at: `https://www.ibm.com/docs/en/cloud-paks/cloud-pak-watson-aiops/3.1.1?topic=requirements-storage-considerations#portworx`

7

Designing and Implementing Networking in Hybrid Cloud Infrastructure

If application code does not follow specific characteristics for efficient and effective cloud infrastructures, it can become impossible to design a secure and high-performing networking communication platform. The success of the cloud mainly depends on the network design of the target platform. If we adopt lift-and-shift or rehost migration patterns and migrate them without refactoring, the cloud target platform might provide poor latency and throughput. Often, the cloud is blamed for the failure. However, in most cases, the legacy application implementation and the target platform's networking design are the main reasons for poor performance. Therefore, this chapter discusses the main challenges and requirements for efficient network communication.

In this chapter, we will cover the following main topics:

- Planning an efficient network solution

- Exploring a reference solution for networking a containerized application

- Exploring **IBM Cloud Pak for Network Automation (ICP4NA)**

- Implementing edge computing with IBM Cloud Satellite

We will gain an understanding of the detailed requirements for cloud solution networking and the different capabilities that are available on the IBM Cloud platform to design solutions for those requirements. Additionally, we will explore the reference architectures for an efficient networking solution on the IBM Cloud platform.

Planning an efficient network solution

An efficient network solution needs to analyze each layer's requirement in the **Open Service Gateway Initiative (OSGi)** model, as shown in *Figure 7.1*. Different layers have different components and characteristics; therefore, they require different mechanisms alongside different levels of services and components. Therefore, planning for efficient network solutions should include functional and non-functional requirements for different layers of the network platform:

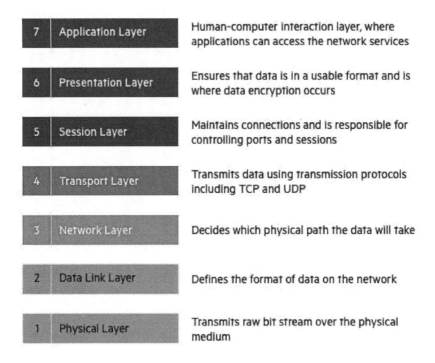

Figure 7.1 – Different layers of networks

The network solution for any cloud application's architecture on IBM Cloud or any other cloud should provide a robust defense against anticipated threats alongside a fast and highly available connection. Furthermore, the network solution should combine a perimeter for defenses, network segmentations, and internal security controls to protect information and data processing. The following section focuses on the different functional requirements of cloud networking solutions.

Functional requirements

Let's get familiar with the functional requirements of network solutions for cloud modernization and migration:

- The ability to connect the cloud platform with an enterprise network through a private network.

- The ability to access an activity directory for the **Single Sign-On** of a user.

- The ability to maintain IP addresses – **Bring Your Own IP (BYOIP)**

- The ability to enable private network connectivity between apps and cloud services. Often, inside a cluster or application deployment environment, applications access services using private service endpoints. Most cloud services have both public and private service endpoints. Additionally, services are accessible over private and public connections.

- Access to applications: Apps are exposed to the public network. Therefore, additional data encryption in motion should be applied to establish a secure connection between the end users and the applications. That way, data can be secured in motion.

- The ability to map a domain name to an IP address using domain services.

Non-functional requirements

Before designing the networking solution of a cloud platform, it is necessary to identify the non-functional requirements. A list of non-functional requirements for the networking of a cloud solution can be found in *Table 7.1*:

Network virtualization and network operations	The ability to design hierarchical network infrastructure components and layouts prior to deploying any compute instances on the cloud platform, such as the following: • Firewalls and ACLs • Subnets or **virtual local area networks (VLANs)** • Routing • VPNs • **Network address translation (NAT)** • Load balancing
Virtual network interface	The ability to enable multiple virtual **network interface cards (vNICs)**, each with its own **media access control (MAC)** address.

IP address management	The ability to provide support for private IP addresses so that customers can mix public IP addresses and private IP addresses on the same compute instance.
Network segmentation and isolation	The ability to support a single entity with multiple virtual network segments without using third-party software to build an overlay.
	The ability to allow the entity to create multiple subnets per virtual network and enable micro-segmentation.
	The ability to support virtual networks that are fully isolated and not routable externally. Instance configurations must exist within the isolated virtual networks without having any public IP addresses or internet routing to avoid security breaches.
Static and dynamic IP address management	The ability to provide support for the assignment of static and dynamic IP addresses. The IP addresses must move between compute instances or load balancing pools and persist if the entity wants.
	The ability to define a customized RFC1918 IP address space within the cloud service environment.
	The ability to provide multiple IP addresses that are independently routed for all VMs deployed on the cloud platform.
	The ability to support both IP versions (IPv4 and IPv6) at either the gateway or instance level and expose this functionality.
Redundancy and distribution	The target cloud network architecture provides capabilities to define virtual networks that span two or more physical data center locations.
Private WAN connection	The ability to support two or more private WAN connections per entity and geographic location. At a minimum, the service capabilities (such as the routing features) must support two scenarios: • Organizations with multiple offices that do not want to backhaul all traffic via a private WAN connection. • Organizations that can leverage private WAN connectivity from multiple carriers in a single location to achieve redundancy.
Gateway	The ability to define a gateway and custom routing for each virtual network. At a minimum, we need to enable the entity to route all traffic to compute instances on the virtual network through a virtual appliance such as a firewall.

Load balancing	The ability to route traffic between two virtual networks that belong to the same entity. If the virtual networks use private IP addresses, the traffic must be routable between the two virtual networks without leaving private IP space (that is, the traffic must not cross the public internet).
	The ability to provide a frontend load balancing service capability. At a minimum, the platform should support the load balancing of HTTP, HTTPS traffic, SSL offloading and passthrough, server health checks, and app rules for programmability and traffic manipulation.
	The ability to provide a backend load balancing service capability. At a minimum, the platform should support the load balancing of HTTP, HTTPS traffic, SSL offloading and passthrough, server health checks, and app rules for programmability and traffic manipulation.
	The ability to support session affinity features within the load balancing service.
	The ability to configure global load balancing via a self-service capability, where requests can be directed to endpoints located in different data centers (usually, this is a DNS-based service).
Health monitoring	The ability to support endpoint health check routing for cloud services.
Latency-based request routing	The cloud service must support latency-based request routing where the request is directed to the endpoint with the lowest latency between the requestor and the location.
Geographic distribution	The cloud service must support geographic request routing, where the request is directed to the endpoint based on the location of the request's origin.
	The ability to provide simultaneous support for multiple virtual networks or routing segments per entity and geographic location.
Private networking	The ability to provide a mechanism to communicate between all the cloud data centers via the private network. This service offering must route data center-to-data center traffic, including traffic across geographic locations, over a private network.
	The ability to support two or more private network connections, such as VPNs, MPLS, and Direct Connect, per virtual network.

Network performance management	The ability to provide the option to purchase an explicit network performance target or performance tier within the cloud service, such as a specific guarantee of latency, jitter, packet loss, or bandwidth throughput.
DNS service	The ability to map a domain name with its corresponding IP address.
Monitoring	The ability to provide a real-time network performance visibility dashboard.
Network isolation	The ability to support multiple networks using security groups.
Enterprise connectivity	The ability to provide a site-to-site VPN that supports multiple subnets.
	The ability to provide support for link bandwidth of greater than 500 Mbps and jumbo frames with a latency of less than 5 ms.
	The ability to provide VPN backend connectivity.
	The ability to provide enterprise connectivity for higher bandwidth requirements.
	All traffic between the cloud platform's data centers should be automatically accelerated using WAN optimization technology.
	All WAN traffic between the cloud data centers must be encrypted, regardless of the protocols for internal connectivity.
	All LAN traffic between the compute instances within the data center must be encrypted in transit and at rest.
	The ability to enable private WAN connections in the cloud service from their data centers.
Operations	Networking requires continuous maintenance, including event monitoring, activity monitoring, security operations, health monitoring, and other operations.

Table 7.1 – Networking requirements for the solution

Now that we understand the functional and non-functional requirements of network solutions in different areas such as communication, connectivity, security, and operations, we will explore a reference solution for networking on a cloud platform.

Exploring a reference network solution

This section will explore a reference solution for cloud modernization, focusing on the networking components. The cloud provider often provides basic connectivity. However, it can also provide capabilities and services for connectivity, security, reliability, and operations. An efficient network reference solution needs to include essential components or services from cloud service providers to ensure a solution for all functional and non-functional requirements, as discussed in the previous section of this chapter. For example, *Figure 7.2* shows the different network components and services used in the cloud solution provided by IBM Cloud. IBM recommends several services for network solutions based on different customer requirements:

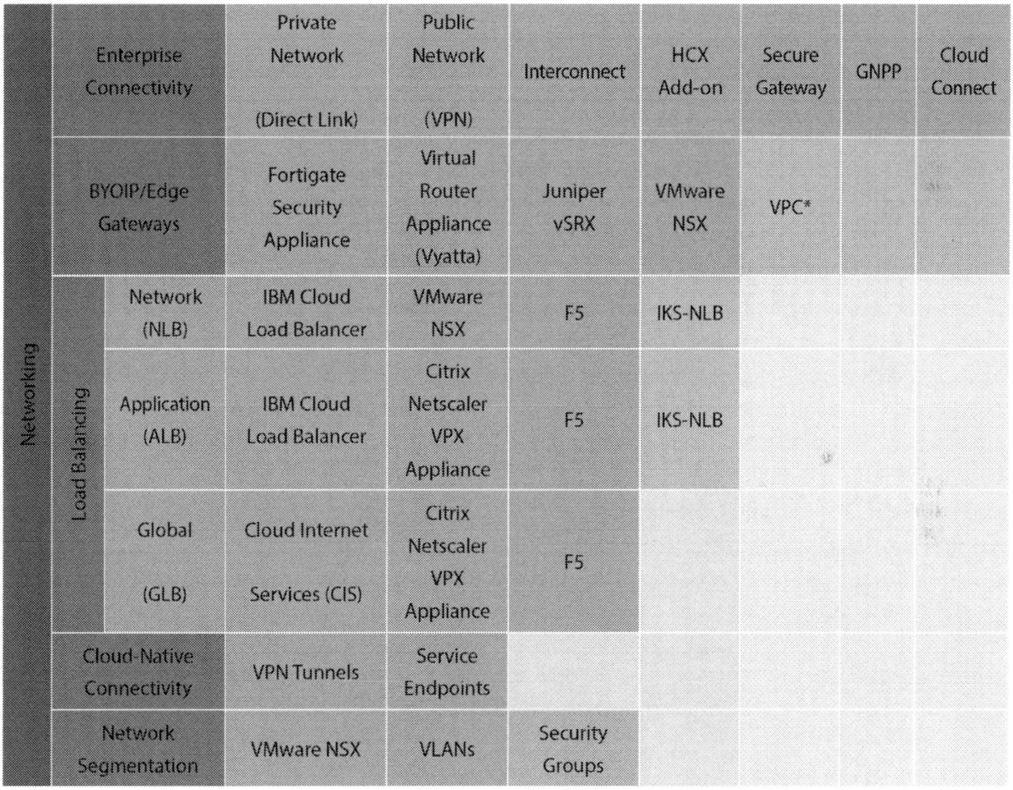

Enterprise Connectivity	Private Network (Direct Link)	Public Network (VPN)	Interconnect	HCX Add-on	Secure Gateway	GNPP	Cloud Connect
BYOIP/Edge Gateways	Fortigate Security Appliance	Virtual Router Appliance (Vyatta)	Juniper vSRX	VMware NSX	VPC*		
Network (NLB)	IBM Cloud Load Balancer	VMware NSX	F5	IKS-NLB			
Application (ALB)	IBM Cloud Load Balancer	Citrix Netscaler VPX Appliance	F5	IKS-NLB			
Global (GLB)	Cloud Internet Services (CIS)	Citrix Netscaler VPX Appliance	F5				
Cloud-Native Connectivity	VPN Tunnels	Service Endpoints					
Network Segmentation	VMware NSX	VLANs	Security Groups				

Figure 7.2 – IBM Cloud services for network solutions

A network reference solution should include components for the following topics:

- Virtualization to enable virtual network functions

- Reliable connectivity with fault tolerance capability and redundancy

- Highly available connectivity

- Security and segmentation

- Network functions such as load balancing, DNS, and more

In the following sections, we will discuss these essential components of a network solution. Let's start with virtualization.

Network virtualization

In this book, we have been primarily discussing cloud-native applications. However, for the **Linux on IBM Power** system, IBM also provides hybrid network virtualization. Firewalls, load balancers, segmentations, and other network components are virtualized on the IBM Cloud platform. *Figure 7.3* shows a multi-region, multi-zone deployment of the IBM ROKS cluster. The production **Virtual Private Cloud** (**VPC**) is replicated over two zones in each region. In addition to the VPC load balancer for multi-zone deployment, this solution also has **Cloud Internet Service** (**CIS**) as a **global load balancer** (**GLB**) for network load balancing between two separate regions. The IBM Cloud services are connected to the ROKS cluster on the production VPC using private service endpoints. The end user can access applications over the internet. There are multiple subnets for frontend applications, backend applications, and middleware such as Kafka, DevOps pipelines, and other middleware components. These application and middleware components communicate with each other using private endpoints. Additionally, there is a single-zone management VPC in each region. The next section of this chapter describes the detailed architectural decisions for this reference solution. However, before we go into the detailed architecture decisions, let's look at the different capabilities provided by IBM Cloud for designing networking solutions:

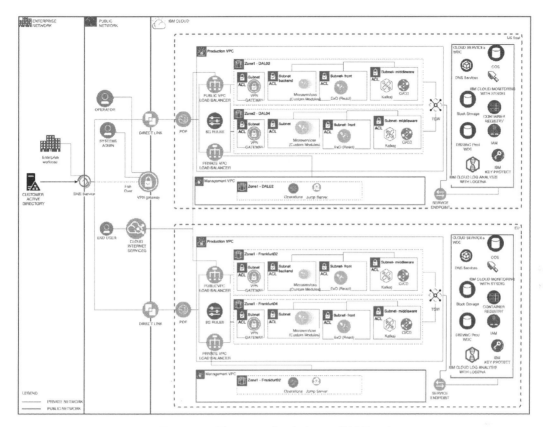

Figure 7.3 – The network solution on IBM Cloud

A VPC provides a logically isolated, secure platform. It can be configured with a virtual firewall. Each instance can have multiple subnets, and embedded security groups ensure protection. A VPC can be created at any distributed location worldwide and can be associated with any IP range. So, besides the IBM IP address pool, an organization can bring its IP address and attach that to the VPC. Both private connectivity and public connectivity are available for each VPC. Therefore, this can provide hybrid connectivity. In *Figure 7.3*, the end users are connected to the applications over public connections, whereas the operator and administrator are connected to the VPC through private connections. A VPC can be deployed on a single geographic location and stretched over multiple geo-locations. It also provides capabilities for observability and other operations. In a cloud environment, the VPC is a self-contained private cloud platform. Therefore, they are popular with organizations that require security and regulations, such as financial and government organizations.

Redundancy and distribution

The selection of the correct geographic location pattern for networking is crucial. Often, users need geographic dispersion in a cloud solution. In our reference solution, as depicted in *Figure 7.3*, a multi-region, multi-zone networking topology is chosen to ensure high availability and geographic connectivity. One of the regions is based in the US, and the other deployment region is in Frankfurt. *Figure 7.4* shows a decision tree that can be used to select the geographic location pattern for deployment:

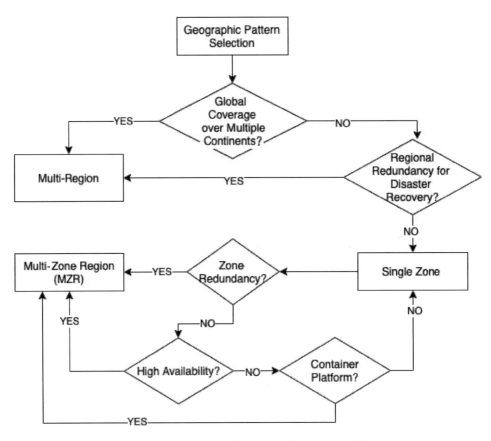

Figure 7.4 – A decision tree for geographic pattern selection

Multi-zone regions (MZRs)

MZRs are composed of three or more zones that are independent of each other to ensure that single-failure events only affect a single zone. MZRs provide low latency (< 2 ms of latency) and high bandwidth (> 1,000 Gbps) connectivity across zones.

The advantage of an MZR is that it provides consistent cloud services across different zones, better resiliency, high availability, and higher interconnect speeds between data centers for resources. These features can be critical to applications. For example, deploying applications in an MZR rather than a **Single Zone Region (SZR)** can increase availability from 99.9% to 99.99%. In addition, IBM has over 60 private interaction **Points of Presence (POPs)**:

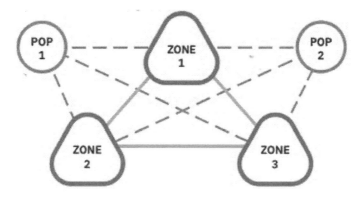

Figure 7.5 – IBM Cloud MZRs delivering availability and resiliency within a region

Each IBM MZR has three or more availability zones that ensure high availability and resiliency within the region, and that allow ACID data consistency for business services. There are three or more data centers within, approximately, 6 miles of each other with low latency between them. Each zone is independent of any electrical, mechanical, or network components. Each zone ensures high availability by having redundant physical resources across zones and avoiding a single point of hardware failure. Each MZR offers a complete and consistent set of IaaS and PaaS services to support highly available, enterprise-class workloads. *Figure 7.5* shows that these zones are connected to two POPs, which provides WAN resiliency.

Enterprise connectivity

Often, in a hybrid cloud platform, cloud connectivity is not enough. Cloud workloads need to communicate with legacy or latency-focused workloads in on-premises locations. In addition, enterprise connectivity between operator networks and cloud networks is essential for a platform's management and operations. Here is a list of questions that can help you to identify the various requirements for enterprise connectivity:

- Speed/bandwidth requirements: for example, < 1 Gbps, 1–5 Gbps, or > 5 Gbps.

- What should the preferred location be? Is there a provider available?

- What is the tenancy requirement (dedicated versus shared)?

- Do we need different environments for production versus non-production workloads?

- What is the scalability, that is, the *speed-on-demand* requirement?

- Where is the traffic going? To a local **Domain Controller** (**DC**) or global DCs?

- What is the availability requirement? Is redundancy required? Is dynamic failover required?

- What is the network latency requirement?

- What is the current network architecture (for example, the WAN topology, data center location, and network carrier of the intranet)?

- Does the customer have an MZR requirement?

- Does the customer have connectivity to other cloud services? Which network provider is used for this purpose?

- Does the cloud DC need to be connected to the current DC as an extension?

- Does the cloud DC need to be directly connected to the customer's current private WAN network (MPLS) as a new site?

- Does the customer need to leverage their current connectivity to IBM CMS to connect to the IBM Cloud platform?

- Does the traffic between on-premises and the cloud need to be encrypted?

- Does the customer have multiple network providers that need to be woven together as one network?

IBM Cloud provides enterprise connectivity for different Direct Link platforms for both classical and VPC platforms. Usually, Direct Link 1.0 is used for classical infrastructures, and IBM Cloud Direct Link 2.0 is used for VPCs and modern platforms to ensure enterprise connectivity:

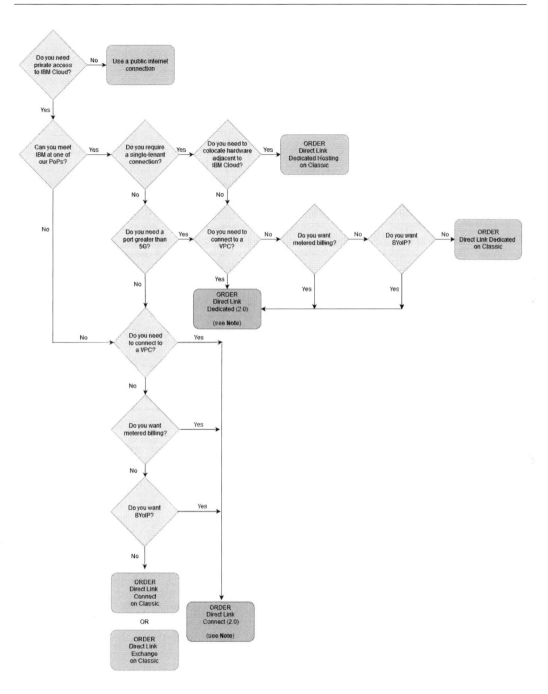

Figure 7.6 – A decision matrix for IBM Cloud Direct Link selection to ensure
enterprise connectivity (credit: IBM Cloud documentation)

Next, we need to understand the fundamentals of network isolation or segmentation, which is essential for the security controls of a cloud platform. Therefore, in the following section, we describe network segmentation's fundamental characteristics and some best practices for the implementation of network segmentation.

Network segmentation

Network segmentation is required to ensure security and isolation between different **IaaS underlay components**. The following requirements/constraints govern network segmentation requirements when creating an efficient network solution. For example, if the answer to the following question set is *Yes* for one or more items, we need to incorporate network segmentation into the solution:

Feature	Required?
Enterprise connectivity	Yes/no
BYOIP	Yes/no
Workload isolation	Yes/no
Public routes to access native cloud services	Yes/no
Private routes to access native cloud services	Yes/no
Firewall-based segmentation	Yes/no
Security groups-based segmentation	Yes/no
Hybrid clouds	Yes/no
Multiple cloud connectivity	Yes/no

Table 7.2 – The requirements for network segmentation

Table 7.3 shows the different services available on IBM Cloud to ensure network segmentation:

Segmentation components	Description	Positioning/use cases	Limitations
VLANs with traditional firewalls\ Edge GW	IBM Cloud uses VLANs to isolate traffic underlaying public and private networks. VLANs are assigned as needed, and additional VLANs can be ordered for additional segmentation purposes.	You need to order additional VLANs for segmentation purposes; for example, an n-tiered application requiring isolation between tiers.	• VLANs are specific to the routers used in IBM Cloud data centers; therefore, the VLAN/Edge GW combination only controls the traffic on the underlay network. • Any attempt to order a VLAN might be prevented due to capacity restrictions in the location that has been selected.
Security groups	Network segmentation can be implemented using security groups. A security group is a set of IP filter rules that define how to handle ingress and egress traffic to a **virtual server instance** (**VSI**)'s public and private interface.	Simple/low-complexity segmentation with a minimal set of VSIs needs to be segmented.	
NSX	Connect isolated VXLANs and stub networks to shared underlay networks by providing standard gateway services such as a DHCP, VPN, NAT, dynamic routing, and load balancing.	Use additional VMware VXLANs and FW rulesets to provide additional network segmentation on the overlay network.	This can only be used to segment the overlay network. However, it can communicate with the underlay (VLANs).

Table 7.3 – Cloud services for network segmentation

Next, we will discuss the implementation of network segmentation in a VPC.

Network segmentation using VPCs

There are different use cases for network segmentation inside a VPC. For example, a subnet can be an efficient solution to isolate the backend microservices in the production VPC from the middleware, such as the DevOps pipeline, so that the developer has no access to the production VPC:

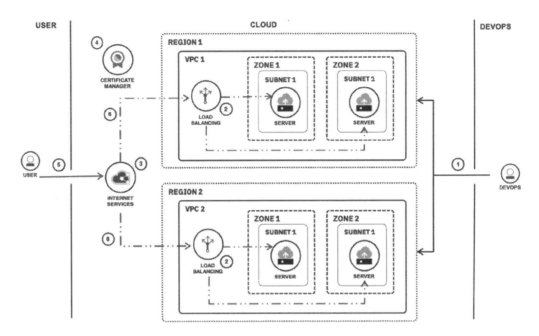

Figure 7.7 – Network segmentation for IBM VPC (credit: IBM Cloud documentation)

Table 7.4 describes some solutions for network isolation using VPCs:

Category	Requirement	Solution
Geographical distribution	Global communication is required in different regions such as Europe and the USA.	Multiple regions are used to enable geographic distribution across two different regions. Figure 7.7 shows a deployment model with two different regions.
	High availability and zone redundancy are required for workload protection and performance.	Multiple zones are used in each of the MZRs. The **High Availability** (**HA**)-enforced deployment model requires multi-zone deployment. Figure 7.7 shows a deployment model with two zones per region.
Private network	For disaster recovery, the private network must distinguish between production and non-production workloads, geographic dispersion, security, and regulation.	An individual VPC is deployed within a region. A VPC can have any topology for geographical distribution. Figure 7.7 shows that each region has its own VPC.
Isolation	Different kinds of workloads such as frontend and backend applications need to be isolated.	There are multiple subnets across the availability zones. Each subnet can have an ACL list to determine the policy for allowing connections from different sources and destinations.
Global load balancing	Workloads are deployed in multiple geo-locations and for geographic coverage or failover. So, the load balancer needs to balance requests globally.	Global load balancing is crucial for two different regions. IBM CIS provides the global load balancing capability and **Distributed Denial of Service** (**DDoS**) mitigation and detection service. Figure 7.7 shows that IBM CIS is set up to be a secure connection and provides **Global Load Balancing** (**GLB**) between two regions.
Zonal load balancing	In each region, there are multiple zones, and they are replicas of each other. The MZR load balancer ensures the proper distribution of requests among different zones.	Each VPC provides a personal load balancing capability to enable load balancing across available zones.

Table 7.4 – How to enable segmentation using VPCs

Another network segmentation implementation technique uses security groups within a VPC. In the next section, we will discuss the use of security groups for the implementation of network segmentation in detail.

Network segmentation using security groups

For this use case, the frontend and backend applications need to be isolated from each other. Each application is deployed within a subnet with related security. Therefore, even the applications are in the same zone. However, they are isolated in two different locations. Security groups and ACL help to configure an IP address for inbound and outbound requests. For example, in *Figure 7.8*, different subnets are created for frontend and backend applications. Each subnet can allow specific IP addresses or all IP addresses, and similarly, subnets can be configured to deny access from a particular IP address or all IP addresses:

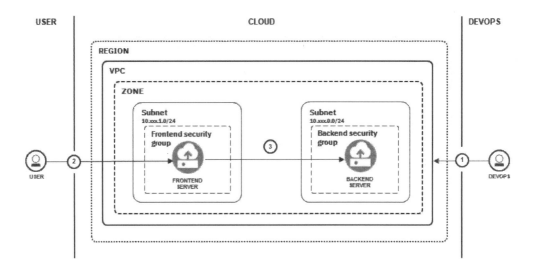

Figure 7.8 – Network isolation between frontend and backend
applications (credit: IBM Cloud documentation)

We can enforce ACL lists for subnets, as shown in *Table 7.5*, using security groups on both subnets for two different security groups for frontend and backend applications:

ACL list	ACL	IP address	Impact
Inbound	Deny	0.0.0.0/0	Deny HTTP traffic from the internet.
Inbound	Allow	192.27.1.27/32	Only an admin from the 192.10.10.10 IP address can access the backend application.
Outbound	Allow	172.06.0.0/20	The frontend application can access the backend application.
Outbound	Allow	192.27.1.27/32	An admin can receive an outgoing response from the backend application.
Outbound	Allow	172.06.0.0/20	The backend application can access the frontend application.
Outbound	Deny	0.0.0.0	All other outbound access is restricted for the backend application.

Table 7.5 – A sample ACL list for the backend application to enforce security group-based isolation

Additionally, we can also implement network segmentation using network policies on the Kubernetes container platform. The following section will discuss the network policies to implement network segmentation.

Network segmentation using network policies

A container platform such as Kubernetes and Red Hat OpenShift provides multiple ways in which to enable network segmentation. The following lists well-known methods to enable network isolation for different workloads deployed on the Red Hat OpenShift container platform:

- Using default and built-in network policies enforces the isolation of different projects in the same cluster.

- Customizing network policies to enable isolation between application pods. Red Hat OpenShift provides configuration capabilities to configure target nodes for different workloads and, therefore, ensures physical isolation among applications.

- Each project has an ingress controller to allow a specific project to expose services.

- VLANs are another valuable way to enable network segmentation. VLANs can isolate different components by isolating them on different Ethernet broadcast domains. For example, each Red Hat OpenShift container platform project is allocated a specific VLAN by default. Therefore, services from different projects are exposed through different VLANs. A single load balancer listens to the different VLANs. When a request comes to the load balancer on a VLAN, the load balancer forwards the request to the corresponding ingress controller.

For the OpenShift container platform, a network policy helps create segmentation for frontend and backend applications. The following is a network policy to isolate frontend applications from another workload. This network policy only allows HTTP and HTTPS calls with specific TCP protocols. In addition, `podSelector` ensures that only frontend applications are selected for this network policy. Finally, here is a `NetworkPolicy` example for an OpenShift cluster to ensure network segmentation within the same cluster:

```
kind: NetworkPolicy
apiVersion: networking.k8s.io/v1
metadata:
  name: allow-http-and-https
spec:
  podSelector:
    matchLabels:
      role: frontend
  ingress:
  - ports:
    - protocol: TCP
      port: 80
    - protocol: TCP
      port: 443
```

Network solutions should also include essential network functions, such as load balancing, intrusion detection, predictions, and mitigation. We will discuss some of the essential network functions in the following sections. That said, first, let's explore load balancing.

Load balancing

Here is a list of questions to understand the requirements for load balancing. If the answer to the following question set is *Yes* for one or more items, load balancing is required in multiple layers, such as the application, the network, or the VPC:

Feature	Required?
High SLA (over 95%) requirement for network communication for different workloads.	Yes/No
The application platform is the container.	Yes/No
Multiple geographic locations.	Yes/No
Load balancing between the cloud and co-locations.	Yes/No
Automatic disaster recovery failover.	Yes/No
The average throughput/bandwidth is high.	Yes/No

Table 7.6 – The requirements for load balancing

IBM Cloud has several services available for load balancing capabilities. *Table 7.7* shows the different load balancing services available on the IBM Cloud platform:

Load balancing components	Description	Positioning/use cases	Limitations
IBM Cloud load balancers	Load balance internet-facing traffic by forwarding traffic to healthy instances. This provides a variety of load balancing methods: **round-robin (RR)**, weighted RR, and least connections.	<ul><li>Load balancing among VSIs and bare metal compute instances.</li><li>Layer-4 load balancing by application port – HTTP, HTTPS, and TCP.</li><li>Public (internet-facing) load balancer only.</li><li>MZR support.</li></ul>	It might be possible to configure an intermediary (NSX GW) that has a SoftLayer private address as the backend server to the load balancer (with the actual servers being VMs attached to the network(s) managed by NSX).
IBM **Cloud Internet Service (CIS)**	An internet-facing GLB ensures traffic reliability, security, and performance at the network edge. Three editions will be covered in the comparison matrix later.	You need GLB services across multiple regions for different service such as DDoS protection, **web application firewall (WAF)**, TLS security, DNS operations, caching, page rules, and innovative routing options and CDN configuration.	Known limitations

Citrix NetScaler VPX	A dedicated virtual software appliance that provides load balancing on both public and private networks. Two editions are available and will be covered in the comparison matrix.	TCP optimization, compressing, caching, and WAF. The allows the reporting of the client's source IP instead of NetScaler.	Application firewalls with SSL offloading can decrease throughput. This requires appliance(s) for each site implementation. This requires appliance(s) for each site implementation.
F5	Intelligent L4–L7 load balancing and traffic management services are required locally and globally, robust network and WAF protection, and secure and federated application access.	TCP optimization, compressing, caching, WAF, and DDoS	F5 limits the appliance throughput based on the maximum bandwidth. However, because network performance is affected by many factors, not all configurations and topologies would be able to achieve maximum bandwidth.
NSX	This enables network traffic to follow multiple paths to a specific destination on the NSX overlay network.	There is no need for advanced features. Local to the VMware instance.	It can only load balance over the overlay network.

Table 7.7 – The load balancing services available on IBM Cloud

DNS service

The IBM DNS service provides the capability to manage IP addresses and associated domain name records. It also provides user access control management for different DNS records. In addition, the IBM DNS service has its own worldwide set of resolvers.

Network protection

Network connections must be secured and regulated. This section will explain the **Intrusion Prevention Service** (**IPS**) and **Intrusion Detection Service** (**IDS**) requirements for the cloud solution. Next, we will discuss some services that are available on IBM Cloud for network protection. In the following subsections, we will focus on firewalls and DDOS protection.

Firewalls

IBM's network services solution includes NGFW at the cloud perimeter and robust Layer-3 and Layer-7 filtering in the Cloudflare cloud solution. In addition, there are two different types of firewalls and virtual firewalls available on the IBM Cloud platform.

Perimeter firewalls

Perimeter firewalls within the cloud infrastructure (Palo Alto virtual firewalls) protect the cloud from external threats and provide encrypted communications with external entities. They provide the following:

- Stateful content inspection/filtering up to Layer-7

- DDoS protection

- Intrusion detection and protection

- Malware protection

- **Data leakage prevention** (**DLP**)

- A reverse proxy

- Site-to-site VPNs

In addition, IBM CIS will provide DDoS protection to build a comprehensive security solution.

Interior firewalls

Internal firewalls (Juniper vSRX) provide segmentation and secure connectivity between the Power Systems VS network segments and the VMware network segments, as permitted by the security policy. The servers within the cloud are either VMware VMs or bare metal. For the VMs, NSX-T provides secure networking with a distributed firewall.

The IBM Cloud Gateway Appliance supports the following capabilities:

Stateful packet inspection	NAT support
Public network protection	SSL/IPSec VPN termination
Private network protection	Open VPN termination
Ingress rules	HA option
Egress rules	Manage from the API and portal
VLAN protection	10 Gbps support
Multi-VLAN support	NGFW add-ons (IPS, AV, and WF)

Table 7.8 – The IBM Cloud Gateway Appliance supported capabilities

DDoS

An efficient solution features an offering called IBM CIS that includes comprehensive DDoS protection for internet-facing applications, endpoints, and interfaces. IBM CIS is powered by Cloudflare and is designed to protect anything connected to the internet:

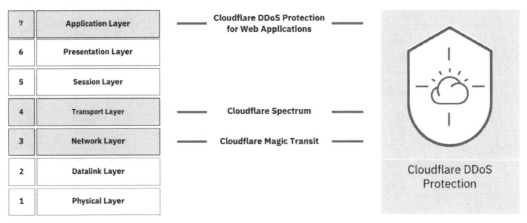

Figure 7.9 – DDoS prevention with IBM CIS in different attack layers

Different solutions are required for different layers to protect the workload from DDoS. The following subsections will discuss different DDoS protection solutions for different layers.

Application layer

IBM Cloud provides always-on DDoS protection for web assets (HTTP/HTTPS), powered by the intelligence harnessed from Cloudflare's always-learning global network. Cloudflare DDoS protection works with our cloud WAF, bot management, and other Layer-3/Layer-4 security services to protect assets from cyber threats.

Transport layer

Cloudflare Spectrum is a reverse proxy service that provides DDoS protection for any application (not just web applications), such as FTP, SSH, VoIP, gaming, or any application running over a TCP/UDP protocol. In addition, Spectrum comes with built-in load balancing and traffic acceleration for L4 traffic.

Network layer

Cloudflare Magic Transit provides BGP-based DDoS protection for network infrastructures, either in always-on or on-demand deployment modes. In addition, data centers in all 250 cities across 100 countries announce customer subnets to ingest network traffic and mitigate threats close to the source of an attack. Therefore, Cloudflare can ensure protection with more significant potential.

Next, we will discuss the architectural decisions for a secure and reliable network solution on the cloud platform.

Architecture decisions

The reference solution needs to provide capabilities mentioned in this chapter's *Functional and Non-functional requirements* section. There are different ways to enable those capabilities mentioned in the previous section. Here is a list of selections or decisions for designing a modern networking platform that enables different capabilities. *Table 7.9* shows different architectural decisions for the solution:

Requirement	Alternatives	Component decision	Reason
Enterprise connectivity On-premises connectivity	Direct Link 2.0 VPC VPN gateway	Direct Link 2.0 VPC VPN gateway	Provide a private connection between the cloud platform and the on-premises location. This link can be either single-tenant or multi-tenant. The direct link is preferred, especially for effective data communication and regulated workloads with strict network isolation requirements. In the case of failure, a secondary IPsec VPN is established between the cloud platform and on-premises location. A VPC VPN provides a secure tunnel for communication, but it has a limitation, as it cannot transmit more than 100 GB. Under normal conditions, a VPN gateway is used for operations and management, and in times of failure, it provides a failover communication channel.

Requirement	Alternatives	Component decision	Reason
Cloud-native connectivity	IBM Cloud service endpoints Public network endpoints	IBM Cloud service endpoints	IBM services are exposed to public and private service endpoints.
Network segmentation	VPCs Subnets Security groups ACLs Container network policies	VPCs, subnets, security groups, ACLs, and container network policies	• IBM VPCs provide secure, isolated virtual networks. By default, all resources within the same VPC can communicate over the private network. VPCs are divided into subnets that use a range of private IP addresses. • Security groups define groups of resources (which might be in different subnets) and assign uniform access rules. Security groups can be used as virtual firewalls to control traffic flow to/from worker nodes. • ACLs define a list of rules that limit who can access a subnet within a VPC. ACLs can be used to control traffic flow to and from the OpenShift cluster subnets. • Container network policies restrict egress/ingress traffic and communication between applications.
Application load balancing	OpenShift route Ingress controller Load balancer	OpenShift route	• Since the OpenShift cluster is created with a private service endpoint only, a public OpenShift route is needed to create public routes for selected applications. • The public OpenShift router functions as an application load balancer and exposes apps to the public network.

Requirement	Alternatives	Component decision	Reason
Local load balancing	VPC load balancer	Private load balancing	<ul><li>When the OpenShift multi-zone cluster with a private service endpoint is created, a private VPC load balancer is created by default.</li><li>The private VPC load balancer distributes traffic among the worker nodes across the zones.</li></ul>
		Public load balancing	<ul><li>When a public OpenShift router is added (to expose selected apps to the public internet), a public VPC load balancer is created by default.</li><li>The public VPC load balancer distributes the traffic among the worker nodes across the zones.</li></ul>

Table 7.9 – Architecture decisions for the network solution

Once we design and build the network solution in our cloud platform, we need to ensure continuous management of the network solution. First, we need to consider the network components deployed and built in the cloud. Then, we need to ensure the network components are continuously monitored and supported. Finally, to enforce continuous management, we need to enable different operations. The following section will discuss ICP4NA and its capabilities for different operations.

Exploring IBM Cloud Pak for Network Automation

ICP4NA enables the automation of different network operations for Telco cloud platforms using AI and automation frameworks. As a result, **cloud service providers** (**CSPs**) can transform their networks. The main goal is to provide zero-touch operations for the underlying platform and network operations to reduce OPEX and deliver services faster. ICP4NA allows for the automation and virtualization of business support services and operation services. In addition, ICP4NA enables automating and optimizing network operations and network component monitoring and management.

Figure 7.10 shows the logical architecture of ICP4NA. The core capabilities of ICP4NA are described as follows:

- Pattern recognition: Discover hidden patterns and trends to continuously fine-tune network operations and performance. These patterns help to identify intrusions, vulnerabilities, and threats.

- Operation: Automate network and service designs, deployments, and operations with intent-driven orchestration and closed-loop operations.

- Optimization: Detect and remediate incidents proactively to improve customer SLAs and experience.

- Intent-driven orchestration: This capability enables a different model state of the operation. This helps to be independent of predefined workflows. As a result, ICP4NA also enables you to perform network operation orchestration.

- Normalized life cycle modeling: With the modernization of software-defined network components, it is essential to standardize operations for all network functions (xNFs). ICP4NA enables model-driven automation with **continuous integration and continuous delivery (CI/CD)** toolchains. Therefore, any automations for change or new functions in the networking components can be tested in a lower environment and deployed to the production environment without downtime or manual interaction. These automation capabilities increase the performance of different network operations.

- Service design and testing: This is essential to keep the system's performance up to the desired level. ICP4NA provides the automation of different changes and network operations for preproduction, and production environments.

- Dynamic service assurance: Network communication happens in real time. Therefore, the automation framework provides real-time monitoring of network and cloud infrastructures using AI. It can also make decisions and fine-tune process automation based on the available information.

- Closed-loop operations: ICP4NA also provides automated feedback in a loop between assurance and orchestration so that it is possible to validate the steps and run smooth and zero-touch operations.

Now that we have a good picture of the different capabilities of ICP4NA, in the next section, let's discuss the reference architecture for ICP4NA.

Reference architecture for ICP4NA

ICP4NA is a set of applications and automation frameworks deployed by the Red Hat OpenShift platform on any cloud or on premises. *Figure 7.10* shows the logical architectural diagram for ICP4NA. IBM Watson AIOPs are the core components of ICP4NA, enabling the automation capabilities required to execute different network operations. As a result, the automation framework has different capabilities, as shown in *Figure 7.10*:

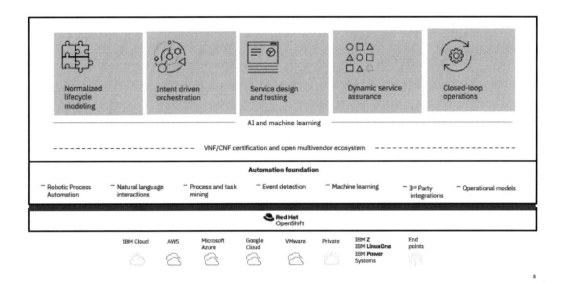

Figure 7.10 – An architecture diagram for ICP4NA

The core components of the ICP4NA are the Red Hat OpenShift container platform and IBM Watson AIOPs. IBM and Red Hat's open source industry allows CSPs to rapidly onboard certified **virtualized network functions** (**VNFs**) and **containerized network functions** (**CNFs**). ICP4NA is already being recognized for reducing the cost and time to market of 5G and 6G innovation projects.

Reference use cases for ICP4NA

ICP4NA enables automated and zero-touch network operation automation with the help of AIOPs, machine learning, automation, and optimization. Here is a list of business challenges that can be solved using ICP4NA:

- To roll out a fully virtualized, fully automated multi-vendor 5G service built on an open platform.

- Network slicing and the potential to extend to orchestration and site deployment for ORA.

- An orchestration and assurance partner can onboard and validate vendor workloads in the lower (development and test) environments and then automatically deploy them into the production environment.

- You can reduce costs to operate at the lowest cost per unit for any wireless carrier globally via real-time service deployment. Anomaly detection, intent-defined orchestration, real-time health, and utilization checking help to optimize performance and reduce costs in real time. In addition, automated network operation and real-time change management by using ICP4NA enables secure ROI for further spending on cloud services by the organizations.

- ICP4NA is deployed on the Red Hat OpenShift container platform. Therefore, it can be easily extendable. ICP4NA helps an organization build an automated, cloud-native, green-field network to scale.

- By utilizing IBM's AI-powered automation and intent-driven network orchestration capabilities, telecommunication organizations can accelerate the time to market for new innovative services to keep up with 5G and 6G services and develop an agile network that is also secure, automated, and intelligent.

In the next section, we will discuss edge computing. Edge computing is becoming popular as it enables private cloud or data center-based organizations to leverage the benefits of managed services and the security of private clouds on the same platform.

Implementing edge computing with IBM Cloud Satellite

Cloud modernization is a complex problem. Moving workloads to the cloud may not be possible on many occasions. However, having some workloads in the cloud and others on premises, organizations require a hybrid model for integration, operation, and standardization. It is inefficient to have different topologies for monitoring, operations, and development. In addition, the new platform on the cloud needs to be managed alongside workloads on on-premises locations from an integrated and central control pane. Finally, establishing a common standard to monitor, measure, and manage cloud service consumption is a must to manage platforms effectively.

As shown in *Figure 7.11*, IBM services can be deployed at any location, including other cloud platforms or data centers. IBM Cloud Satellite enables organizations to enjoy managed IaaS or PaaS facilities without moving to the cloud. Many IaaS or PaaS options can be deployed to the designated location. IBM provides these services as managed service. This reduces the cost and time of modernization. The organization does not need to move latency-dependent workloads or databases to the public cloud; instead, they can enjoy a managed DBaaS deployed on their on-premises location as a managed service:

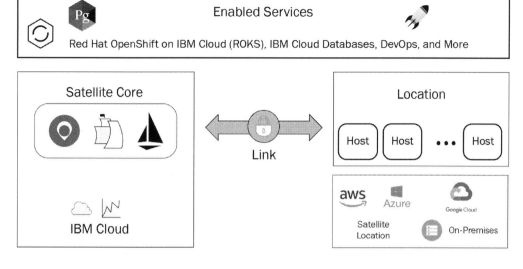

Figure 7.11 – IBM Cloud Satellite for workloads in any location

Here is a list of major architecture decisions for developing an IBM Cloud Satellite platform:

- **Locations**: IBM Cloud Satellite brings consistent experiences across the hybrid cloud landscape on AWS, Azure, GCP, and on-premises locations, along with security patches/upgrades governed by the IBM Cloud SRE team. The client provides an infrastructure that is managed with shared responsibilities between the client and IBM Cloud.

- **The number of hosts**: To produce IBM Cloud Satellite clusters, the minimum recommended number of control nodes is three.

- **Specification of the host machine**: The size of the hosts that run the control plane affects the number of clusters and worker nodes that can be present at the location; for example, 4 vCPU and 16 GB RAM or 16 vCPU and 64 GB RAM.

- **Storage**:

  - Hosts must have a boot disk with sufficient space to boot the host and run the operating system.

  - Hosts must have an additional disk attached, which provides a minimum of 100 GB of unmounted and unformatted disk space.

  - For hosts, the attached storage device must have at least 1,000 IOPS. The required IOPS varies with the number of clusters and the activity of the master nodes for those clusters.

  - Hosts cannot have a device mounted to `/var/data`.

  - For AWS, it will be ESB.

- Persistent storage depends on the application workload requirement. It can either be SDS or remote storage such as object storage.

- IBM Cloud Satellite storage templates are provided and tested by IBM or third-party vendors.

- **Network**:

  - Host IP addresses must remain static and cannot change over time due to a reboot or other potential infrastructure updates.

  - Hosts must have minimum network bandwidth connectivity of 100 Mbps, with 1 Gbps preferred.

  - Hosts can have multiple IPv4 network interfaces. However, the eth0, ens0, or bond0 network interface must serve as the default route.

- **Compute capacity**: The IBM Cloud Satellite monitors the available compute capacity of the location. A proper threshold should be set to trigger a "Warning" event at 70% CPU usage and a "Critical" event at 80% CPU usage, indicating the requirement of more hosts at the location. Also, it is essential to plan to keep at least three extra hosts attached and unassigned to the corresponding location. When there are extra hosts, IBM can automatically assign the hosts to your Satellite location control plane when the location reaches the warning capacity threshold, or an unhealthy host needs to be replaced.

- **Image registry**: The OpenShift image registry does not run in the Satellite IBM-managed OpenShift cluster, as no storage is set up. Therefore, if the pod or worker node is restarted, the stored data will be deleted and unrecoverable. It is recommended to use the IBM Cloud Container Registry on IBM Cloud Satellite for image storage.

- **Satellite Link**:

  - Satellite Link is used for the management of plane traffic.

  - The client has complete control and visibility over what goes into the links.

  - Satellite Link uses Kubernetes to provide three redundant connections for each location.

  - All data transported over Satellite Link is encrypted using TLS 1.3.

  - It supports encryption using signed certificates from IBM Cloud Satellite.

IBM Satellite ensures IBM Cloud services are available anywhere the client needs them, delivered as a service from a single pane of glass controlled through the public cloud.

Summary

Networking is a complex concept and component of cloud solution design. Therefore, it needs planning, understanding, requirement analysis, and the right decisions to be made for different requirements in the solution. In this chapter, we touched upon the different services provided by IBM Cloud to design a solution with different requirements, including connectivity, isolation, security, and operations. This chapter only discussed the fundamentals; however, we recommend looking at the official IBM Cloud documentation to clarify the different concepts, services, and reference architectures that were mentioned.

In the next chapter, we will discuss the core component of a cloud solution: *security*. We will try to understand the different requirements for security in a cloud solution. We will also become familiar with the different services available on IBM Cloud to design a secured solution.

Further reading

For more information about the different topics discussed in this chapter, check out the following materials:

1. *Getting started with IBM Cloud Satellite*; this resource is available at `https://cloud.ibm.com/docs/satellite?topic=satellite-getting-started`.

2. *IBM Cloud Pak for Network Automation*; this resource is available at `https://www.ibm.com/cloud/cloud-pak-for-network-automation/features`.

3. *Getting started with IBM Cloud Direct Link on Classic*; this resource is available at `https://cloud.ibm.com/docs/direct-link?topic=direct-link-get-started-with-ibm-cloud-direct-link`.

4. *Getting started with IBM Cloud Direct Link (2.0)*; this resource is available at `https://cloud.ibm.com/docs/dl?topic=dl-get-started-with-ibm-cloud-dl`.

5. *Direct Link (2.0) docs*; this resource is available at `https://cloud.ibm.com/docs/dl/getting-started`.

6. VPC VPN gateways; the resource is available at `https://cloud.ibm.com/docs/vpc?topic=vpc-using-vpn`.

7. IBM Cloud service endpoints; the resource is available at `https://cloud.ibm.com/docs/account?topic=account-service-endpoints-overview`.

8. Container network policies; the resource is available at `https://cloud.ibm.com/docs/openshift?topic=openshift-network_policies`.

9. Ingress controllers; the resource is available at `https://cloud.ibm.com/docs/openshift?topic=openshift-ingress-about-roks4`.

10. VPC load balancers; the resource is available at `https://cloud.ibm.com/docs/vpc?topic=vpc-load-balancers`.

8
Understanding Security in Action

Security is the fundamental component of any cloud-native enterprise workload. Therefore, organizations' main obstacle to adopting a cloud strategy is security. This chapter will focus on the practice, methods, tools, and platforms you can use to enforce secure platforms and communication with the target platform. Therefore, each layer of the application and cloud platform should be secured. Security must be implemented at an early point. Implementing security just once is not enough to protect the system from threats. Security should be part of your design, implementation, and practice. A secure reference architecture must be followed to design an architecture and establish an implementation method that enforces security controls at every phase of modernization. Similarly, a practice for continuously monitoring the platform's security and performing different security operations to manage the platform must be in place.

In this chapter, we will cover the following topics:

- Planning for the adoption of security as a culture
- Solution design – security in action
- Exploring the reference security architecture
- Getting familiar with Cloud Pak for Security as a Service on IBM Cloud
- Understanding continuous security review readiness

Planning for the adoption of security as a culture

Organizations need to establish engineering policies for their data and systems. It is essential to establish the necessary standards and policies to ensure the confidentiality, integrity, and availability of information. The implementation process should follow standards and policies. Organizations need to classify each system based on their corresponding security sensitivity. These systems must be installed, configured, administered, and maintained at the corresponding security levels. They must follow industry security best practices to safeguard against accidental or malicious loss, damage, theft, unauthorized access, or destruction.

In addition, the system should be designed while the security and confidentiality of the systems are considered to achieve security by design, all while ensuring balance among risk, performance, accessibility, and business functionality. The core goals of adopting security as a culture are as follows:

- Employ the correct standards, processes, and procedures, as defined by the company.

- Ensure that the confidentiality, integrity, and availability of information flow through the different communication channels of the IT system.

- Classify the different components and systems of the organization based on their corresponding security levels.

- Define the minimum system requirements.

- Implement policies, standards, services, assessments, and evaluations and orchestrate or adhere to them when deploying or managing IT systems.

- Verify your system's configuration requirements and specifications. Specifications are designed and implemented explicitly for information systems based on their risk assessment and while following the relevant legal, regulatory controls, executive orders, directives, policies, or standards that are appropriate to your business needs.

We need certain engineering principles to be established, and security must be adopted as a culture to achieve the aforementioned goals. Next, the organization must apply procedures and policies to achieve security by designing in-house systems and activities while balancing the need for business functionality, performance, accessibility, and associated risks. Here are some best practices you will need to follow to ensure the policies and procedures for the adoption of security as a culture are established:

- Each system and technology of the organization will be assessed against a set of security policies that have been defined by the organization.

- The defined policies protect the organization's system and technologies against known attack vectors, patterns, and threat actors.

- These policies are managed through a dynamic system that can be updated periodically.

- The policies should be saved in a knowledge store or catalog with AI capabilities to extract insights, create new policies, or update existing ones based on the system's state and requirements.

- This knowledge catalog for the policy will be used for automation and assessment.

- Continuous monitoring should be established to identify any violation of these defined policies, and the corresponding action should be automated for immediate execution.

- Some of the most well-known policies are as follows:

  A. Regular processes must be developed to apply applicable security patches that are in line with legal, regulatory, and operational requirements. This process should be automated, and a single truth will be used to maintain the system's consistency. For example, for a cluster of 50,000 core VMs, a single golden image will be used to upgrade all the VMs through an automated process.

  B. The organization will commit to securing the use and deployment of technology within the corporate operating environment and the system's boundaries. Therefore, it is essential to identify the boundaries for each system in each environment.

  C. Authentication and authorization should be everywhere when accessing any system within the IT ecosystem of the organization. Any sensitive information, such as the descriptions of applications, processes, procedures, system setup and configurations, authorization processes, and other components, must be protected from unauthorized access, alteration, viewing, or destruction. In addition, these standard best practices and policies must be classified according to the data management function information classification policy defined by the organization.

- Hardware, systems, and software/applications that are used in business operations are usually recorded in an inventory of assets.

- The organization will develop, document, and implement system configurations, security controls, and operational procedures while following business needs and regulatory requirements that are subject to risk assessment, vulnerability, and validation testing.

- Formal agreements will be established to interconnect networks and exchange information or software between the organization and any third party, as specified in the organization's **information security network security policy**.

- Information describing the design and implementation of systems and security controls employed will be given in sufficient detail to permit detailed analysis, threat models, and appropriate testing and validation of controls.

- The security standard of an organization should follow the required industry standards, as shown in the following table:

Standards	Reference
Information Technology – Security Techniques – Information Security Management Systems	ISO27001:2013
Information Technology – Security Techniques – Code of Practice for Information Security Controls	ISO27002:2013
Cyber Security Risk – Governance and Management Specification	PAS 555:2013
Information Technology – Security Techniques – Information Security Incident Management	ISO27035:2011
Payment Card Industry Data Security Standards	PCI DSS Current version
The Data Protection Act 1998	DPA 1998
Business Continuity Management Systems – Requirements	ISO22301:2012
Data Protection – Specification for a Personal Information Management System	BS10012:2009
Copyright Designs & Patents Act 1998	CDPA 1998
Computer Misuse Act 1990	CMA 1990
Regulation of Investigatory Powers Act 2000	RIPA 2000

Table 8.1 – The industry standard for security policies

Along with standards, policies, and best practices, it is also essential to identify different actors for the security framework of the cloud platform to ensure the successful adoption of security as a culture. The following diagram shows the system context of the system and security actors:

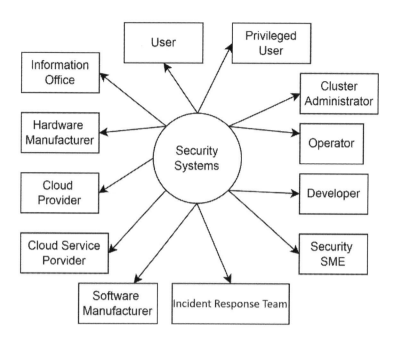

Figure 8.1 – Actors for security culture adoption

A secure solution needs secure communication between its systems and users, such as developers and operators. In addition, users such as cloud providers, service providers, software and hardware manufacturers, the information office, and administrators with privileged access should be able to access the system with the proper authorization and authentication.

For application development and IT system management, these best practices are essential. In addition, different activities for *building, running,* and *management* need to adopt these best practices. Let's look at some activities where security should be adopted as part of the culture and discuss some best practices for mission-critical systems on the cloud.

Systems that are essential for business-critical functionality are known as **business-critical** or **mission-critical systems**. The organization should define the size baseline, user base, data classification, business function, revenue impact, integration, communication, and other features for each mission-critical system. Some of the essential features of a potential mission-critical system are as follows:

- The security policies and their settings should be configured in the system's hardware specification based on the security level that's been allocated to the system. This will be addressed as part of the specification and procurement process.

- The system should be resilient by design to avoid loss due to failure. Technology will be resilient, providing automatic redundancy and failover.

- In addition to software, services, data, and applications, the organization should establish a set of **information security physical** and **environmental security** policies. In addition, the inbound and outbound communication of the system must be controlled with the appropriate entry controls to restrict and monitor access. Finally, creating a comprehensive threat model for the system specifies the vulnerable and weak points of the system. Each point must be protected against the threat.

- Mission-critical systems are physically installed and connected while following the manufacturer's guidelines. They need reasonable environmental controls for the specification of the system's manufacturer.

- Each system must be evaluated with periodic hardware audits as part of its procurement while following the **information security asset management policy** and **information security asset management process**, as well as the **information security change management policy** and **information security change management process**.

- Include the architecture, physical and logical connections, and data flows as part of a corporate network diagram that's maintained and kept up to date.

Security is essential for any workload on the cloud, regardless of its type. However, the scope for security differs for different types of workloads, such as mission-critical versus experiment workloads. In this section, we discussed some major architecture decisions and the best practices that are required for designing security at different layers of cloud infrastructure.

In the next section, we will discuss the security design process for different use cases and explain how we can implement the best practices to design a secure cloud infrastructure.

Solution design – security in action

Security needs to be designed, implemented, and practiced on every platform component, including the hardware, middleware, software, and containers. The following subsections will discuss the different controls that are used to manage and support access to the client's systems, production environment, personal information, sensitive personal information, and business-sensitive information.

Change management and planning

Security should be started from the bottom layer, which is *hardware*. Standard policies must be defined to enforce change management and access control management to establish the proper structure for security management. Here is a list of best practices for secure operations:

- Use a set of standard **information security change management policy** controls to make any changes to the specification or configuration of a system's hardware or software component. These policies define the life cycle of any change in the underlying platform, data, applications, users, and more.

- **Separation of duty** will identify the actor to apply server hardware or software changes to. In addition, an authorized operator or administrator from the organization should oversee and review the changes that are made by the operator. Where practical and possible, conflicting duties and responsibilities will be segregated to reduce the opportunity for unauthorized or unintentional modification or misuse of business assets and information processing systems.

- An end-to-end change request approval and governance process is essential to enforce sustainability. In addition, organizations should define service delivery and change management interlocks for control configurations and changes.

- Each change and configuration needs to be validated and processed, and there must be an isolated development, testing, and production systems environment for experimenting with and testing changes.

- Hardware and software need to be monitored continuously for vulnerabilities. In the event of vulnerabilities, patches and fixes must be applied to all the systems as quickly as possible, adopting a risk-based approach to implementation.

Secure landing zone

The infrastructure must be secure and fault tolerant. Security weaknesses and vulnerabilities within applications and infrastructure can lead to security breaches that impact confidentiality, integrity, and the availability of applications, systems, and data. This can pose significant risks to safety, reliability, and business continuity. Avoiding introducing weaknesses and vulnerabilities, frequent security testing, and timely remediation of these weaknesses and vulnerabilities is critical to helping minimize risk and mitigating its impacts. Here are some architecture decisions you should make to ensure landing zone infrastructure security:

- Information systems, applications, operating systems, and data processing equipment must be built, hardened, and configured while following the relevant **Center for Internet Security** (**CIS**) benchmark or NCSC guidelines for the specific system platform before it's deployed to the corporate environment. In addition, server/system build standards must implement security-by-design practices, as prescribed by the applied benchmark for the technology.

- **Private key infrastructure** (**PKI**) services must be available for certificate and key life cycle management to enforce encrypted communications for data and processes.

- When a vendor operating system end-of-life notification is received, an upgrade plan must be developed and implemented on time. Sunset dates are to be factored into system design and development life cycles.

- Application servers should be configured with only one primary function – for example, databases, web services, emails, and so on.

- Unnecessary and insecure services, applications, protocols, and functions should not be installed; they must be disabled or removed.

- Utility programs that might be capable of overriding systems and application controls will be restricted and tightly controlled.

- When used inside the corporate network, remote control software for systems management will be configured to ensure that only legitimate system administrators can gain open access to the system.

- Administrative access to systems from trusted sources should enforce multi-factor authentication.

- Administrative access to systems from external or untrusted sources will require at least two authentication factors that, where practical, occur over encrypted channels.

- Network segmentation and firewall services must be part of a reference architecture for network traffic that's in line with the identified security and compliance configurations. In addition, antivirus software should be installed.

- All systems must align with the security best practices and have user and security auditing facilities enabled and configured to log, at a minimum, all access attempts, whether they're successful or otherwise.

- Auditing additional activities and automatic system alerts should be enabled where the functionality is available, and a relevant business justification/requirement exists.

- Logfile rotation and retention should be configured to maintain the continuity of the logged events without imposing an undue load on the system, thereby affecting its business use cases.

System testing, maintenance, and monitoring

Security testing involves performing comprehensively automated and manual tests across applicable cloud platform layers, including application **steady state** time, application source code, application libraries, middleware, infrastructure, and networks, all while following strict engagement rules and standards, such as security configuration scanning, vulnerability scanning, and penetration testing. Here are some design guidelines or security architecture decisions:

- There will be defined acceptance criteria for new information systems, system upgrades, and versions that are promoted through development, testing, and operations.

- New and updated systems will be thoroughly tested and verified during the development process.

- Operating system and application layer security patches or fixes must be tested and applied to critical systems. In addition, they must be applied to all other systems and applications as quickly as possible, thereby adopting a risk-based approach to implementation.

- Schedule, perform, document, and review maintenance and repair records on information system components while following manufacturer/vendor specifications and business operational requirements.

- Systems that are no longer supported by the vendor and no longer have critical security patches released will be decommissioned or upgraded to a supported version.

- Network resources, systems, and application users will be monitored, tuned, and used to predict future capacity requirements to maintain critical business system performance.

- Access to and the use of company systems will be subject to auditing and monitoring by authorized members of the IT department or authorized third parties.

- Systems that are scanned or monitored by any employee outside designated members of the **security testing** team are expressly forbidden, except when third parties or members within the IT department are contracted to manage those services.

- Internal vulnerability assessments must be conducted at least quarterly.

- Internal and external penetration testing at both the network and application layers must be conducted at least annually or after any significant changes (for example, an operating system upgrade or a subnetwork or web server has been added to the environment) to the infrastructure to make sure there is no adverse impact on the organization's business operations or security posture.

- Vulnerability and penetration testing assessment tools should be regularly updated to test for newly identified threats and any high-risk vulnerability that's identified on any server system.

- There must be remediation processes, such as a **corrective action plan (CAP)**, to correct weaknesses and deficiencies that have been identified during any security testing and evaluation process. The CAP must be part of and tracked by the **change management board**.

- The **security reference** architecture must include network- and host-based intrusion detection and prevention systems to monitor critical systems. A specific requirement is to monitor network traffic associated with cardholder, critical business, or personnel (sensitive personal) data.

- All systems' access and audit logs must be actively running and regularly reviewed to identify potential unauthorized use or attacks. In addition, any anomalies must be appropriately investigated.

- The following table shows a set of essential security testing for preproduction and production environments, along with the corresponding recommended frequency:

Security Testing Targets	Security Test Type	Phase	Frequency (Best Practice)
Cloud-provisioned services and networks	Infrastructure penetration testing (internally facing and externally facing)	Transition	One-time
	Infrastructure penetration testing (internally facing and externally facing)	Steady-state	Annual
	Network vulnerability scanning	Transition	Quarterly
	Network vulnerability scanning	Steady-state	Quarterly
Cloud-hosted virtual servers and operating systems	Server vulnerability scanning	Transition	Quarterly
	Server vulnerability scanning	Steady-state	Quarterly
Cloud-hosted container hosts, images, and repositories	Container vulnerability scanning	Transition	Optional
	Container vulnerability scanning	Steady-state	Optional
Cloud-hosted middleware	Vulnerability scanning	Transition	Optional
	Vulnerability scanning	Steady-state	Optional
Application source code and libraries	**Static Application Security Testing (SAST) for Security and software composition security analysis (SCA)** scanning	Transition	One-time
	SAST and SCA Scanning	Steady-state	Optional
Cloud-hosted applications	**Dynamic application security scanning (DAST)**	Transition	One-time
	DAST	Steady-state	Optional
	Application penetration testing	Transition	Optional
	Application penetration testing	Steady-state	Optional
	Post-exploitation pivot and attack surface discovery	Transition	Optional
	Post-exploitation pivot and attack surface discovery	Steady-state	Optional

Table 8.2 – List of security testing targets for production and preproduction environments

Authentication process

A well-established procedure must be established to control identity and access control management for different users. This procedure will include an onboarding and management component. As a result, all users accessing corporate IT systems will be adequately authenticated before gaining access to systems, applications, or the information contained therein. Here are some recommended design guidelines for the security reference architecture:

- Each user must be identified by a unique ID that is created following receipt of an authorization form signed by the appropriate business manager.

- Users will be allocated an initial passcode that they are required to change when logging in for the first time to one of their choosing. It must comply with the requirements for password complexity.

- Based on the security level of any system, additional authentication processes, such as multi-factor authentication, bio identification, and other processes, can be included to allow users to access the corresponding system.

- Each step in the authentication process should be well defined and associated with an appropriate message for easy and definite execution. For example, once users log on to a system, they should be notified that their actions will be monitored and recorded.

Violations

Detecting and analyzing violations is crucial for the security design of cloud infrastructure. Identifying the potential attack vectors and related incident detection and response strategy must be included in the security reference architecture design. Here are some architecture decisions for security reference architecture design:

- Security monitoring should identify any violations regarding policies or regulations and trigger automated alerts and remediation processes to be executed.

- Periodic reports for violations should be published and shared with the system administrator, security administrator, and information security officer.

- Violations should be investigated while following the **information security incident management policy** that's been defined by the organization and must also be dealt with while following the company's disciplinary and dismissal procedures.

Responsibilities

Separation of duty should be applied at each layer. The activity of each user should be tracked and monitored. Operators, developers, and administrator users must be accountable for their compliance with the policy that's been defined by the organization. Any breach of this policy may be dealt with following the company's disciplinary procedure or equivalent for non-employees. In addition, standard policies that have been defined by the organization must be communicated to all employees and other privileged users. Regular training and exercises should be conducted so that they understand their responsibilities and become familiar with the necessary policy. Finally, regular audits and internal process reviews must be undertaken to confirm adherence to this policy.

Threat modeling for applications and cloud services

The cloud is so vulnerable that it is mandatory to strengthen it before starting your cloud journey. Organizations should be aware of the scope of their workload and the weaklings. One of the easiest and most efficient ways is to define the *threat scope* or *model* for each application. This section discusses a sample threat model for a web application. This sample threat modeling can be used for the security readiness review for the corresponding application. Let's consider a web application for this task. The following subsections describe the threat model evaluation process for the application.

Security objective

The first step of the **threat model** evaluation process is identifying the security objectives to be achieved. Some examples of security objectives are as follows:

- Protect data and applications by identifying threat actors and threat vectors across different assets.

- Prevent malicious users from accessing information about any other users.

Key scenarios

To design a threat model or plan the threat protection process, we need to identify a simple set of use case scenarios that are simple but provide a better end-to-end view of data communication. These scenarios need to cover all the critical business transactions. Here are some use case scenarios for the threat model evaluation process:

- User login web portal.

- User chats with the chatbot of the application for the help desk.

- The user must navigate the supported materials/URLs/links by conversing.

- Users must provide names and other **personally identifiable information (PII)**.

Technologies

The next step is to identify the underlying technologies, development stack, and cloud services that will be used in application development to identify the technical threat vector quickly. Various technologies are used to develop a web application, such as IBM Red Hat, OpenShift Managed Service, Spring Boot, Angular, IBM Cloudant, IBM Watson Assistant, and IBM Cloud.

Application security mechanisms

Applications must have standard security embedded in their design. The application development process requires a set of controls and tools, libraries, and best practices to enforce application security. The most crucial application security mechanisms, known at the time of writing, are as follows:

- HTTPS/TLS encryption is used between the browser and web application.
- HTTPS/TLS encryption is used between the application server and all services (Watson and Cloudant).
- JWT authentication between backend API calls.
- The user can log into the application using SSO via the portal's OAuth authentication.
- Security operations and testing must be part of the DevOps pipeline, so limited time for container deployment must be available to ensure the security test isn't ignored.
- The communication channel among containers must be authenticated. Otherwise, one affected container or application can impact others.
- Enforce compliance metadata at the container level to reduce the threat.

Application decomposition

This section describes the trust boundaries, entry points, exit points, and data flows. First, we must identify a set of trust boundaries, as follows:

- Only allow inbound HTTPS traffic over port 443 into the OpenShift ingress controller.
- Only outgoing calls from the application server and **IBM Watson Conversation chat server** to recognized hosts should be allowed, such as the cloud and conversation services.
- Calls must be made between the chat server and backend REST API server.
- The REST API server must validate the JWT from the web portal.

There are corresponding entry and exit points for each threat boundary, as shown in *Figure 8.2*, such as the cloud and the user's machine. For example, in the threat model shown in *Figure 8.2*, each external data flow enters the cloud boundary using port 443 for HTTPS requests; a firewall restricts all other ports.

Based on the critical scenarios, we also need to identify a crucial data flow, as follows:

1. Users are authenticated by a web portal and then access the application via a browser over HTTPS.

2. The user communicates with a chatbot on the chat server.

3. Text or commands are sent from the browser to the web application over HTTPS (Ajax).

4. The application sends a text to the IBM Watson conversation service and Alchemy service for parsing and response.

5. The application stores the user's utterance in the IBM Cloudant database.

6. The application accesses the database, filters, and results for the user.

7. The application processes users' PII/SPI data and stores it in the IBM Cloudant database.

8. The application fetches PII/SPI data from the IBM Cloudant database.

Threat modeling

The main goal of threat modeling is to analyze the baseline threats and requirements and identify threats, threat actors, and vectors that apply to the applications and services within the target architecture and environments. Threat modeling also enforces collecting and analyzing standards and compliance-driven requirements, as well as identifying additional control requirements that are necessary for mitigation. For example, the following threats could affect the application:

- Cross-site scripting, which occurs when an attacker succeeds in injecting script code in the chat window through WebSocket communication.

- Network eavesdropping, which occurs between the browser and web server to capture clients' data.

- The server's information and sensitive exception details are revealed to the client.

- An attacker manages to take control of the web server, gain unauthorized access to the database, and run commands against the database.

- A malicious user obtains access to data encryption keys, which are used to access sensitive data in the database.

- Distributed denial of service attacks can cause potential failure.

- An attacker may fetch power user information to request the JWT generation server, acquire JWT information, and gain unauthorized access to backend application servers.

The following diagram shows the threat model for the application described here. Similarly, threat assessment and modeling for other applications will help you understand the cloud platform's weak points, which will help you design a secure landing zone for these applications:

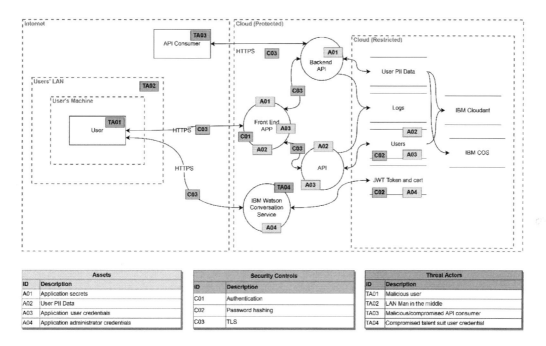

Figure 8.2 – Threat model for web applications

Assets	
ID	Description
A01	Application secrets
A02	User PII Data
A03	Application user credentials
A04	Application administrator credentials

Security Controls	
ID	Description
C01	Authentication
C02	Password hashing
C03	TLS

Threat Actors	
ID	Description
TA01	Malicious user
TA02	LAN Man in the middle
TA03	Malicious/compromised API consumer
TA04	Compromised talent suit user credential

As you can see, threats are evaluated against planned security controls to identify gaps in availability, as well as security requirements. These are also evaluated to measure the efficacy of security controls for the identified compliance and regulation requirements. These identified performance metrics are used to update existing security controls or create new ones to protect applications, environments, and infrastructure and strengthen the security posture of the analyzed applications and environments.

Vulnerability management

Organizations must establish a **vulnerability management** process to identify any known as well as new vulnerabilities within the business application, system, equipment, devices, machines, and services as soon as possible and take corresponding mitigation actions. A centrally governed vulnerability management solution includes vulnerability assessments, analysis, and mitigation. A vulnerability management solution must have the following components:

- **Vulnerability identification**: Organizations must establish a process to identify all the vulnerabilities in different systems. Regularly scanning for vulnerabilities using software applications should be scheduled. In addition, they must collect information regarding vulnerabilities from multiple sources, such as vendors, threat intelligence, or some global database subscription. There must be a database storing correlation between application and their corresponding vulnerabilities, infrastructure, systems, and tools. This information should be managed and refreshed regularly.

- **Vulnerability analysis**: The next step is to analyze the collected vulnerability information based on the threat model. Vulnerabilities must be classified based on their threat boundary, vectors, and their corresponding impact on the system. Analysis should also determine the remediation mechanism for different classes of vulnerability.

- **Vulnerability remediation**: A vulnerability treatment or remediation plan for each of the different vulnerabilities must be executed while following a process. If any of the vulnerabilities can't be mitigated over time, there must be a corresponding risk assessment, and a corresponding risk mitigation plan should be executed to reduce the impact. The acceptable risk should also be agreed upon in the case of unavailable feasible vulnerability remediation plans for any vulnerability. One well-known remediation is applying minor or major patches for affected software or hardware tools. There must be a change control process to schedule and manage the patching activities. Once the patching is done, it must be verified in every step using other security testing and penetration testing mechanisms.

In the next section, we will discuss the security reference architecture, which follows how you should control hardware, the landing zone, the test framework, and authentication to ensure security for hardware, networks, compute, storage, data, applications, endpoints, containers, and other workloads in the hybrid cloud platform.

Exploring the reference security architecture

In this section, we'll discuss the security reference architecture for IBM Cloud. First, we will discuss the essential requirements for security in the case of the cloud platform. The following table shows the core requirements for the security reference architecture:

Category	Requirement
Network security	Network components should be isolated and monitored. Then, they can easily be configured with security controls and policies.
	Intrusion should be continuously assessed using pattern recognition and other intrusion detection and prevention methods.
	Data in motion must be secured.
	Connections between any two components in the cloud must be secured.
Compute security	Compute components must be isolated and monitored for vulnerabilities.
	The integrity of each compute component must be intact.
	The runtime should be protected against threats using encryption.
Storage security	Storage components must be isolated and monitored for vulnerabilities.
	Data must be encrypted at rest.
Cloud infrastructure	Each network, compute, and storage component must be accessed with proper authentication and authorization. In addition, they must be protected against unauthorized access.
Identity and access control	Each cloud provider provides an identity and access control management system at a fine-grained level for each type of resource.
Role-based/ attribute-based access	In IBM Cloud, a user can be assigned to multiple access groups and act as a role. An individual user can also be controlled using different policies and attributes, such as the service name or resource group name. Therefore, providing any user with fine-grained access/least-privilege access is essential.
Authentication and federation	Users can be authenticated using different procedures, such as multi-factor authentication or single sign-on.
Vulnerability management	Hardware, software, services, and applications must be scanned for vulnerabilities regularly. Found vulnerabilities must be mitigated by applying patches as soon as possible.
Threat protection	Define the threat model for each application and service and design the protection system.
Data security	Data must be encrypted in motion and at rest.
Encryption algorithm	The data encryption algorithm must be AES256.
Data encryption key management	Data encryption keys must be managed bya small group of people, and they must be rotated regularly.

Category	Requirement
Data access	All the data in the system must be protected from unauthorized access.
Identity governance	A governance framework for the identities must be applied to the cloud platform.
Risk-based access	Privilege or administrator access is very risky and vulnerable. Therefore, there must be a well-defined privilege identity access control management solution.
App scanning	Applications will be scanned in each deployment as part of the quality gate of the CI/CD pipelines.
Activity monitoring	Any activity, such as logging in, listing cloud services, accessing an object in cloud storage, provisioning new services, or deleting existing resources, must be monitored and tracked.
Data classification and governance	Sensitive and insensitive data must be identified and classified.
Endpoint protection	The endpoint must be protected. Endpoint security consists of two categories: • Authenticating identities and rights to access • Integrity and confidentiality of data transferred between entities
Security monitoring	Continuous monitoring for security control actions should be enforced.
Threat management	Once the threats of the platforms have been identified and a protection system has been built, they need to be managed continuously with observability, policies, governance, and change management.
Incident response	A vigilant incident response framework should be established with the proper tools, processes, policies, and experts.
Visibility	An integrated dashboard containing the current security state, potential threats, and other advice must be available to the operation teams.

Table 8.3 – Basic requirements for security on IBM Cloud

The architecture shown in *Figure 8.3* shows the main activities that must be followed for security solutions, such as container security and endpoint security. This *reference architecture for security* focuses on the requirements described in *Table 8.3*.

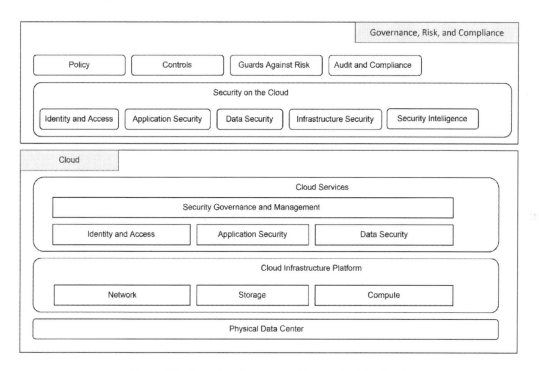

Figure 8.3 – Security reference architecture for IBM Cloud

Now let's look at the recommended components mentioned in the reference architecture of security shown in *Figure 8.3* in the following sub sections.

Identity and access management

Identity and access management should ensure that no unauthorized access is allowed in the cloud platform. In addition to that, it also requires **privileged user identity and access management and monitoring, end user identity and access control management**, **single sign-on**, and other user authentication.

Security intelligence and Operation Center (SOC)

The main activities you must complete to ensure **security intelligence** are as follows:

- SIEM and threat management.

- Incident response and intelligence.

- Infrastructure management.

- Define and enforce controls based on corporate and regulatory requirements.

Data security

Data is the core part of any platform. The following are specific security controls you can implement to ensure data security:

- Data in the platform must be encrypted in *transit* and at *rest*.

- Data encryption keys should be managed using *key management*.

- Continuous monitoring must be conducted through *data activity monitoring*.

- Data loss prevention.

- Secret management.

Container security

The container contains a pod for one or more applications. The following controls must be in place to ensure container security:

- Images must be trusted, signed with a verified signature, and encrypted.

- Reduce clutter.

- Enforce secret management.

- Introduce multiple isolated segments in the network.

- Authenticate users and enforce role-based access.

- Scan for vulnerabilities regularly and mitigate them as soon as possible.

- Harden the operating system.

- Govern operations.

- Implement intrusion detection and prevention mechanisms.

- Enable container security governance, IT policy management, and enforcement.

- Utilize time-based checks to monitor the health and availability of managed devices.

- Store both raw and normalized logs/events for a minimum of 1 year.

Application security

Application security needs to ensure the following:

- Application threat modeling

- Build validation and code scanning

- Static and dynamic application security testing

- Image compliance and vulnerability scanning

- Application deployment protection

- Application firewalls

Infrastructure security

Network, compute, and storage must be secured. Here are the main components for security:

- Provide security connectivity.

- Enforce micro-segmentation.

- Protect the hypervisor and virtualization layer.

- Identify native security and additional controls.

Endpoint protection

Endpoints serve as access points to an enterprise network and create points of entry that malicious actors can exploit:

- Protect the operating system level, hardening, and kernel security.

- RHEL CoreOS and SELinux.

IBM Cloud has multiple security services, as shown in the following diagram:

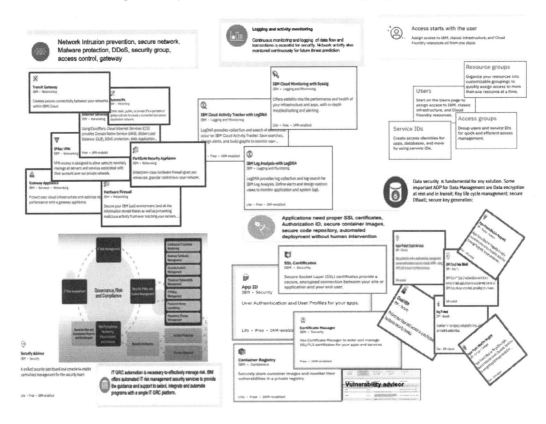

Figure 8.4 – IBM services for security

In the next section, we will focus on the security readiness review you must conduct for any target platform. Finally, we will discuss a process you must follow to enforce a security review at each release for each component or application on the target cloud platform.

Getting familiar with Cloud Pak for Security as a Service on IBM Cloud

Organizations' workloads, such as data and applications, are attacked every day. Unfortunately, many organizations cannot detect and remediate attacks that quickly. Often, particular skills and **subject matter experts** (**SMEs**) are needed to investigate such attacks and resolve them accordingly. Therefore, security threats are one of the primary areas where organizations face extensive loss.

Cloud Pak for Security (CP4S) can put the information that security SMEs need at their fingertips to mitigate threats, including four key areas of capability: **visibility**, **detect**, **investigate**, and **respond**. It provides necessary information in a more comprehensive visualization and acts autonomously to disconnect compromised systems once they have been identified via automated checking and investigation. CP4S works with a wide variety of IBM and non-IBM security tools, including Splunk, ArcSight, Microsoft Azure, Amazon CloudWatch, and Carbon Black, to name a few.

How does it work?

Visibility, detect, investigate, and respond are part of IBM CP4S. It has a fully integrated set of tools from IBM, including **Threat Intelligence Insights (TII)**, **User Behavior Analytics (UBA)**, Case Manager, Threat Investigator, Data Explorer, and Risk Manager. CP4S can be deployed on any platform on a hybrid cloud (IBM Cloud, AWS, Azure, and so on, including on-premises locations) to provide threat management, data security, identity and access management, and **Security information and event management (SIEM)**.

The following is the typical workstream for CP4S.

Review several threat investigator attack graphs generated using anomaly detection, pattern recognition, behavior analysis, and other technologies to investigate the incident and its scope and impact across the organization. It uses single query language from **Structured Threat Information eXpression (STIX™)** to investigate threats, patterns, and behavior across all data sources.

1. Visualize the security incident's scope, cause, and impact on a dashboard to help the SME.

2. Remove the compromised system from the network to prevent further compromise.

3. Integrate with IT service management tools to create a ticket for the incident and help SMEs collaborate with the necessary instructions as a recommended remedy.

Benefits

CP4S brings a complete set of integrated tools and services to enable organizations to succeed in taking care of their infrastructure. Here are some core benefits of CP4S:

- **Zero trust**: Any organization's IT system is a combination of devices, processes, tools, software, hardware, and people. Measuring trust is impossible for such a complex system. Therefore, zero trust is essential to design and manage the system with the mantra of *"never trust, always monitor, and enforce least privilege."* Implementing zero trust requires an end-to-end framework for implementation, verification, auditing, changes in roles, and accessing multiple identities on multiple resources. CP4S provides continuous monitoring and automation to manage zero trust.

- **Hybrid cloud**: Organizations need a single plane of glass to integrate services that are deployed on the public cloud, private cloud, and on-premises locations. The security control framework needs to be single and unified but flexible to customize based on their requirements. CP4S is a suitable solution for this requirement, enabling the organization to control its growing IT systems.

- **Security orchestration with automation**: CP4S is developed with cloud-native and AI technologies, which enable it to monitor behaviors and generate alerts, perform root cause analysis, and execute notifications automatically. Often, organizations have minimal visibility of their security control framework across their hybrid and multi-cloud environments. Real-time data for analysis is often segregated across multiple data storage areas, making security event correlation and analysis very expensive and time consuming. It also needs a whole list of tools to be connected to it, which makes the process even more expensive. In addition, almost every task is manual and repetitive in a traditional security control framework. Often, organizations also suffer from a lack of skills and automation.

- **SIEM**: Using IBM Security QRadar as a core component of CP4S, you can manage logs, information, and events with real-time analytics and take autonomous action to mitigate the risk.

- **Threat intelligence**: CP4S identifies and acts on threats that are active in the environment by performing continuous automated searching across different system components based on their relevance, severity, penetration, impact, and environments.

Now that we know about the tools and techniques we can use to implement secure cloud infrastructure, we need to establish a design review authority for the continuous security design and implementation of the infrastructure. In the next section, we will learn how to design authority to review the security readiness of any cloud infrastructure.

Understanding continuous security review readiness

Each development and release team must establish a **security readiness review** for an application, software, hardware, or service before each release.

The following subsections discuss a checklist of evidence that's required to assess the security readiness of the release of an application. It is recommended to automate the validation of the following evidence evaluation and integrate its automation with the DevOps pipeline.

Multiple areas should be evaluated for the security readiness review for each release. Those areas and the corresponding checklist of evidence that is required to assess it will be discussed in detail. In addition, each criterion requires a set of evidence to establish whether the platform is compliant with the corresponding criteria.

Authentication and access management

We need to enforce authentication and access control on all public interfaces and service components, including password complexity and the password change cycle, to protect the workloads from different threats. The following is a set of evidence that must be provided to verify the controls for authentication and identity and access controls:

- All internal UTC endpoints must be protected by TAI and JWT services.
- Several basic auth roles must be defined in WebSphere Liberty Server for access to admin-privileged APIs.
- All external APIs must be protected by basic auth and API tokens over TLS.
- IAM for service-level authentication and access control must be used.
- Clearly defined roles that allow you to implement least-privilege operations must be maintained on the endpoint levels, as well as at the UI application levels.

Secrets management

All sensitive and confidential secrets for applications, systems, and platforms must be stored and managed securely. The following is a set of evidence for compliance:

- IBM Key Protect must be used to store encryption keys per tenant.
- PKI certificates must be used in TLS.
- The properties service must be used to access application properties in their encrypted states.
- Properties must be saved in the corresponding environment.
- No plain text properties must be used in the source code, the configuration file in GitHub, or any other system.

Least-privilege operation

Always operate at the lowest level of privilege that's required to execute tasks effectively (do not run processes as the root user). The following is a set of evidence of compliance that can help you verify the necessary controls for privilege access control management:

- The access control hub manages the root password for the DB2 database.
- Only a few users have read access to the DB2 database and VMs.
- The data can only be inserted through a segmented API with a proper API token.

Compute isolation

Isolating critical processes and untrusted code at the compute level is essential for any secure infrastructure. Therefore, we need to manage a set of artifacts to enforce that each threat boundary is either physically or logically separated from the compute level. To verify the essential security controls for compute-level isolation, we can use the following evidence of compliance:

- The architecture diagram must be secured.

- Solution design document.

- The underlying component must be a decoupled component that's exposed as a microservice.

- The service components must run in physical machines.

- No untrusted code should be executed.

- Valid credentials must be used to access Artifactory and generated tokens to allow the use of the base image.

- The service must run in a specific namespace or environment.

Network isolation

You must group related systems into network segments that are isolated from unrelated systems, adding additional isolation for high-risk systems. The continuous release security monitoring systems and personnel must verify the following evidence of compliance before each release:

- Network diagram.

- Threat model diagram.

- The specific hosting management team must manage all the VMs.

- All authorized users must be identified, and their roles must be defined.

- Firewall (Juniper, FortiGate), Calico, and Kubernetes network policies must be revalidated annually for validity and business purposes and at least quarterly for correctness (no drift/ changes in comparison to GitHub/a change management system) with evidence maintained.

- Data in motion must be encrypted using TLS 1.2.

- Certificate refresh after expiration must be automated through the DevOps pipeline.

- Monitoring for enterprise connectivity, such as DirectLink and VPN, must be enabled.

- Firewall policies must be periodically re-evaluated.

- Network segmentation must be implemented.

Encryption at rest and secure deletion

The continuous security readiness review board must ensure that all sensitive data is encrypted at rest. At the same time, proper encryption should be used for data encryption. For verification purposes, the board can use the following evidence of compliance:

- The API must enforce sensitive data encryption, which is an *AES256 encryption* algorithm.

- DBaaS must provide data at *rest* encryption.

- The second layer of data encryption must be done on the DBaaS to protect the data from **Data Admin** view access for sensitive data.

- Users with only the role must have access to download data using the appropriate endpoint.

- Data in temporary download and caching storage must be encrypted.

- Standard encryption libraries must be used, that is, Java JCE in CDP AES256 using Key Protect.

- Hashing must be done with SHA-256.

- Active encryption must be implemented with envelope encryption using a wrapper key from the key management service to wrap/unwrap data encryption key.

- No custom encryption schemes must be used, such as MD5.

Logging and non-repudiation

Application, as well as system, logs are part of one of the major threat vectors. Sensitive information should not be exposed to logs, so they must be stored securely. Logs must be reviewed and analyzed using logging services. Here are some best practices that must be followed and verified during the security readiness review for release:

- Integrate with any log analysis service, such as IBM Cloud LogDNA.

- All CRUD operations must be logged and tracked.

- All user operations must be logged (they need to be checked).

- All system administration operations must be logged outside the application, and performed by the hosting.

- API logs must be parameterized by customer/tenant ID to ensure distributed tracing for multiple tenants.

- Logs must be stored off-system so that they cannot be manipulated on-system.

- Logs must be sent to visualization and analysis services, such as the ELK stack.

- Audited or flow logs for a **virtual server instance** must be enabled to track the system log.

- Automation to identify violations and vulnerabilities must be implemented and integrated.

- Credentials or other secrets must never be included in logs.

- PII must never be included in logs. If PII needs to be logged due to business requirements, it must be masked.

- Code reviews and merges include manual as well as automated validating to verify that credentials or other secrets are not logged.

Injection prevention

Prevent **injection vulnerabilities** by continuously validating user input, using language-specific safe libraries and APIs, performing periodic application vulnerability scans, and applying a corresponding remediation plan for different vulnerabilities. Once the remediation is executed, such as a minor patch being applied to the affected systems, the following verification steps must be taken:

1. Development tests must be executed after each API implementation.

2. Penetration tests must be executed periodically. Therefore, each release needs the corresponding penetration test result report to be associated as evidence.

3. Issues that have been found in the pentest must be fixed.

4. Safelisting helps to validate the input validation.

5. Untrusted input must always be validated on the server side.

6. Language-specific safe functionality (such as parameterized queries) must be used to construct queries, commands, and web content.

7. Templating engines and frameworks that do automatic context-sensitive escaping must be used.

8. Automated scanners (SonarQube) must be used to scan for injection vulnerabilities on each *pull request*.

9. A static and dynamic code scan must be performed, where SME reviews the result.

Secure development practices

The goal is to make the platform secure by design. Security must be built into all the phases of the software development life cycle and cloud modernization program. Some of the following evidence of compliance can help the review process verify that the platform is secured by design:

- The development team must have a security focal person.

- Static and dynamic analysis must be performed with **application security** on the cloud or other static analysis, or dynamic analysis must be used – a tool called **App Scan** can be used here.

- Pentesting must be run periodically.

Updates and secure configuration

Threats are continuously generated in the platform and come from external settings. Therefore, to protect the platform, the best practice is to ensure that all aspects of the service are updated regularly and securely configured. Here is a list of evidence of compliance that can help you verify the configuration:

- OWASP Dependency-Check is integrated into the DevOps pipeline. Therefore, each pull request is verified.

  Every change that's made to any software or hardware of the application platform is reviewed and verified.

- Vulnerability Advisor, Health Checking and Patching tools, or other alternatives can be implemented to scan for missing security fixes and patches.

- Reports of third-party dependencies can be made via tools such as Gradle and npm.

- Nessus scanning can be implemented.

- SOS Health Checking and Patching, CIS Benchmarks, and IBM tech spec can be used to perform health checks.

- SOS Vulnerability Scanning with separate Nessus, which is a proprietary vulnerability scanner developed by Tenable, or similar can be used to perform network scanning.

- It must be compliant with CIS Benchmarks.

- The code library and other dependencies can be checked during the build of each pull request to verify them.

Business continuity planning (BCP)

Every production environment must be protected from failures, such as cyber-attacks or other disasters. In addition to designing a fault-tolerant platform, we should also design a verified BCP that demonstrates the expected RPO and RTO. There must be a periodic test for disaster and other failure exercises.

Data classification

The data in each environment is classified. Evidence should be provided to ensure that the data classification process is accurate based on the underlying host system's security level. Here are some artifacts you can use to verify that all the data components in the classes are compliant and have the appropriate compliance:

- Non-protected data
- Electronic health record

- Personal credit card data (PCI)

- Personal information

- Sensitive personal information

- Highly confidential information

Known issues

A list of known issues should be reviewed to help you understand the different risks with the implementation. This helps you understand the risk so that the necessary steps can be planned ahead of time for mitigation. In addition, the review board must verify the following evidence of compliance:

- A RAID log for existing issues and their corresponding mitigation plans

- A strategy for unknown risk issues and their mitigation process

Central information security officer

A dedicated authority should be established for the continuous security review plan. A **central information security officer** (**CISO**) should be responsible for enforcing a continuous review of security controls, policies, settings, user activity, and other aspects of security. The reviewal process must be regular. Even though the responsibility of the CISO is to enable best practices and enforce reviews for them, the responsibility and accountability of building a secure platform are shared among application developers, workload owners, platform architects, and others. Therefore, the CISO must establish an anti-pattern alongside the best practices and share it among the different teams so that they're aware of the vulnerabilities.

This section has taught us how to establish a continuous security review so that we can plan for each release. Security needs to be operated regularly using practices, processes, operations, and authority.

Summary

Security is a fundamental part of the cloud platform. If the workload is not secured, the solution has no value to organizations. Therefore, applications, data, endpoints, containers, networks, storage, and compute must be secured and protected. This chapter discussed the core components of the security framework for cloud platforms.

In the next chapter, we will discuss the reliability, high availability, and resiliency of cloud platforms.

Further reading

To learn more about the topics that were covered in this chapter, take a look at the following resources:

- *Enterprise Security Solutions*. Available at `https://www.ibm.com/security`.
- *IBM Cloud Pak for Security*. Available at `https://www.ibm.com/products/cloud-pak-for-security`.

9
Designing a Resilient Platform for Cloud Migration

A cloud migration solution should ensure **business continuity** (**BC**). Therefore, resiliency is one of the fundamental characteristics of the cloud. Resiliency enforces **high availability** (**HA**), auto-scaling, workload backup and restore, failover, and **disaster recovery** (**DR**) to ensure the ecosystem is fault-tolerant and BC is verified in the target state after cloud migration. The core characteristics of resiliency are noted here:

- **HA** is achieved when the organization's data, system, and environment are available to end users.
- Backup and restore focus on copying data, systems, and environment multiple times and restoring them to the corresponding system to ensure their availability for recovery.
- **DR** ensures the built-in redundancy of the system with defined failover at the time of failure.

In this chapter, we will discuss the following topics:

- Planning to build a resilient platform
- Implementing HA
- Implementing reliability
- Implementing DR as a service (**DRaaS**)
- Implementing cyber resilience
- Implementing observability and governance

Planning to build a resilient platform

This section will design a solution for the application platform on IBM Cloud. BC refers to the capabilities of any mission-critical workload in that it can never go down or be unavailable for any reason. In addition, there are some other expectations, as follows:

- The business will not be hampered due to the unavailability of systems.

- End users will receive immediate responses at all times.

- For end users, the failure will not be visible. In the case of any system being unavailable, it will be possible to respond to the end user seamlessly by using alternative systems.

- For mission-critical workloads for the end user, there will be zero downtime. We can define a mission-critical workload as one where the application, database, or web server meets at least one of the following criteria:

  - HA architecture such as *clustering* and *hot standby*.

  - 24/7 support and callouts for both **phase 1 (P1)** and **phase 2 (P2)** problems.

  - Support prioritized above all non-critical images.

  - Changes are implemented as and when required.

  - The underlying cloud or physical platform will provide four (99.99%) or five (99.999%) nines of uptime for **service-level agreements (SLAs)**.

- Any system hosting mission-critical workloads will have the following characteristics by design:

  - Backup and restore

  - HA

  - Disaster avoidance or transparency

  - DR in a few minutes

  - Always-On or **continuous availability (CA)**

  - Chaos-defined availability

IBM Cloud supports several services for designing scalable, highly available, and resilient solutions, as follows:

- Multiple geo locations for container platforms

- **Virtual Private Cloud (VPC)** load balancers

- **Availability Zones (AZs)**

Resiliency ensures the agility at which a platform/service can continue to be available for **input and output (I/O)** operations, even when the integrated critical components have suffered a disruption. In simple terms, a resilient system is highly available, fault-tolerant, and provides BC even during a time of disaster. Building a resilient system needs some specific design constraints in the platform architecture. The following table shows a checklist of design constraints to enable resiliency for the cloud platform:

1	Ensure HA by eliminating potential points of failure in **information technology (IT)** infrastructure.
2	Include multiple AZs for the platform.
3	Enable geo-redundancy by including multiple regions for the cloud service.
4	Include a global load balancer to ensure geo dispersion and deployment over more than one AZ .
5	Ensure DBaaS with storage backup or synchronized replication to avoid failure.
6	Enforce backup policies for the correct backup pattern for the proper application or workload.
7	Use multiple AZs to deploy applications on the container platform and DBaaS with replication, eventual or strong consistency, and a cross-region storage class.
8	Use a cross-region storage class for IBM Cloud Object Storage.
9	Enforce observability rules, policies, alerts, and notifications for proactive and reactive monitoring.
10	Ensure Always-On or CA for mission-critical workloads.
11	Define **key performance indicators (KPIs)** for continuous resiliency testing and evaluation.
12	Ensure a detection, prevention, and recovery mechanism for a cyber crisis.
13	Ensure protection against total AZ failure.
14	Ensure network communication channel redundancy to protect against network channel failure.
15	Enforce network policies and configuration to enable data as well as communication protection.
16	Ensure protection against physical infrastructure failure.

Table 9.1 – Checklist for planning resiliency for the platform

Resiliency is a complex subject; it has several domains, as shown in *Figure 9.1*. The core domain of resiliency looks like this:

1. HA

2. Backup and recovery for applications, the **operating system (OS)**, images, and data

3. Zero downtime/Always On or other patterns for CA

4. Observability

5. Reliability

6. BC

    I.   DR

    II. Cyber resilience

7. Continuous evaluation or a readiness test for resiliency

The different domains are presented in the following diagram:

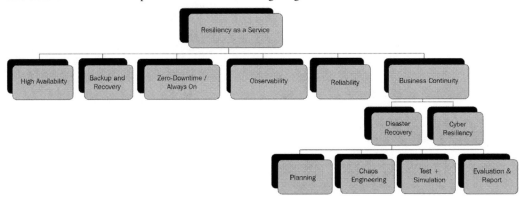

Figure 9.1 – Different domains of reliability

In this chapter, we will discuss these seven domains in detail. However, before taking a deep dive into those domains, we need to understand how we can measure the resiliency of platforms.

Workload severity

There are multiple KPIs for measuring the reliability and resiliency of the infrastructure and cloud platform. Different workloads require different service levels, such as HA, resilience, and DR. Based on the nature of the workload, there can be different components, as shown in the following table:

Workload type	Definitions
Real-time and mission-critical (A)	Applications, databases, or web servers that meet at least one of the following criteria: • HA architecture such as clustering and hot standby • 24/7 support with 24/7 callouts for both P1 and P2 problems • Support prioritized above all non-critical images • Changes implemented as and when required

Workload type	Definitions
Mission-critical (B)	Applications, databases, or web servers that meet at least one of the following criteria: • 24/7 support with 24/7 callouts for P1 only • Lower than P1 priority callouts are handled the next business day • Frequent application or system changes • Support prioritized above medium and simple images • Changes implemented on an extended-hours basis—that is, up to midnight
Complex (C)	Any server that does not meet the critical, standard, or simple definitions can fall under the category of a complex system. These systems are usually less crucial than mission-critical systems but more critical than standard systems, with the following criteria needing to be met: • These servers will receive 24/7 monitoring. • Callouts will be during the next business day, regardless of priority level. • Changes will be implemented on an extended-hours basis—that is, up to 10 P.M.
Standard (D)	The server is used for infrastructure purposes (file, print, firewall, **Domain Name System** (**DNS**), network) or used in development or test environments that meet all of the following characteristics: • Supported during 5x8 business service hours • Support prioritized below all other images • A limited number of changes and during supported hours only
Simple (E)	Non-production or development platform. This kind of platform does not store any essential data. In the case of disaster or failure, they can be restored from backup or using **infrastructure as code** (**IaC**). No additional support is required for this platform except when new provisions are rebuilt after failure.

Table 9.2 – Different types of workloads

For backup and restore, the standard KPIs are **Recovery Point Objective (RPO)** and **Recovery Time Objective (RTO)**.

RPO

RPO defines the age of data that must be recovered from backup storage for normal operations to resume after a system failure or disaster. The RPO is expressed backward in time (in the past) from the time of the failure and indicates the maximum amount of data loss for the data recovery process to be effective. When using database snapshots, the frequency of snapshots determines the worst RPO achievable – for example, a database snapshot is taken every 24 hours, and a disaster takes place after the last database snapshot and before the following one. In this scenario, depending on the database activity and the failure time, up to 24 hours of data could be lost when the database is brought back online after the snapshot restore process. A factor to consider in choosing a cloud data warehouse provider is whether the client has a choice to take a user-defined snapshot, can use a combination of system (automatic) snapshots and user-defined snapshots, or is restricted to system (automatic) snapshots only. The choice of snapshots available to the data warehouse will impact the RPO in a system failure or disaster.

RTO

This is the maximum time it can take to do a database restore operation, and its duration is the time from the database failure occurring until the database is fully restored and available to connect to applications after the restore process. Generally, the RTO depends on the time to start the recovery operation after a failure and how fast the database can be restored during the recovery process. In addition, the overall database size and I/O rate for the database recovery media determine the overall RTO for the database.

Different workloads require different RTOs and RPOs; therefore, it is essential to classify the environment and workload based on their RTO and RPO. For example, the following table shows four different categories of workload based on their required RTO and RPO:

Category	RTO	RPO	Disaster Recovery Pattern
A	5 minutes	5 minutes	Active-active synchronous with restoration
		15 minutes	Active-active asynchronous
B	15 minutes or less	5 minutes	Active-active synchronous with restoration
		15 minutes or less	Hot standby
C	Less than 4 hours	15-60 minutes	Restore backup snapshot
		15 minutes or less	Warm standby with continuous replication
D	4-24 hours	>24 hours	Cold standby
E	>24 hours	>24 hours	Restore backup snapshot

Table 9.3 – RPOs and RTOs for different kinds of workloads

The following figure shows reliability trends in 2020. These trends have identified different reasons for system failure. A resilient solution should have protection against these different system failure triggers:

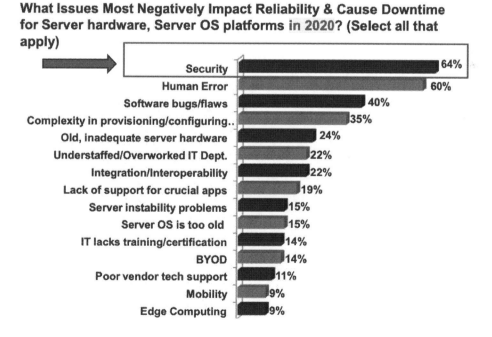

Figure 9.2 – Reliability trends in 2020

Figure 9.3 shows an overview of different issues and failures caused in 2021 for various reasons according to the **Gremlin** 2021 reliability state report. This report clearly states that there are different vulnerable actors and components in any cloud platform. Resiliency ensures protection against different kinds of issues exposed in *Figure 9.3*; therefore, it is essential to plan accordingly. The core activities for planning are listed here:

1. Understanding the requirement for HA, availability patterns, observability, reliability, fault tolerance, DR, and cyber resilience.

2. Understanding classification for workloads, such as mission-critical, standard, development, and experiment. Different kinds of workloads require a different pattern for the resiliency of the platform.

3. Setting up controls and configuration for the required resiliency pattern.

4. Designing the required resiliency pattern.

5. Continuously managing and monitoring the platform.

6. Enforcing governance and continuous testing or evaluation for the platform.

An extract from Gremlin's 2021 reliability state report is presented here:

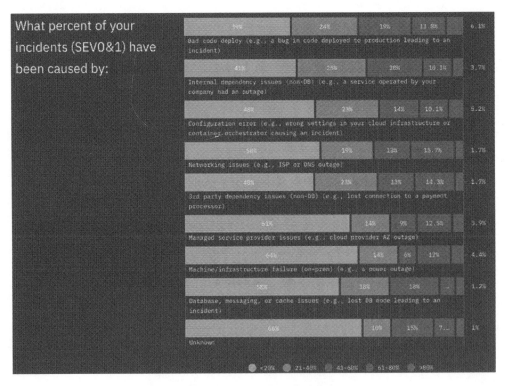

Figure 9.3 – Gremlin's 2021 state of reliability report

In the following section, we will discuss the implementation of different aspects of resiliency, such as HA, observability, reliability, DR, and cyber recovery.

Implementing HA

HA is a capability of a cloud solution that enables the solution to perform well as the number of access requests increases. To design a highly available solution, the organization must determine the characteristics of their HA requirement, which is crucial for any cloud solution. This section discusses the benefits of HA, steps for planning and understanding the requirement for a HA design for a platform, and steps for designing HA.

Benefits of HA

HA is a crucial characteristic of any platform to achieve resiliency. Most of the time, applications, data, and services deployed on the target platform should be available to end users. HA is designed by making a redundant copy of the system, data, and applications. The main benefits of HA are listed here:

- HA ensures that systems can be taken offline for planned maintenance and unplanned outages while their corresponding mirror system continues to work. For example, in the Landorous use case, the organization lost millions of United States dollars (**USD**) in the weekly development maintenance window. All fixes and new features were released on Saturday, and during that time, all interconnected systems remained shut down for 6-8 hours. In today's world, where users prefer to do online shopping, this is not acceptable for BC. HA can reduce the impact of and time for planned outages.

- HA also ensures that DR, redundancy by design, and a backup solution can protect the system from loss in unplanned outages and disasters.

- HA is enforced to ensure load balancing among mirror or redundant solutions. This load balancing also improves the performance as access requests for any data and applications can be controlled in a balanced way.

Requirements for designing for HA

Different systems exhibit different behaviors—for example, a mission-critical workload has higher business value for HA, and therefore, it is essential to design the HA solution based on the requirement of the underlying system. The following table shows the recommended features as input for a highly available solution design:

Criteria	Description
Business value	Before designing any HA solution, it is essential to calculate the business value. As HA is expensive and often designed by applying redundancy in the workload, it is essential to balance the desired HA state for the workload and cost to achieve optimum business value.
Uptime requirement	The total time that the system is available for end-use applications per hour drives the HA for any solution.
Outage coverage	HA will ensure that the workload can survive any event such as backup window reduction, planned maintenance, unplanned outages, or site disasters.
Resiliency nature	Organizations must identify a need to protect the system during an outage. In addition, the set of applications, data, and system environments should be identified as those needing resiliency.
Failover	An organization should also define the level of control conducted by automation during unplanned outages and failures. In addition, the time for execution of the automation should also be determined. For example, in a given scenario, the organization determines that as soon as all parties are on deck to run some manual tasks such as selection and manual approval, the automated script should take 15 minutes to fail over to the secondary site.
Distance or geographic coverage	Geographic dispersion between systems protects against disaster. Usually, the protection level remains higher if the sites are far apart.
Number of systems required to back up	Backup policies regarding frequency and amount of data to be backed up should be defined and identified.
Frequency of access to secondary data	Access to backup dataset requirements indicates the level of access required for secondary copies of the data for other work activities offloaded from primary copies, such as saves and queries/reports. Therefore, the backup solution needs to consider the frequency, duration, and access needed for the backup copy of the data.
Performance	Performance implications should be governed by business value for HA of the cloud workload.
SLA	The **cloud service provider** (CSP) should provide the SLA for the underlying cloud. *Table 9.2* shows the definition of SLAs for different kinds of disaster patterns.
Data resiliency methods	*Table 9.2* describes some primary resiliency methods for data.

Table 9.4 – HA criteria for a cloud solution

The following table shows the relationship between mission-critical workloads and SLAs and DR patterns for cloud workloads:

	A	B	C	D
SLA for cloud and infrastructure	99.0%	99.9%	99.99%	99.999%
Downtime per month	7h 12m	43m	4m	4s
Downtime per year	3d 15h 36m	8h 46m	52m	5m
Number of AZs	1	2	3	3
Application deployment pattern	Monolithic	Monolithic	Multi-active microservice in multi-regions	Multi-active microservice in multi-regions
Deployment pattern	Waterfall	Waterfall	Frequent	**Continuous integration/ continuous deployment (CI/ CD)** and GitOps
Zero downtime capability	No	No	Partially Yes	Yes
Resiliency method	DR	HA Stretched HA	CA Cloud-enabled Always on	CA Cloud-native Always on

Table 9.5 – Characteristics of different workloads

Now that we are familiar with the basic requirements for the HA of a system, we need to understand the building blocks for a highly available platform. Therefore, in the next section, we will discuss the design parameters for the HA of a platform.

Designing HA

As depicted in the following diagram, each platform layer should be highly available for a standard, highly available platform. Therefore, we need to understand the requirements for designing HA for each layer. In addition, it's essential to design HA in each layer shown here:

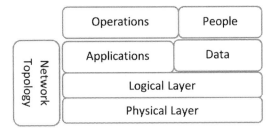

Figure 9.4 – HA at different layers

The following table shows the mechanism to ensure HA for different components at different layers:

Physical layer	Machines at the physical layer should provide sufficient memory and storage to enable reliable response times, expected throughput, latency, and other performance parameters.
	Physical machines should be redundant. Therefore, in the case of the failure of any machine within a particular machine set, there is always a backup or additional machine to replace the faulty one. Moreover, physical machines should be independent components to be easily removed, or new ones can be added to the machine set.
	Multiple AZs or data centers with the required physical machines connected over secured connections and proper load balancing will ensure HA.
Storage	Storage should be redundant. Storage must be classified for different workloads, such as development or mission-critical, and mission-critical workloads must be backed up.
Logical layer	Ensure each application has multiple replicas in any one of the AZs, which will protect the applications from zonal failure.

Network topology	Ensure geographic dispersion by applying multi-active regions, as follows: • **Share-Nothing, Stretch-Nothing, Cluster-Nothing** • Service parallelism bypassing failures • No manual failovers • No manual workflows • No service recovery delays • Limited blast radius
Application	Follow the extended Twelve-Factor methodology described in *Chapter 4, Cloud-Native Development*.
	By developing a clean contract between the application and the platform, applications must be self-resilient, built to manage, and designed for failure mitigation.
Data	Apply to write anywhere to achieve optimum consistency and integrity by following different concepts: • Transactional swimlanes • The **consistency, availability, and partition tolerance (CAP)** and PACELC theorems, indicating that if the system is **partioned (P)**, we should follow CAP and select **availability (A)** and **consistency (C)**, and **else (E)**, we should select **latency (L)** and consistency • Eventual or strong data consistency • NewSQL capabilities
Message	Follow modern architecture patterns for a message- or event-based service, such as the following: • Event-driven architecture • Distributed patterns for consistency • Patterns: **Command and Query Responsibility Segregation (CQRS)**/Event sourcing/Outbox
Operations	Operations and management for the system should also be highly available.

Table 9.6 – Configurations for HA platform

In addition to HA, cloud platforms should also provide **Continuous Availability (CA)** to meet a higher (5 nines) SLA. CA (also known as **Always On**) ensures the prevention of failures by applying a zero downtime strategy. Here are some well-known principles to ensure the Always On concept:

- Architecting the application to be self-resilient and fail gracefully.

- Hosting the application in multiple active and separated clusters or regions (three are recommended for the highest availability **service-level objectives (SLOs)** and cost efficiency).

- Stretched clusters are not to be used. Instead, deploy separate clusters in all regions.

- Bypassing component and regional failure.

- Applying GitOps practices to rebuild environments instead of restoring from a versioned Git repository.

- Applying **disaster transparency** instead of DR.

- Performing application releases, updates, and patches one active cluster/region at a time.

- They are embracing database-level eventual consistency.

Among different availability patterns, the most crucial one is Always On. The Always On concept aims to ensure that the replication among the mirrors of a system to provide fault tolerance happens in real time and the RTO and RPO can be described as several minutes. We will get familiar with the Always On concept in detail in the following subsections.

Implementing Always On

The main characteristic of the Always On concept is the following mantra:

Everything fails, and we design an easy solution to resolve those failures.

Any production system comprises hundreds of dependencies, applications, services, and databases. Therefore, the probability of system failure at any given time is moderate, and the art of managing such production systems at scale lies in embracing failure. The Always On concept requires adaptive risk management, change management, problem management, and incident management based on systems thinking, transparency, experimentation, robust automation, self-healing, and fast-feedback loops.

In order to design an Always On system, we need to follow the guidelines in the next subsections.

Ensure disaster transparency

Different system and component failures should be considered to design a non-disruptive solution and enable disaster transparency.

Follow the extended Twelve-Factor method

Applications should be developed and deployed following the extended Twelve-Factor methodology. Legacy application development and deployment are no longer applicable for cloud solutions.

Enforce the idea of "keeping it simple"

The solution should be designed with the theorem of "*keeping it simple.*" Complexity adds obfuscation and prolonged service recovery. Therefore, the solution should be designed with a simple structure and components.

Concurrent versioning

At any moment, the entire system should be able to run at least two different versions of different components. This feature enables these systems to run a blue/green test. Therefore, in the case of maintenance or unplanned outages, the system should still run with a different version.

Continuous operations

Designing in-platform concurrency to enable non-disruptive changes will ensure the system's continuity. In addition, continuous monitoring, management, incident management, problem management, change management, and **site reliability engineering** (**SRE**) will ensure the platform's health.

Do it once and repeat

First, a resilient landing zone needs to be developed following the fundamental concept of resiliency. Then, repeat the same process through automation and configuration in different geographic locations, either an AZ or a region, to build the same landing zone. Each cloud region will be identical due to automation.

Fail small

As the core concept of the cloud platform is that everything breaks, the blast radius should be minimal in the design so that if there is a failure, it will impact the entire ecosystem minimally.

Virtualize or containerize everything

Virtualization and containerization provide flexibility and mobility. Container platforms are designed to ensure built-in resiliency; therefore, it follows the Keep It Simple, Stupid (KISS) concept, and anyone can maintain the resiliency of the overall solution. On the other hand, a legacy physical machine-based solution requires additional complex effort and design to ensure resiliency in the overall solution. Similarly, virtualization allows the definition of different software-defined compute, storage, and network components that are easily configurable to ensure resilience.

Automate nearly everything

Figure 9.2 shows that human error and inconsistency are significant reasons for system failure. Automation can reduce this error. For example, declarative provisioning such as IaC, CI/CD, **artificial intelligence for IT operations (AIOPs)**, GitOps, and other automation mechanisms reduces errors and failures.

Design for failure

Failure cannot be avoided. Continuous monitoring will ensure that failures are detected and evaluated to understand how they work and break the system under different conditions and states. Once they are known, necessary automation must be developed to mitigate failures automatically. Therefore, a pervasive **root cause analysis (RCA)** process should be established to ensure the cause of failures is captured and evaluated to design an automation framework to mitigate those failures.

Designed for failure

Applications must be designed for failure. Applications should be designed so that they fail gracefully and minimize the impact on the consumer. Different disaster patterns such as Circuit Breaker and Bulkheads should be adopted during application development.

Avoid HA takeover

Redundancy and geographic dispersion enable service parallelism, making the system more reliable and efficient.

Peer clouds provide availability

On hybrid or multi-cloud solutions, failure in one cloud should not impact the others. The fault domain is isolated to each cloud, and the service is still functional in others. A fault-modeling solution should be designed to identify the failure actor and domain to design a fault-tolerant system.

Share nothing

Each cloud must provide the business service independently, perhaps with reduced capacity. The central concept of *share nothing* is that each zone, region, or cloud will be independent of each other and isolated. Therefore, services are not shared among them, so in the case of failure in one location, it will not impact the other locations.

Availability Zones

HA environments have architectural requirements and change windows. In the case of DR, the applications and data should avoid the entire region or AZ, even for a single component failure.

Service discovery

Add global traffic management and service discovery to the ecosystem.

Security is mandatory, not optional

Backup, geographic locations, network topology, applications, data, platform, and middleware must be secured and protected.

Manage state

According to the Twelve-Factor methodology, applications should preferably be stateless. However, if an application must maintain a state across clouds, it should use an in-memory application grid. In addition, applications should be designed to be fast and fault-tolerant. Finally, sessions must be small to take advantage of this technology or not use sessions beyond a personal cloud.

Application-level data replication

Applications and data should be replicated among independent replicated systems. Any changes in data or applications should be captured and applied to all peers. To provide fast failover or transparent service bypass, logical data replication is required, which will also help to avoid human tasks. A bidirectional peer-to-peer setup for applications and data allows the *write anywhere* concept and ensures eventual data consistency out of the region.

Stretch nothing, cluster nothing

Stretching a cluster across multiple clouds extends the fault domain beyond an individual cloud. Therefore, the solution becomes very complex. Furthermore, different parts of the same cluster will require different services and mechanisms to ensure fault tolerance in this kind of solution. Therefore, the *keeping it simple* concept is violated in the case of stretching a cluster across multiple clouds.

Performance is vital

Embrace performance engineering as a mandatory part of application development, infrastructure design, and data management. Businesses must make development and operations aware of any planned events that may bring "flash mobs." Continuous monitoring of the golden signal will ensure that the system can proactively detect failure and performance degradation.

Formulate SLOs

Incorporate resiliency and BC and assign **service-level indicators** (**SLIs**) to track metrics across the entire service. A well-defined formula to measure the service level at any period, such as a month or a week, can help determine whether the complementary services maintain the predefined SLO.

Ensure data consistency

Consider moving from the **two-phase commit protocol** (**2PC**) to Saga patterns with rollbacks and compensating transactions to ensure data consistency and integrity.

Automated start and stop of applications

Stopping the application or restarting traffic should be automated by implementing readiness, liveness probes, and circuit breakers. This helps to gracefully redirect users to the live system from failed systems.

Distributed storage

Workloads – including source code, **virtual machine (VM)** templates, Dockerfiles, Helm charts, database schemas, IaC, and declarative deployment files – should be stored in distributed repositories and with proper versioning. Static files should not be stored in **Server Message Block (SMB)** / **Network File System (NFS)** or local disks. External services such as multi-regional distributed object storage can be more suitable for storage. These externally managed storage services provide built-in fault tolerance.

Zero downtime

There are different ways to achieve zero downtime application releases. To enforce zero downtime for any cloud-native application, it is essential to define the number of concurrent disruptions that are in the corresponding application experience, known as the disruption budget in the knowledge domain of Kubernetes. The disruption budget is defined using two main parameters, as follows: `maxSurge` defines the maximum number of Pods that can be created over the desired number of Pods, even in the absence of the evicted Pod, and `maxUnavailable` defines the number of Pods from that set that can be unavailable after the eviction. For example, `maxUnavailable=1` states that evictions are allowed as long as they leave behind one or more healthy Pods, and `maxSurge=1` states that one more Pod can be created than the desired number of Pods. The following table shows three different disruption budget patterns for zero downtime settings:

Pattern 01	maxUnavailable=0	maxSurge=1
Pattern 10	maxUnavailable=1	maxSurge=0
Pattern 11	maxUnavailable=1	maxSurge=1

Table 9.7 – Disruption budget patterns for zero downtime

Now that we understand the building blocks and settings for a highly available platform, we should also ensure that the platform's availability level is well managed and monitored continuously.

Once a resilient platform is built, it should be maintained and continuously monitored. In the next section, we will discuss the governance and monitoring of the platform.

Implementing reliability

Reliability can be defined as the ability of a system or component to function under stated conditions for a specified period. Reliability focuses on preventing failures during the lifetime of the product or system, from commissioning to decommissioning. There are different patterns for reliability, as detailed next.

Redundant resources

This is an expensive pattern for reliability. In this pattern, the target platform is replicated in multiple geographic locations. Each of the components in the target platform is replicated multiple times, as illustrated in the following diagram:

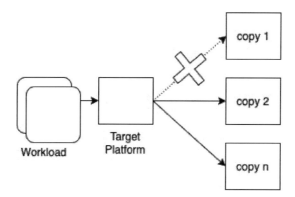

Figure 9.5 – Redundancy of resources in multiple locations

Figure 9.5 shows a reliable system where the redundancy-of-resources concept is applied. This kind of system is robust and can survive individual failure. If any one of the replicas of the target platform is unavailable, another system can be used.

Retrying until N times

In this pattern, the user can retry the same request multiple times. There is a threshold for the number of retries. Therefore, any system or user can retry accessing the target platform until the request is successful or the number of retries reaches the threshold of *N*:

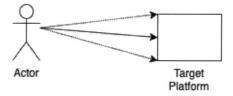

Figure 9.6 – Retry pattern

Using sidecars

Instead of implementing reliability in the source code or infrastructure as in the previous pattern, this pattern offloads the operations and activity to ensure the reliability of other services, as follows:

- Load balancing

- Encryption

- Observability

- Traceability

- Authentication and authorization

- Dynamic request routing

- Deployment and release strategies such as canary, A/B testing, and blue/green deployments

- Support for the Circuit Breaker pattern

The following diagram represents that workloads are deployed on the target platform, and the platform is continuously monitored, secured, evaluated, and tested for reliability using different sidecars:

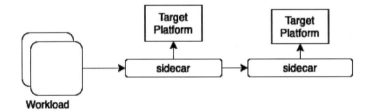

Figure 9.7 – Utilizing sidecars for reliability

Auto-scaling for growth

The target platform should have the capabilities to grow on demand. Robust and autonomous scaling capabilities will ensure seamless scaling in the platform. Similarly, an automated process will also ease the reallocation of unused space by the OS.

Waterfall

In this pattern, multiple instances of a transaction are executed, and the best response is returned to the end user. For example, the response with the best quality or the first response can be selected as the response to a transaction. Other transactions are discarded following the compensating transaction. The core concept of the waterfall pattern is an *idempotent* operation that is usually called more than once with the same input parameters and is expected to return the same or similar output. Each transaction is identified with an **identifier** (**ID**). Multiple instances of the same transaction are sent to the system, and the system processes the transaction if a transaction with the same ID has not been processed yet.

Different reliability patterns are discussed in this section. Based on the nature of different components, a different pattern can be used to ensure reliability across those components. The following section will explore the design and requirements for DR to protect systems against any failures.

Implementing Disaster Recovery as a Service (DRaaS)

A *disaster* can be explained as any disruption to the standard or regular business of any components in the platform. To reduce loss, a mission-critical production environment must be protected against such disruptions. Mission-critical production environments need BC, and therefore they need to be recoverable from any failures. DR ensures that systems are fault-tolerant and can recover from any failures. In this section, we will understand the concepts of **Disaster Recovery as a Service** (**DRaaS**). The IBM *ITBC127* standard defines a disaster as a sudden, unplanned calamitous event causing significant damage or loss. Some other characteristics of disasters are presented here:

- Any event that creates an inability on an organization's part to provide critical business functions for some unscheduled period.

- In the business environment, any event that creates an inability on an organization's part to provide critical business functions for some predetermined period.

- Management decides to divert from normal production responses and exercises its DR plan.

On the other hand, *recovery* is a process that enables a system to recover its activities in the shortest time possible after a disaster has been declared. Recovery planning is the ongoing effort of planning, developing, implementing, and exercising processes and procedures to ensure the efficient and effective resumption of the offering in the event of a disaster.

Two essential characteristics drive a DR solution, as outlined here:

- Ensuring effective orchestration for DR

- Ensuring continuous testing to enforce disaster transparency

This section will discuss these two characteristics of any DR solution.

DR services

A DR service should provide orchestration for DR for any workload, as described in *Table 9.2*. Here are some characteristics of an effective DR service:

- Automation is the core of this service as time is crucial for DR. Therefore, the main goal of a DR service is to ensure the restoration of workload within a predefined time. For example, *Table 9.3* shows that workload of category type *A* can only be down for a few minutes. Therefore, to ensure BC and protect an organization from the loss of millions of USD, the DR service should be autonomous and configurable.

- DR services must ensure quick and flawless provisioning or restoring of services, storage, and applications to reduce risks.

- DR services must have an integrated readiness testing and validation process that ensures restoration and recovery are successful.

- The DR service categorizes workloads into different categories, as shown in *Table 9.2*, and adopts a risk-regulated approach to enforce optimized resiliency.

- DR services should be insight- and data-driven; therefore, validating the process against risk can be measured and changed along with the evolution of the cloud platform.

Disaster transparency with chaos engineering

When planning for **chaos engineering**, there are three basic scenarios while performing activities that we need to consider, and they play a vital role in running experiments successfully. These scenarios are presented here:

- **Blast radius**
- **Magnitude**
- **Abort conditions**

A blast radius is the proportion of hosts and containerization-based worker nodes where we run the experiment – for example, start with one single host and run the experiment, then increase the radius and run the experiment with multiple hosts. This is a centrally important concept because we must minimize experiments' potential impact on users and the environment. The main point is to start with a minimal blast radius such as one host or one worker node (this could be a container) and then increase the blast radius as we learn more and get comfortable with the experiment. This is an important parameter to consider while running experiments regardless of the environment – **quality assurance staging (QA staging)**, **pre-production (pre-prod)**, or **user acceptance testing (UAT)**.

Magnitude is the amount of stress or disruption we apply to individual hosts or containers. For example, if we are testing the effect of a **central processing unit** (**CPU**) attack against a web server running Apache or nginx, we might start by adding 30% more CPU load (the magnitude) and increase that over time. We can observe different metrics that can affect CPU load, such as the response time, and then determine how large the chaos attack could be so that the system can withstand it before performance becomes unacceptable.

Abort conditions are conditions that cause us to halt the experiment – for example, when we are testing a container that has reached the peak of its CPU or memory load, we abort the test and try to understand the scenario of the attack. It is always good to have an understanding of the effects on the system that make an experiment too disruptive to continue. These could be related to more errors or latency, or high-priority alerts raised by the monitoring tool. These abort conditions vary in experiments.

IBM has a set of recommended chaos engineering principles, as follows:

- Strengthen reliability disciplines.
- Understand the system.
- Experiment with every component.
- Strive for production.
- Contain the impact.
- Measure, learn, and improve.
- Increase complexity gradually.
- Socialize continuously.

Chaos engineering as a service

Different cloud service providers offer chaos engineering *as a service* – for example, Netflix has Chaos Monkey, which shuts down servers randomly to test the disaster tolerance and transparency of the system. This simulator creates different templates for systems with a set of predefined states of different systems – for example, some systems are active while others fail. These templates help deploy a different state of the infrastructure randomly. Fault actions are defined in these templates. The simulator triggers fault actions to shut down random target systems such as **Elastic Compute Cloud** (**EC2**), **Relational Database Service** (**RDS**), and so on. Once the tests are completed, the experiment is stopped with necessary reports and events. The result of these experiments is published as a report.

Disaster transparency and tolerance are essential for the mission-critical platform. In this section, we have highlighted the core components of DR. We have also discussed methods and practices to ensure continuous tests and evaluation for DR.

Cyberattacks can also trigger fault tolerance. In recent times, system failure due to cyberattacks has been widespread. In the next section, we will discuss the main components required for designing a cyber-resilient platform.

Implementing cyber resilience

Organizations face cyberattacks in regular patterns. Cyber resiliency is no longer a *nice-to-have* feature for organizations – it is a *must-have* feature. However, most organizations worldwide are not prepared for cyberattacks. Due to a lack of skills, knowledge, planning, the non-existence of proper governance and resilient platforms, and inconsistent **incident response** (**IR**) and recovery solutions, protecting a system against cyberattacks is a very challenging job. During the pandemic, the healthcare system faced cyberattacks at an exponential level. The threat landscape is growing every day, and so is the complexity of designing protection against attacks. Here are some critical features of a cyber-resilient platform:

- Ensure the platform is highly available and resilient against any failures.

- Ensure air-gap protection of configurations of devices, VMs, and bare-metal systems for immutable storage with **IBM Resiliency Orchestration** replication.

- Enforce swift identification of cyber breaches in configuration files and enable response with Resiliency Orchestration built-in intelligence.

- Ensure rapid restoration of device configurations and VMs on production infrastructure through Resiliency Orchestration.

- Ensure testing capability by testing the solution frequently without impacting the production landscape. At the same time, security controls should be tested through regular penetration testing.

- Provide continuous visibility and reporting in the process to ensure compliance and readiness.

- Enforce a practice among processes, tools, and people to identify gaps and improve resiliency strategies.

- Improve security controls with governance and risk management processes.

- Implement a realistic *cyber-crisis simulation* to identify gaps and cyber penetrations.

Implementing a cyber-resilient system is not enough if it is not continuously monitored and managed. Therefore, governance and risk management should be implemented and practiced. Cyber resilience is not a one-time setting, and it should be practiced at each layer of the platform and monitored continuously.

Implementing observability and governance

Monitoring and observability are the most effective ways to understand the state of the platform at any time. Therefore, each component, service, application, and piece of data should be monitored continuously. Here are some requirements for different component monitoring:

Capabilities	Activities
Application monitoring	• Application throughput monitoring. • Application or microservice health monitoring. Each microservice or application should have an **application programming interface (API)** exposed that returns 200 in the case of a healthy state and 404 in the case of unavailability. • Each transaction should have a **unique ID (UID)** so it can be traced. • Application configuration changes should be monitored and governed with acceptable predefined policies.
Log aggregation	Different applications and services all together define the business characteristics of an organization. Therefore, central government must maintain the quality and drive common goals. Aggregating the log from a different application, service, and data platform ensures log governance, search governance, and data access governance and also helps to define policies.
Activity monitoring	• Define rules, roles, access, and other activity policies. • Organize periodic validation, change, and risk assessment for current policies. Based on the result of the assessment, change the policies. • Continuously monitor activity for each cloud service. • Define alerts and notifications for different activities.
Synthetic and end-user monitoring	• Capture end-user behavior as well as experience using internal and external bots. • Change the application configuration to improve the experience based on monitoring information.
Change monitoring	• Monitor policies and readiness. • Monitor consistency. • Monitor impact.

Capabilities	Activities
Performance monitoring	<ul><li>Monitor hardware failures.</li><li>Monitor OS services and processes.</li><li>Monitor hypervisor availability.</li><li>Monitor the OS event log.</li><li>Monitor the HA cluster status and resource group status, and correct problems identified wherever applicable.</li><li>Publish periodic reports for different KPIs based on the technical agreement with the client.</li><li>Leverage the console and tools provided by the target cloud and a predefined toolchain.</li><li>Monitor the resource usage of runtime environments of the application components (for example, memory monitoring) and changes in the cluster configuration for potential performance degradation and optimization.</li></ul>
Infrastructure monitoring	Monitor the resource usage of runtime environments of application components (for example, memory monitoring).
Capacity monitoring and management	<ul><li>Monitor the workload status and provide reports periodically.</li><li>Optimize cloud rate and cloud usage.</li><li>Manage cost observability and optimization.</li><li>Manage IT compliance governance.</li><li>Provide rightsizing for platform workload.</li><li>Ensure the transparency of cloud usage with anomaly detection and an observability report.</li><li>Provide detailed budget planning and forecasting.</li><li>Enforce resource group-level budgeting and tracking.</li></ul>
Workload monitoring	<ul><li>Monitor the workload status and provide reports periodically.</li><li>Monitor the resource usage of runtime environments of application components (for example, memory monitoring).</li><li>Manage cluster configuration for potential performance degradation and optimization.</li><li>Perform RCA for any performance incident.</li></ul>

Table 9.8 – List of activities for observability implementation of a modern cloud infrastructure

All these activities need to be managed and monitored from a central location so that it is possible to enforce proper governance; otherwise, there will be chaos. A central visualization for all different fundamental aspects of *observability* and *governance* can ensure better effectiveness and efficiency. The next section will discuss having a central *dashboard* for observability and governance.

Dashboard

A central visualization of the health of the entire platform is essential for the cloud platform. It provides the overall state of the platform's health from a management, operations, applications, security, and resiliency point of view. Some of the essential characteristics of a dashboard are noted here:

- A dashboard focuses on resource utilization.

- Moving a dashboard across four SRE golden signals is required.

- A central overview is essential.

- SLI and SLA dashboards can improve performance monitoring by indicating the following features along with the UID:

  - Service name

  - Method

  - API version

  - Credential ID

  - Location

  - Protocol (**Hypertext Transfer Protocol (HTTP)** / **Google Remote Procedure Call (gRPC)**)

  - HTTP response code (for example, 402)

  - HTTP response code class (for example, 4xx)

  - gRPC status code

The following screenshot shows a heatmap containing different data points essential to ensure an efficient visualization and central monitoring dashboard for the cloud platform:

Aspects	Domains							
Planning	Self-Service	Terraform workflow	Security	Automation	Notice Board	Service Catalogue		
Platform	Compute Health	Storage Health	Network Health	Container Platform Health	Performance	Multi Cluster Management	Multi Tenant Management	Geo Location
SRE	SLOs and SLIs	error budgets	4 Golden Signal (e.g., Latency)	Anti-fragility				
Finance	Expense by Instance (compute, network, storage)	Expense by application / multiple tenants and other Categorical Expense	Expense by operations and other Categorical Expense	Budget Analysis	Proactive Recommendation	FinOps Frequency	Affected resources/ asset	Expense Correlation
Compliance	Compliance Health	Activity related to Resolution	Task/ Risk Board	UI based Report				
Regulation	Regulation Health	Activity related to Resolution	Task/ Risk Board	UI based Report				
Policy	Policy Health	Activity related to Resolution	Task/ Risk Board	UI based Report				
Application	Application Performance	Transaction	Distributed Tracing					
Inventory	Self Service	Asset Health	Assets Inventory Multi Tenancy					
AI Insight	Predictive Monitoring	Proactive Alert	Consumption trend analysis & prediction					
Operation	Frequency of run	Affected resources/ asset						
User	Activity	Audit	Report	Digital Behavior (Click + AI based)				
Security	Health	SecOps frequency	SecOps affection on asset/ resources	Violation	Report publication			
Cloud	Multi Cloud	Edge Computing						

Figure 9.8 – Heatmap for dashboard data points

Monitoring a platform with proper observability settings, visualization or a dashboard, logging, and continuous monitoring is crucial to maintain the platform's HA and resiliency. In this section, we discussed the essentials and some best practices to ensure continuous platform monitoring.

Summary

It is essential to understand the system's resiliency at any given time. Therefore, there must be a systematic evaluation process to ensure that the underlying platform provides the required availability to continue business operations without any disruption. This chapter has discussed different domains of resiliency for a cloud platform. We discussed the resiliency of cloud platforms by designing HA, backup and restore, cyber recovery, and DR with the means of architecture design and continuous operations.

In the next chapter, we will discuss some essential operation practices to ensure a platform's resilience.

Further reading

- *Use the Always On pattern to achieve zero downtime during outages*: `https://www.ibm.com/cloud/architecture/architecture/practices/achieve-zero-downtime/`

- *Always On. Considerations When Adopting the Cloud*: `https://www.redbooks.ibm.com/abstracts/redp5297.html?Open`

10
Managing Operations in Hybrid Cloud Infrastructure

Building a cloud platform and moving all workloads to the platform is not enough. The cloud platform needs *continuous management*. Each cloud provider provides a wide range of managed services that the cloud provider manages. However, organizations still need to take care of a range of responsibilities to ensure the cloud platform works smoothly.

In this chapter, we will discuss the major areas of operations on the cloud. Here is a list of topics that we will cover:

- Understanding the pillars of **Site Reliability Engineering** (**SRE**)
- Exploring the platform engineering service
- Understanding **Key Performance Indicators** (**KPIs**) for the platform service
- Understanding FinOps
- Understanding reference architectures for MLOps
- Understanding the IBM reference architecture for incident management
- Understanding the IBM reference architecture for problem management
- Measuring **Operational Readiness Reviews** (**ORRs**)

Understanding the pillars of SRE

The fundamental principle of SRE is to work more innovatively and effectively through automation. In the following subsections, we will discuss the eight pillars of SRE.

Leadership and culture

One of the crucial activities of SRE is **Root Cause Analysis (RCA)**, where we examine all mistakes and problems to determine the root causes and contributing factors to any negative consequences. A key element is to have a blameless postmortem culture to manifest trust among all stakeholders.

Work sharing

SRE is designed to support the entire software development life cycle, ensuring the service meets the agreed-upon quality characteristics. As organizational silos are broken down, site reliability engineers share responsibility with other stakeholders such as the **product owner, architect**, and **developer**. Only strong collaboration across teams can lead to the targeted outcome.

Monitoring

Dumping all logs onto the log aggregator causes the log server to become exhausted and overloaded. Therefore, it is essential to enforce AI insights to remove any noise from the log and only focus on the relevant information that will help to identify root causes and incidents. Although monitoring does not need to be automated, AI can enforce the following to improve observability:

- Anomaly detection

- Fault localization

- Similar incident detection

- Change detection

- Content creation

- Content mapping

- Issue routing

- Causality analysis

- Factfinding

- Augmented intelligence

- Next action

- Escalation

SLOs and SLIs

Service quality or reliability needs to be monitored and measured against a goal. Often, service providers must face the consequences if the goal has not been met. Three different service-level metrics are used to measure the quality of management and service operations for the cloud. The first indicator is a metric to measure the quality and reliability of the services and operations, which is called the **Service-Level Indicator (SLI)**. SLIs range between 0% and 100%. Next, SLIs are measured against a **Service-Level Objective (SLO)** goal. SLOs need to fit the business values and priorities. Critical business uses cases define the priority for different SLIs. SLOs must be realistic and achievable. SLOs connect reliability metrics to business KPIs. In addition, to reflect on the consequences, the third metric, known as the **Service-Level Agreement (SLA)**, indicates the penalty that the service provider has to pay if the SLOs are not met. SLIs, SLOs, and SLAs must be clearly defined and precisely measured. The different types of SLIs are shown in *Table 10.1*:

Request/ response	Availability	The proportion of valid requests served successfully
	Latency	The percentage of valid requests served faster than a threshold
	Quality	The proportion of valid requests served without degrading the quality
Data processing	Coverage	The proportion of valid data processed successfully
	Correctness	The proportion of valid data producing correct output
	Freshness	The percentage of valid data updated more recently than a threshold
	Throughput	The percentage of time where the data processing rate is faster than a threshold
Storage	Durability	The proportion of valid data that can be successfully read even after failure
Scheduled execution	Skew	The percentage of executions that start within an acceptable window of the expected start time
	Duration	The percentage of executions that complete within the acceptable duration window

Table 10.1 – Different types of SLIs

Now that we have some SLIs, the next step is to define the goals or SLOs. Here is a list of some best practices with which to establish a set of SLOs:

- Identify the system boundaries and scope for the services.
- Define the capabilities required for each system in the environment, such as availability, because different systems might have different levels of availability.
- Define technical SLIs for each SLI type.
- Monitor SLIs continuously and measure them against the SLOs.

Error budget

An *error budget* is the maximum volume that a technical system can afford to fail without contractual consequences or business discontinuation. The error budget controls the velocity of new feature releases or existing system changes, maintenance, or planned outages. It helps teams stay vigilant and find the right balance between innovation and reliability.

Toil reduction

Toil refers to the repetitive, manual, predictable, and constant stream of tasks related to maintaining a service that tends to scale linearly as the service grows. Once such a task has been identified; it needs to be automated as soon as possible to reduce the amount of effort taken and auto-scale the services without complexity. Each identified piece of toil must be monitored, and appropriate planning to automate it should be in place, which might help to reduce errors and the time taken for resolution. Innovation needs to meet reality in terms of budgets and costs, and an error budget is a common incentive for product teams and SREs to find the right balance.

Incident management

A well-integrated single plane of glass is essential for *incident management*. Later in this chapter, we will discuss the reference architecture in detail. Blameless incident management is essential for successful SRE adoption. Blameless incident management requires the incident task force members to frequently collaborate with each other in a central designated room or over a Zoom call, known as a *War Room*, to focus on the following items instead of who owns the management of the system in question:

- Events
- Actions
- The execution time of those actions
- The effect of actions

- The expectations and errors in the standard execution path of actions

- The key assumptions

- The associated events surrounding the actions and execution time

There are different efficient practices to adopt for efficient incident management. For successful incident management, we need automation and event correlation. During each second within the IT landscape, thousands of events are triggered from logs, activities, systems, networks, manual interventions, and other sources. An intelligent event collaboration system collaborates with related events and automates the process of identifying the probable cause of any incident by classifying related events. There are different event management tools, such as IBM Watson AIOPs, IBM **Cloud Event Management** (**CEM**) with Netcool Operations Insight, and more. *Figure 10.1* shows the standard capabilities of an intelligent event management solution:

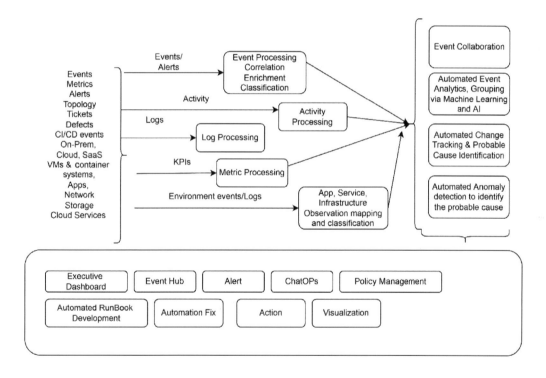

Figure 10.1 – Event management

Events from multiple heterogeneous sources are collected and processed to correlate them using machine learning algorithms or AI analytics. AI analytics help to reduce noise and focus on relevant events for different incidents. After the events and logs are processed and classified, they are analyzed for anomalies to identify the context and probable cause, that is, the insights, from event analysis to improve the collaboration and execution by leveraging automation. In addition, as shown in *Figure 10.1*, a set of automations can be developed to automate some operations using the contextual insights from these events to fix incidents. For example, a central operations executive dashboard can visualize the health of the platform and develop relevant runbooks to resolve incidents and similar actions.

Automation

Automation must be everywhere for each service operation on the cloud. Automation can quickly identify business priorities based on metadata such as tags, commit messages, associated backlog items, context, applications, log analysis, and other information. Additionally, automation can help design a pipeline by identifying business priorities to reduce the deployment time and toil. Automation must be performed during the service's testing, provisioning, deployment, and operations.

SRE is one of the best practices to enforce continuous platform engineering to take care of cloud environments. In the next section, we will discuss platform engineering.

Exploring the platform engineering service

A cloud platform can be divided into the physical platform layers and the cloud platform layers, where all the IaaS and PaaS products are deployed; the middleware layer, where middleware and SaaS solutions are deployed; and finally, the application layer. Each managed service, such as PaaS or IaaS, provided by a cloud provider has its own responsibility matrix, which defines the roles and responsibilities of service providers and organizations. *Figure 10.2* shows the shared responsibilities for IaaS product management between IBM and customers. Therefore, in addition to the service management by the service or cloud provider, organizations should also establish the processes, practices, toolchains, and governance for the service management of different services deployed on the cloud. Usually, the cloud provider manages the physical layers and hypervisor layer.

On the other hand, organizations have some responsibilities for virtual components and middleware layers. In addition, organizations need to manage applications and data. Therefore, a well-defined service management framework for the organization for each layer of the cloud deployment is essential:

Resource	Incident and Operations Management	Change Management	Identity and Access Management	Security and Regulation Compliance	Disaster Recovery
Data	Customer	Customer	Customer	Customer	Customer
Application	Customer	Customer	Customer	Customer	Customer
Operating system	Customer	Customer	Customer	Customer	Customer
Virtual and bare metal servers	Shared	Shared	Shared	Shared	Shared
Virtual storage	Shared	Shared	Shared	Shared	Shared
Virtual network	Shared	Shared	Shared	Shared	Shared
Hypervisor	IBM	IBM	IBM	IBM	IBM
Physical servers and memory	IBM	IBM	Shared	Shared	IBM
Physical storage	IBM	IBM	IBM	IBM	IBM
Physical network and devices	IBM	IBM	IBM	IBM	IBM
Facilities and data centers	IBM	IBM	IBM	IBM	IBM

Figure 10.2 – Shared responsibilities for IaaS products by IBM

Figure 10.3 shows the different activities required to manage the landing zone for the Landorous use cases. Each layer needs administration, governance, security control management, and monitoring as mandatory operations components.

The cloud provider takes care of the physical and hypervisor layers in the **D** layer of *Figure 10.3*. On top of the hypervisor based on the services, the cloud provider provides partial operations as the out-of-the-box add-ons for the managed services. Therefore, the operation owners have their responsibilities. *Figure 10.3* shows different operations required for the infrastructure layer (**C**) and platform service layer (**D**). The middleware layer requires a different kind of operation.

Automation is at the core of all these operations. Infrastructure as code, policy as code, and security by design are all essential for successful platform engineering.

In a hybrid environment, you should take care of the cloud and the on-premises locations. Therefore, a central standard and single plane of glass are essential to enforce the same policy and leverage the benefit of an automation pipeline for services across hybrid platforms:

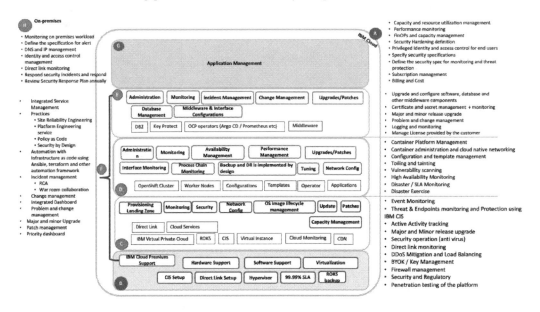

Figure 10.3 – Service management for the different layers of a cloud deployment

Monitoring is the fundamental operation of platform engineering. An integrated dashboard to expose all data points collected by monitoring and insights developed by AI analytics can provide a clear picture regarding the current health of different platforms. In addition to user activities, services, resource utilization, and golden signals, such as latency, traffic, errors, saturation, and requests, **platform engineering** also emphasizes monitoring user experience, SLIs, and the availability of services connections.

Platform engineering enforces a security operation center to manage policies for network security such as intrusion detection and prevention, security policies, and security controls to harden the infrastructure. In addition to infrastructure security, we also need to manage data encryption keys, certificates for applications and middleware, and licenses for software for data and application security.

Platform engineering leverages SRE to establish proper problem management, incident management, and change management.

Aside from skills, processes, practices, and governance, the success of platform engineering is heavily dependent on the toolchain. Therefore, a set of proper tools and automation can reduce the complexity of platform service operations. *Table 10.2* shows the principle categories for platform operations and their corresponding toolchains:

Operations	Toolchain
Infrastructure as Code	Ansible, Terraform, and Git
Service management	ServiceNow and Jira
Alert	PagerDuty
ChatOps	Slack and IBM Watson Conversation
Event correlation	Netcool Insight
Vulnerability scanning	Qualys
Security Event Insight Monitoring (SEIM)	QRadar
Disaster recovery	Zerto for VMware, Azure Site Recovery, and other cloud services
Backup and restore	The cloud Backup and Restore service, Veeam Availability Suite for VMware; Velero for container storage; Portworx for Portworx container storage; and IBM Spectrum Protect for any storage
CI/CD	A cloud CI/CD service such as Tekton; open source CI/CD such as Argo CD
Platform monitoring	Cloud monitoring services such as IBM Cloud Monitoring, Azure Sentinel, AWS Cloudwatch, Instana, and Datadog
Log aggregation for insight and event analysis	Splunk
Application performance monitoring	AppDynamics
Change monitoring	Evolven
End user monitoring, browser experience	Aternity
Synthetic user monitoring	BSM
Inventory and asset management	ServiceNow

Table 10.2 – Toolchains for different platform engineering operations

In the next section, we will discuss some major KPIs for the assessment of platform operations and evaluate the efficiency of the underlying cloud infrastructure.

Understanding KPIs for the platform service

For hybrid cloud operations, we need to define a set of KPIs to measure the efficiency of the underlying cloud platform. Here is a set of KPIs for cloud platform evaluation:

- **Total downtime** indicates the aggregate number of hours within the scheduled operational hours in the reporting period when the infrastructure elements and applications were unavailable for use by the designated end users.

- **Planned downtime** refers to the aggregate number of hours out of the scheduled hours in any reporting period when the supported infrastructure elements and applications were unavailable for use by the designated users due to planned preventive maintenance, upgrades, or changes.

- Response time refers to the time the first resolver group(s) takes to accept a ticket for resolution. For example, this would be the time difference between an incident (ticket) being created to the time the resolver acknowledges the incident (ticket) for action (in the queue).

- **Resolution time** refers to the time taken to resolve the incident or provide an acceptable workaround for the incident.

- **Priority** (or severity) indicates a category that is used to identify the relative importance of an incident. The target resolution time for an incident depends upon the priority (or severity) category it belongs to, as it states the degree of impact that an incident can have on business value. *Table 10.3* shows incidents with different priorities:

Priority level	Description
P1	A critical function or network outage has a high impact on service(s), and no alternative or bypass is available.
P2	A potential high impact or degradation of service of a critical function where no acceptable alternative or bypass is available. A non-critical function causing medium impact to business/corporate operations with no acceptable alternative (for example, multiple user issues with a significant impact on business operations).
P3	A non-critical function (such as a system or an application) or procedure is down, unusable, or difficult to use with medium/low impact, but no immediate impact on service delivery. Additionally, an alternative or bypass is available. Problems that would otherwise be considered priority level 1 or priority level 2 but that have an acceptable alternative or bypass available will also be designated priority level 3 (for example, multiple users with no significant impact on the ability to support the business).
P4	A personal application or procedure is unusable, and either an alternative is available or deferred maintenance is acceptable.

Table 10.3 – Incident priority classification

The response and resolution time of the incident are defined based on their level of priority, as shown in *Table 10.4*:

Priority level	Response time	Resolution time	% SLA
P1	15 minutes	< 3 hours	95%
P2	60 minutes	< 8 hours	95%
P3	4 hours	< 24 hours	95%
P4	12 hours	< 48 hours	95%

Table 10.4 – The response time and the resolution time for different classes of incidents

Similar to incident management, other operations also have their corresponding KPIs, as shown in *Table 10.5*:

Category	Prerequisite	Metric	Reporting period	SLA attainment
Change management	Applicable to all changes in the production environment.	Change success rate	Monthly	98%
High availability	Clustered servers/devices and network elements, high availability with physical redundancy, hardware and network availability of 99.9% or higher.	Measured at the cluster level (service) N + 1 (spare) level redundancy	Monthly	99.9%
Backup and restore	The underlying infrastructure needs to have 99.95% availability. Storage should be adequate to support the backup policy. Network throughput should be adequate to support the backup policy.	Backup success rate	Monthly	95%

Table 10.5 – KPIs for different platform operations

In the next section, we will discuss FinOps to effectively manage the variable spend model of cloud consumption.

Understanding FinOps

- Throughout this book, we have focused on business value as the main driver for any cloud conversation, practice, or program. It is essential to give business value the driving seat to maximize the return on cloud investment for any organization. As the cloud is scalable and easy to grow, it also provides flexibility in adoption. On the other hand, too much focus on cost can limit the advantages of the cloud for organizations. Therefore, balancing cloud adoption and the business value returned on cloud investment is essential. A set of practices leveraging the people, processes, tools, and technologies help to establish the balance between cloud adoption and the business value returned on cloud investment, known as FinOps. According to the **DevOps and Cloud InfoQ Trends Report** from July 2021, as shown in Figure 10.4, FinOps is the trending operation model to maximize the cloud investment guided by business value. FinOps can benefit any organization regardless of its corresponding cloud footprint volume. The best practice is to start small, test different processes, and iterate the successful process throughout the life cycle for continuous improvement.

The FinOps operating framework should be established for small or large cloud platforms and continuously practiced over iterations to improve the result by maximizing cloud investment. FinOps is more of a cultural practice than an operating framework. Here is a list of the building blocks for successful FinOps for any cloud platform:

- **People**: To establish FinOps, the responsibilities and accountabilities should be shared among everyone working on the platform. A clear **Responsibility, Accountability, Consultation, and Information (RACI)** matrix can describe the responsibilities of related parties. Based on the reference architecture described in Figure 10.5, there are multiple operation centers with corresponding squads and a central management and governance team called **FinOPs Office Center (FOC)**. The responsibility to establish FinOPs is shared and should be orchestrated with a well-defined RACI matrix:

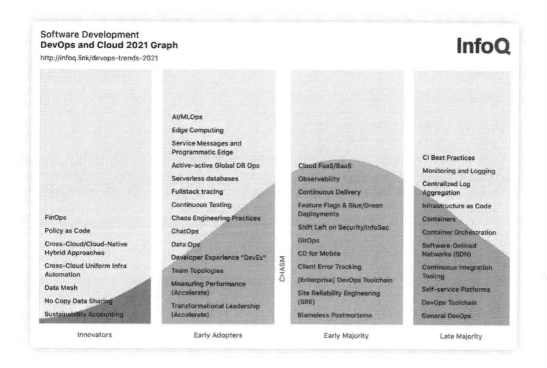

Figure 10.4 – The DevOps and Cloud InfoQ Trends report from July 2021

- **Processes**: A set of KPIs should be established to measure cloud waste and usage. A governance process ensures the team has access to the knowledge domain for FinOps, KPI metrics for measurement, and tools for implementation. This process needs to have workload onboarding capabilities, so each cloud workload is registered and evaluated for capacity management from a specific location with global standards. Additionally, the process should include a continuous capacity evaluation for each workload against the ideal KPI for capacity usage for the corresponding workload. This KPI can change due to any changes in the corresponding workload. Therefore, a well-governed process of KPI change management should be established to reflect those changes to avoid incorrect evaluation. Finally, the trends of the golden signals for each workload should be analyzed to predict future costs and waste.

- **Methods**: Different methods, such as rightsizing, which ensures that the underlying infrastructure is scaled to fit the right intended usage, can improve the quality of FinOps. Continuous monitoring of storage and compute usage by different products helps to estimate the right size for the infrastructure. The on-demand auto-scaling of cloud-native services ensures that they are used when there is a demand. Storage life cycle management is another method that can help with old archive data and deleting unused and unnecessary data, ultimately improving cloud usage.

- **Technology**: Different tools and technology are available to provide a FinOps solution. The main component for any FinOps solution should be (i) the consumption configuration and visualization components, (ii) the operations component to execute different operations to keep the cloud usage within the intended amount, (iii) the AI component for insight and analysis generation, and (iv) the governance component to manage, view, and administrate different aspects of FinOps.

- **Governance with security and compliance**: The last pillar of FinOps is well-defined governance, including people, processes, technology, and best practices. Governance must enforce security and compliance to improve the FinOps adoption quality. For example, if identity and access control management has been defined correctly, it can help enforce policies so that the cloud investment can remain optimized. In addition, security and compliance can be implemented as policies to enforce cost optimization and controls to reduce waste. Also, governance for FinOps requires a regular audit and cost review process to monitor the cloud investment closely.

FinOps reference architecture

The FinOps reference architecture, shown in *Figure 10.5*, has six main operation centers:

- Monitoring

- Planning

- Analysis

- Execution

- Change management

- Configuration management

The monitoring operation center collects information about the cloud ecosystem's financial and technical aspects. The planning operation center focuses on best practice adoption, governance, decision-making, and continuous vigilance of cloud resource utilization. The analysis operations center focuses on optimizing the current practice and utilizing AI insights and optimized decision-making. Finally, the execution operation center executes and changes the configuration to implement the best practices of FinOps to ensure maximum return on cloud investment. Each operation center has a corresponding squad team, and for overall governance, a central and well-integrated FOC should be established. Each operation center should have team members with platform engineering skills, financial skills, and decision-making skills. Besides operations, FinOps is also a practice. Therefore, FOC must establish practices to get the maximum benefits by following best practices for capacity management for the cloud.

Let's look at different components of the reference architecture, shown in *Figure 10.5*:

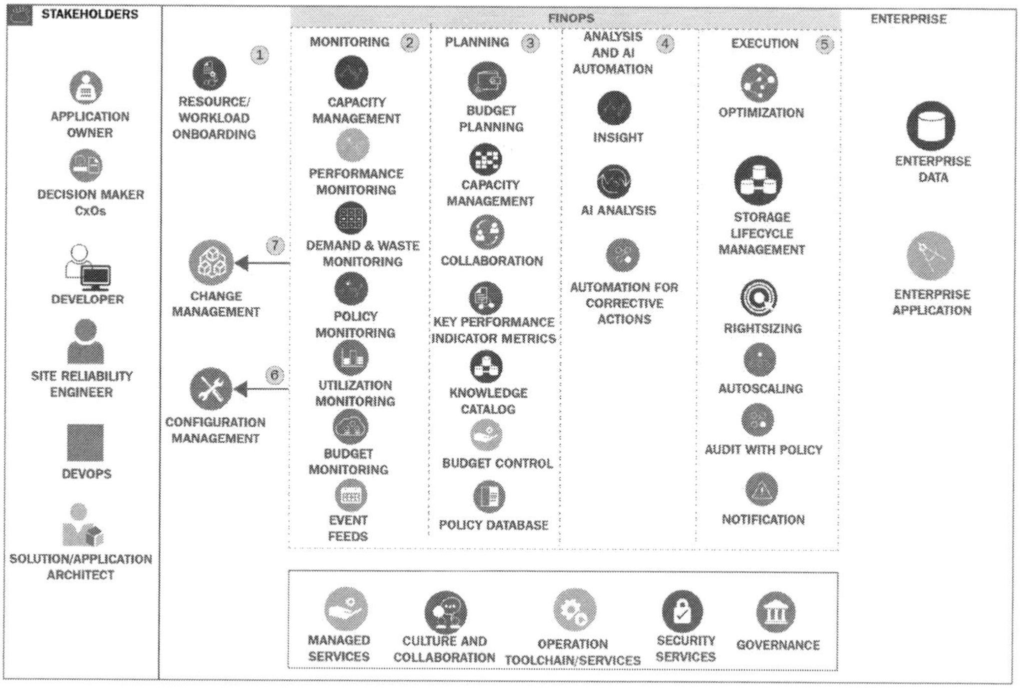

Figure 10.5 – The reference architecture for FinOps

Monitoring

As shown in the reference architecture, a FinOps manager must have the following capabilities:

- Monitor each component in the connected platform, for example, a virtual machine, a network component, an IP address, tags, labels, a worker node, and every other thing deployed on the cloud.

- Monitor demand for each component and service (IaaS, PaaS, and SaaS) to understand the demand, current utilization, and future utilization based on demand trends.

- Monitor the overuse of each service and understand the demand, usage, and waste of cloud resources.

- Monitor the performance of each workload or application deployed on the platform.

- Justify that the current utilization is sufficient to achieve the desired service level and availability. Otherwise, the cloud investment should increase to add more resources to the existing platform.

- Monitor any applied policies and new, incoming policies to understand the impact of cloud consumption on cloud budget and investment.

- Monitor any violation of policies to ensure that the cost and budget constraints are followed by the current cloud consumption.

- Monitor current utilization to establish any trends. Therefore, future costs can be predicted.

- Monitor any other events and correlate them to the platform's capacity, budget, investment, and utilization of cloud resources to identify any insights for capacity management.

Monitoring focuses on data collection and feeds that data to analytics and planning for the successful execution of different FinOps processes.

Planning

There are different operations in the execution phase. These operations should be automated and governed by policies. In the following subsections, we will discuss different FinOps management reference architecture operations. Once the workload, services, or resources are provisioned on the platform, they should be continuously monitored for capacity, demand, performance, waste, and utilization by analyzing a series of events generated by the corresponding workload, services, or resources.

The next step is to define a budget for the cloud that reflects the desired return on the business value of the cloud investment. This budget will also explain different services and corresponding settings to reflect the intended cost of each service. Additionally, a software-defined capacity management framework should be established to manage the cloud budget for the underlying cloud platform along with the dynamic requirements. KPI metrics control the cloud budget and measure the waste in cloud adoption. Therefore, they are essential and should be described in detail with instructions for evaluating them and when to evaluate them. Finally, FinOps is a set of shared responsibilities among all stakeholders, and collaboration between them is essential.

As FinOps is a shared responsibility among all stakeholders, everyone needs to be educated and encouraged to understand the pay-as-you-go nature of cloud consumption with rightsizing, which is a process to control expenses by eliminating obvious waste in instances and storage used.

A single driver to control decisions in a complex cloud environment is often recommended as a business value. When reviewing the FinOps report, it is recommended that you consider how much business value is achieved by the current and future cloud consumption.

Analysis and AI automation

AI analysis and automation are essential to identify the waste and desired size of the platform from the data collected by different monitoring agents. Furthermore, automation can trigger corrective action to reduce waste controlled by KPIs and business values.

Often, FinOps triggers change management to reflect the recommended insight generated by AI analytics in cloud optimization and resource utilization.

One of the core functions of the analysis operation center is to identify influential parameters to identify waste, utilization, significant and heavy workloads, and others. FinOps teams are using these parameters. The analysis operation center analyzes the forecasting for utilization. The future utilization reports are then evaluated against the budget control, and necessary changes in budget control and policies are planned and executed. Utilization, waste, budget, and demand forecasting are continuously based on the information collected by the monitoring tools and agents. FOC runs a regular periodic review of forecasting reports to adjust policies, KPIs, and budget controls. The monitoring agents collect data for AI analytics to understand patterns in demand, usage, waste, utilization, and return on cloud investment and detect anomalies in potential trends and vulnerabilities.

Another essential feature of analytics is to report KPIs, costs, and finances regularly. FOC and other teams need to have access to the complete picture of relevant data to make the right decisions. A single pane of glass or dashboard containing different data for demand, waste, usage, investment, business costs, finance, and value should be at the fingertips of teams for better adoption of FinOps.

Budget control policies and allocation cannot be fixed; they must be iterative. Therefore, policies and control should be implemented as code.

Execution

Execution starts with the optimization of resource utilization and budget control. The primary operation activities are listed as follows:

- Apply different policies, KPIs, and budget controls to the platform.
- Define budget controls.
- Manage alerts and notifications.
- Apply capping and constraints for cloud resource usage to control the return of cloud investment.
- Onboarding or provisioning new resources by following rightsizing and budget policies.
- Regularly review or audit policies and budget controls.
- Validate any new resource onboarding to the platform by validating the request against the budget. In the case of a violation of the policies, alter FOC to mitigate the demand and budget.
- Optimize product efficiency, financial efficiency, and cloud usage enforced by policies and budget controls.
- Distribute the cost between the consumer and the owner to balance budget controls by policies.

Configuration management

To reduce cloud waste and optimize investments, we need to regularly manage the storage life cycle and on-demand auto-scaling for workload, optimization, and configuration management. Configuration management is directly influenced by the policy catalog and AI automation. Configuration changes are the implication of changes in policies on the cloud platform and improve the performance of different AI automation according to the policy changes. Different KPIs and their definitions are controlled by configuration management. The configuration management operation center also implements configurations for insights, such as labeling, tagging, and classifying different cloud resources. In addition, any application, service, or infrastructure can have thousands of applications, services, pieces of software, products, and other components. The same component can provide different capabilities for different use cases based on different configurations. All these components are set up with a specific configuration. Therefore, these configurations are crucial for capabilities, performance, complexity, and productivity. To reduce complexity and maintain the expected performance, a configuration management solution should have the following capabilities:

- Identify different versions of the same configuration.

- Classify related configuration for components, applications, projects, and more.

- Identify the baseline for each configuration to reduce complexity.

- Edit the configuration with flexibility.

- Implement policies as code or infrastructure as code to set up the configuration.

- Branch a different configuration variant from the baseline for different environments to enable parallel development.

- Provide a holistic view of the artifacts for a specific version of components.

- Create a hierarchical structure to reflect different underlying environments, for example, global configuration, test configuration, source code configuration, network policy configuration, and more.

- Enable a CI/CD pipeline for configurations.

- Enable change management for configurations to keep track of different versions or specifications to reduce complexity.

Change management

Changes should also be monitored to make better decisions. Business value should govern changes directly to control the return on cloud investment. Some configurations cannot be changed automatically. An alert is sent to the corresponding authority or FOC to make the changes in those cases. FOC is responsible for making decisions about changes. Here are the steps for a change management process:

1. Request a change with a detailed specification.

2. The *change authority* should review the change request to understand the technical and financial feasibility and make approval or rejection decisions.

3. If the change request is approved, the following will occur:

    I. Plan the implementation for the corresponding change with the timeline.

    II. Design the change implementation.

    III. Build the deployment model.

    IV. Deploy the change to the target platform.

    V. Conduct the final assessment.

    VI. Identify the success instance for the corresponding change.

    VII. Inform the end user about the change.

    VIII. Track and record any problem with the new change.

    IX. If a new problem is found, do the following:

        x. Loop to *step 1* to create a change request for the problem to be fixed.

4. If the change request is rejected, do the following:

    I. The change request is closed.

Security services

Security is essential to enforce FinOps. Different operations teams should work within the access boundary enforced by the identity and access control system.

Culture and collaboration

There is no alternative to Agile as the collaboration choice for FinOps. FOC is responsible for enabling best practices among cloud service consumers and operators. A successful FinOps adoption requires blameless cause analysis. Mistakes are learning opportunities and are not meant for firing employees.

The following section will discuss a reference architecture for MLOps in detail.

Understanding reference architectures for MLOPs

Machine learning jobs are now an essential part of any software and organization. Moreover, machine learning and data analytics components are both dynamic and continuous. Therefore, **Machine Learning Operations** (**MLOps**) is crucial for organizations. *Figure 10.6* shows the reference architecture for MLOps. This section will discuss how IBM Cloud Pak for Data can provide an end-to-end MLOps solution.

Project governance

MLOps mainly needs project governance, security operations such as identity and access control management, and data and network security operations. MLOps starts with project governance, where organizations can manage multiple data analytics and insight projects. Each project has its assets, such as data, Jupyter notebooks, models, people, dashboards, data flows, and more:

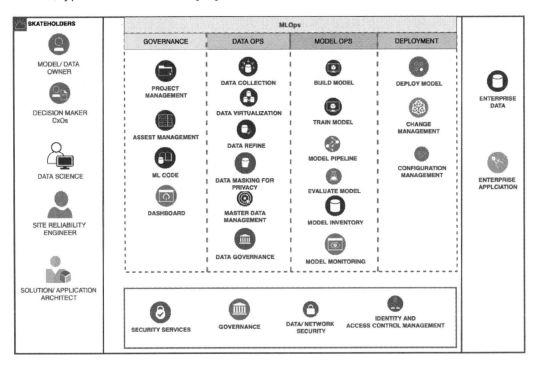

Figure 10.6 – Reference architecture for MLOps

Figure 10.7 shows different assets for a data science project in IBM Cloud Pak for Data:

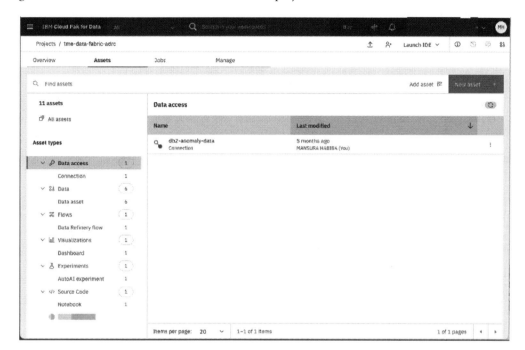

Figure 10.7 – Project management in IBM Cloud Pak for Data

DataOps

DataOps refers to the main operations in an analytic data platform as data is essential for the machine learning platform. Data can be imported into a project and, using data virtualization, IBM Cloud Pak for Data can virtualize the data in external resources such as AWS S3, Azure Files storage, and more. In addition, the IBM Watson Quay service provides data virtualization capabilities that enable connecting with other sources and replicating data to the local cloud object storage bucket so that the model can use them without any latency. The main goal for the data collection phase is to either create a platform connection for data replication or upload data to the machine learning platform so that the model can access the training data without any latency.

Once the data is collected and available on the platform, it needs to be prepared with data governance or refinement. IBM Cloud Pak leverages DataStage to refine the data, clean the data, and process it for model training. *Figure 10.8* shows several predefined templates for data refinement. You can also include different nodes and create templates for IBM Data Refinery:

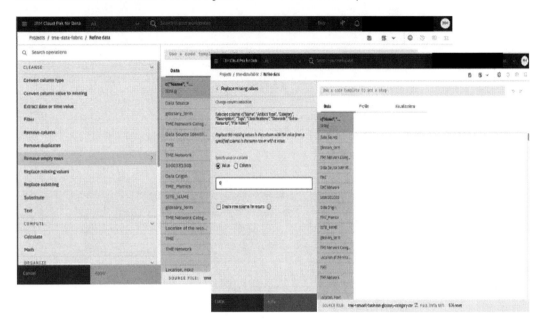

Figure 10.8 – IBM Data Refinery in IBM Cloud Pak for Data

Additionally, there are master data management components that help to save the master data separately and manage the life cycle of the master data.

Data operations must be privacy-conscious. Therefore, different masking approaches are applied to the data during the data preparation phase. Several predefined templates for masking are available on the IBM Cloud Pak for Data platform.

Models

The next phase is to define the model ops to build and manage the model's life cycle. The life cycle of any machine learning model runs through the following steps:

1. Build the model using the different stages of a pipeline.

2. Train the model.

3. Save the model and manage the model inventory.

4. Deploy the model to different target platforms.

5. Monitor the performance and impact of the model.

6. Evaluate the deployment of models for bias.

7. Update the deployment with a better-performing model.

8. Monitor deployments and jobs across the organization.

AutoAI in IBM Cloud Pak for Data runs multiple algorithms on the same dataset and engineers model parameters and features to optimize the performance of each algorithm. AutoAI generates a pipeline for each model in sequence and evaluates and ranks those models. Additionally, IBM Cloud Pak for Data provides an easy and flexible interface to design the pipeline for any AutoAI pipeline. *Figure 10.9* shows the steps for an AutoAI pipeline:

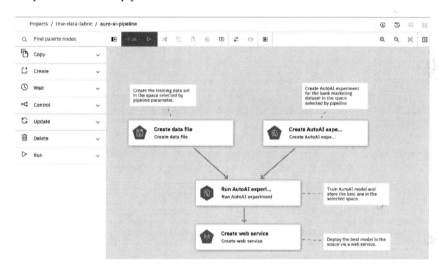

Figure 10.9 – The steps of the AutoAI pipeline

AutoAI helps to choose the correct algorithm with the highest performance. Once the model with the best performance has been identified, it can be exported, saved to the model inventory, or directly deployed to a deployment space inside the IBM Cloud Pak for a data project. The exported model can be configured further using a Jupyter notebook. *Figure 10.10* shows 10 different pipelines created for 10 different algorithms. Each of the pipelines is run individually to improve the performance of the model:

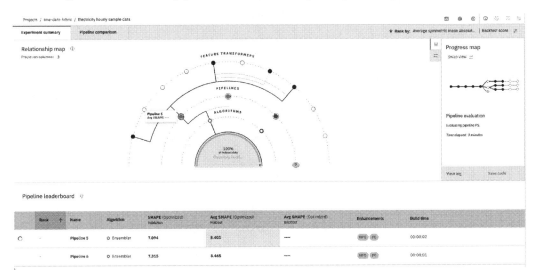

Figure 10.10 – Pipelines for 10 algorithms on time series model training

Additionally, AutoAI provides the comparative performance of all 10 separate models, as shown in *Figure 10.11*. You can also save any of the models in the *Model Inventory*:

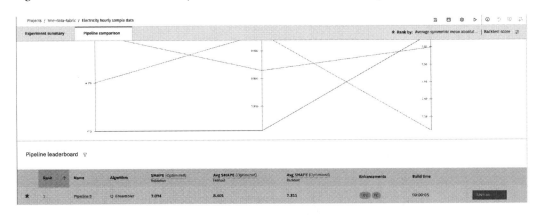

Figure 10.11 – The comparative performance of models

Deployments

Finally, the model can be deployed to the target workspace. Deployed models are continuously monitored for quality and fairness. *Figure 10.12* shows the OpenScale dashboard that collects historical records and measurements for seven days and provides the model's quality:

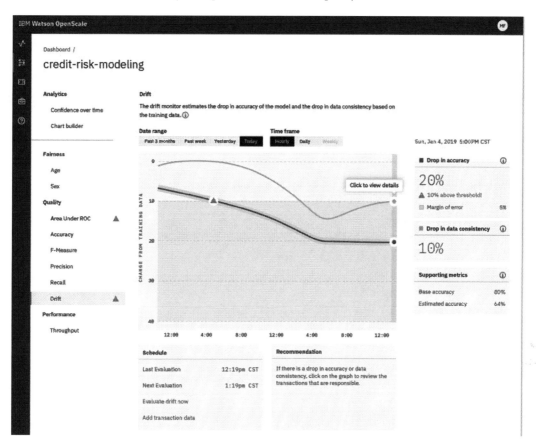

Figure 10.12 – The IBM Watson OpenScale dashboard for model monitoring

Next, we will discuss some IBM reference architectures for incident and problem management. Finally, we will discuss different operations for incident and problem management based on the reference architectures recommended by IBM.

Understanding the IBM reference architecture for incident management

Incident management can be described as restoring the healthy state of a system after an incident affects that system. IBM Architecture Center describes the end-to-end workflow for managing any incident in the reference architecture, as shown in *Figure 10.13*.

Incident management happens in four stages: *monitoring, analyzing, planning*, and *executing*. The primary artifacts for incident management are observability dashboards and runbooks.

The following dashboard shows a typical cloud platform's current IT and business aspects. In addition, it shows the healthy and unhealthy components of the platform and provides visual insights to determine the incident along with its root cause:

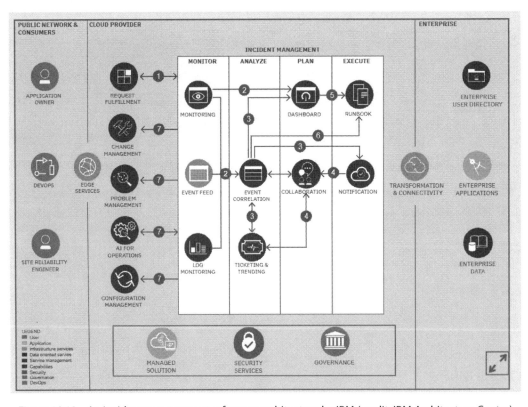

Figure 10.13 – An incident management reference architecture by IBM (credit: IBM Architecture Center)

Runbooks refer to scripts or written instructions that are used by first responders to resolve issues. However, in addition to written instructions or scripts, runbooks can also be automated processes, including automated mitigation processes and notification processes, to reduce incident mitigation and response time.

Monitoring and logging components create event feeds continuously that can be tied together to identify incidents, and corresponding actions can be taken to resolve the incidents. At the same time, notifications for corresponding teams are generated to engage the necessary subject-matter experts who should collaborate to restore the healthy state of the system as soon as possible. The ticketing system tool should create a corresponding ticket for the record and for any future requirements.

Incident management often triggers other processes, as shown in step 7 in *Figure 10.13*, such as changing a database entry with change management and updating a configuration with configuration management. Similarly, incident management can also trigger problem management and AI intelligence feedback.

Understanding the IBM reference architecture for problem management

The IBM problem management reference architecture focuses on the activity and artifacts required for problem management, where the root cause of any incident is identified and resolved. The incident management system triggers problem management. The activities for problem management are mainly completed in three stages: RCA, corrective action identification, and mitigation. There are different well-known processes for RCA, such as the following:

- **Fishbone diagrams**
- **Keppner-Tregoe**
- **5 whys**

Fishbone diagrams

The incident is represented as the fish head, as shown in *Figure 10.14*. Each potential cause and method category is represented as a corresponding branch from the central arrow in a fishbone diagram. These causes are identified by asking the question *Why does this happen?* for each effect:

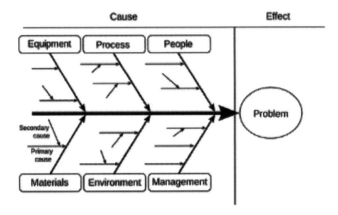

Figure 10.14 – Fishbone analysis for RCA (credit: IBM Architecture Center)

Keppner-Tregoe

In this process, the incident situation is described by asking the following *is and is not* questions:

- What precisely is happening? And what is not happening?
- Where is it impacted? And where is it not?
- When is it happening? And when is it not? Since when has it happened?
- What are the extent and scope? How many are there? What size are they? What is the trend? And what is the inverse of the extent and scope?

The answer to the preceding questions helps to identify the possible cause of the incident. Each possible cause is then verified against a set of metrics. Then, the most probable causes that best explain the evidence are identified.

5 whys

Often, the first layer of observation for any incident fails to provide in-depth details for the probable cause of the incident and, therefore, requires a diagnosis. **5 whys** focuses on the quick dissection of the incident by simply analyzing the close circle connected to the origin of the incident. The technique works as follows:

1. State the issue and ensure that the group agrees with the problem statement.

2. Share any data that was gathered and ask the first why.

3. The group responds. As it answers each question, the group must agree that the answer is correct, supports the question, and leads to the next question.

4. After we determine the contributing factors of the incident, create and assign the corresponding corrective actions.

Here is an example of a 5 whys analysis for an incident where the backend application API returns encrypted data in the database to the frontend applications without decrypting it before showing it to users intermittently:

1. *Why was the frontend application showing data as encrypted instead of decrypted?*

   Answer: The API from the backend application was returning encrypted data without decrypting it.

2. *Why was the API returning encrypted data?*

   Answer: The backend application failed to decrypt the data.

3. *Why did the backend application fail to decrypt the data?*

   Answer: The backend application failed to get the data decryption key from the IBM Key Protect service.

4. *Why did the backend application fail to get the data decryption key?*

   Answer: The IBM Key Protect service was intermittently unavailable.

5. *Why was IBM's Key Protect service unavailable?*

   Answer: The IBM Key Protect service went through a service maintenance window and then failover disaster recovery locations as needed. Sometimes, the caching is reset, so no key is available to return.

Most of the time, 5 whys can identify the root cause with five questions, making this process robust and focused. RCA identifies the corrective actions for the corresponding root cause. To correct the issue if the cause is known, a corresponding runbook might be available. If the cause is new, it is added to the known issue database with details. Often, RCA forces you to change the particular configuration so that the same issue cannot happen in the future. Therefore, problem management can often trigger change or configuration management activities, as shown in step 3 of *Figure 10.15*. Change or configuration management happens for different incidents based on their priority; high-priority incidents are resolved before low-priority ones. Change or configuration management activities for low-priority incidents are logged in the backlog for the future. Later, the items from the backlog are implemented through change management, as shown in step 6 of *Figure 10.15*:

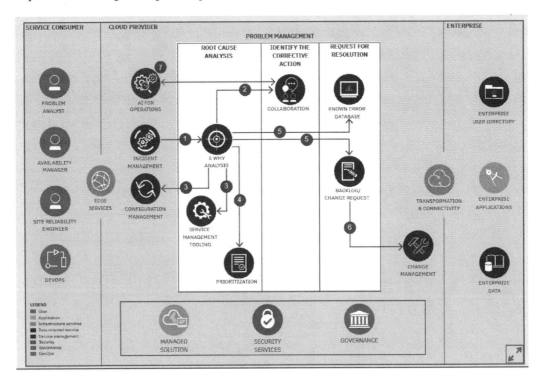

Figure 10.15 – The IBM reference architecture for problem management (credit: IBM Architecture Center)

Incident management, problem management, change management, and configuration management need to be managed closely. Therefore, they need an **umbrella management center** to apply the governance and communication among each management system. The following section will discuss the overall umbrella for the cloud service management reference architecture recommended by IBM Architecture Center.

The cloud service management reference architecture

Service management starts with gathering data for any incident or change request. The incident management processes are triggered for an incident with the correct information. For a change request, change management processes are triggered. Incident management triggers problem management to identify the incident's root cause and corresponding corrective actions. Additionally, an AI solution collects patterns and events over time in central data storage. Different analytical models are trained on that central data and provide additional insights into the root cause identified by the problem management processes. As shown in step 7 of *Figure 10.16*, this AI solution can also recommend preemptive actions to resolve the incident or take precautions against future losses. Additionally, this component also enables you to identify incidents that could happen in the future if the current configuration is not changed. Therefore, the analytic component can trigger configuration management such as incident management and problem management components:

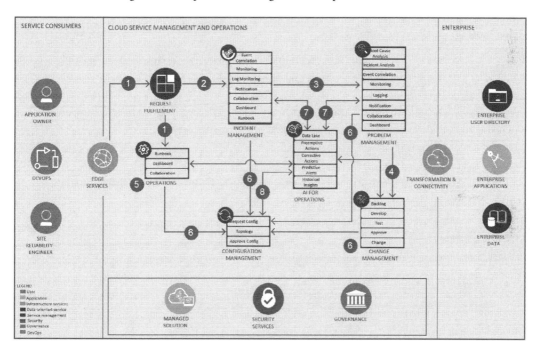

Figure 10.16 – The cloud service management reference architecture (credit: IBM Architecture Center)

Automation is mandatory for each management component in the reference architecture, as shown in *Figure 10.16*. Automation can take precautionary actions and corrective actions without losing any time and, thereby, improve the quality of cloud service management.

Now that we understand different operations and KPIs for those operations, we need to establish a process to ensure that the operations are executed regularly with standard performance. In the next section, we will discuss the continuous ORR process to ensure those different operations are running continuously. Each of these operations is also regularly assessed against associated KPIs.

Measuring ORRs

As organizations adopt a microservices approach to applications, it is essential to establish guidelines and processes to keep the services robust and operational. Service management is the collection of processes that teams must implement to manage the operational aspects of their applications to keep them healthy and troubleshoot them when there are issues. For **service reliability engineers** to manage microservices applications, they implement specific guidelines to build and maintain them. The critical questions for **ORR** are as follows:

- How do we adopt new services?

- How do we ensure the quality, performance, and availability of end user-facing applications?

- What is the behavior we need to request from our services?

We need to understand the guidelines to enforce ORR regularly. Here is a list of some guidelines. Technical guidelines might include one or more of the following:

- Expose the health of services by utilizing health check APIs.

- Expedite rapid incident resolution by providing **First Failure Data Capture** (**FFDC**).

- Make topology information available.

- Ensure services are stateless and can scale horizontally.

- Ensure local files, such as log and configuration files, are not used by services.

- Ensure the latest versions of libraries.

Non-technical guidelines might include one or more of the following:

- Regularly validate backup and restore capability.

- Describe mitigation actions for known issues by providing runbooks.

- Ensure resiliency by implementing chaos testing.

- Define the SRE team that is responsible for operating the service.

- Make service documentation available, including the architecture, key metrics, configuration, and tuning guidelines.

- Define the delivery cadence and the service owner or product manager.

Compliance guidelines or automatic checks can include one or more of the following:

- Build an automated checks model that measures service quality at scale and assists organizations on what to do to improve the quality.
- Define appropriate actions to take if a service doesn't comply with the guidelines.
- Identify incentives that can be implemented for adhering to the guidelines.
- Define additional guidelines to verify that applications are production-ready.

Summary

Running workloads on the cloud has its advantages, but managing the infrastructure platform on the cloud is unique and requires a comprehensive set of cloud-specific services. A central and integrated operations model with proper tooling, an integrated control tower, automated processes and frameworks, insights collected from continuous monitoring, and the right skills can provide a single source of truth to decrease risk and costs while streamlining platform operations.

This chapter discussed SRE principles using deep AI insights and platform operations to speed up incident management, FinOps, MLOps, and problem management, thereby reducing manual interventions. Organizations should enforce a comprehensive operations model with proper skills, processes, practices, technology, toolchains, and overall governance. This chapter mainly focused on the operation and maintenance of cloud platforms, so we discussed different operational activities, processes, practices, and reference architectures to manage a cloud platform with efficiency. Overall, we went through the technical and cultural backgrounds to take good care of cloud environments.

Further reading

- *What is FinOps*: https://www.finops.org/introduction/what-is-finops/
- *FinOps: Evolving Cloud Financial Management*: https://www.ibm.com/cloud/blog/finops-evolving-cloud-financial-management
- *IBM Services DevOps Commander*: https://dc.edst.ibm.com/#/
- *DevOps and Cloud InfoQ Trends Report - July 2021*: https://www.infoq.com/articles/devops-and-cloud-trends-2021/
- The IBM reference architecture for incident management: https://www.ibm.com/cloud/architecture/architectures/incidentManagementDomain/reference-architecture/
- The IBM reference architecture for problem management: https://www.ibm.com/cloud/architecture/architectures/problemManagementDomain/referenceArchitecture/
- *Cloud service management architecture*: https://www.ibm.com/cloud/architecture/architectures/serviceManagementArchitecture/referenceArchitecture/

Appendix A – Application Modernization and Migration Checklist

Now that we have discussed application modernization and migration in depth, we will present a *six-step* journey for **application modernization** and **migration**.

The six steps consist of the following:

- Identifying the key roles
- Discovery and learning
- Determining the KPIs
- Prioritization and planning a roadmap
- Designing and building MVPs or Waves
- Operation at scale

Let's dive in and explore each in detail.

Identifying the key roles

Application modernization and cloud migration are very complex programs. They require concrete planning, so it is essential to identify the right roles. Here are the critical roles of a migration and modernization program:

- **Chief Technical Officer (CTO):**
  - Responsible for making the final decisions on different design and architecture aspects and defining the KPIs
- **Chief Financial Officer (CFO):**
  - Provides knowledge and help for the CTO to define the KPIs

- **Data Architect (DA):**

  - Understands the data insights, data communication pattern, data residency, data security, and compliance, and helps other architects to make the right decisions

  - Designs data operations

- **Application Architect (AA):**

  - Designs applications' architecture and decides the correct migration pattern for different applications

  - Designs **continuous integration**, **continuous deployment** (**CI/CD**), and other operation pipelines for applications

  - Designs an automation framework for data access, security, and a user experience for applications

- **Infrastructure Architect (IA):**

  - Designs the landing zone for applications in the cloud, including compute, storage, and the network

  - Takes input from the AA, the security architect, and the network architect for the platform, and designs end-to-end solutions for the infrastructure

- **Security Architect (SA):**

  - Designs a security framework for data, the application, and the network

  - Designs a component model and makes architecture decisions for security components

  - Designs the regulation and governance for the security of the modern platform

- **Network Architect (NA):**

  - Makes architecture decisions for the network to follow the functional and non-functional communication requirements

- **Automation Engineer (AE):**

  - Designs the automation framework for operations and management

Once the key roles are identified, the next step is to analyze the infrastructures' current state, workload, application, and data storage. In this discovery step, we need to gather as much information and data as possible to learn about the current platform that we intend to modernize.

Discovery and learning

The next step is to assess the cloud maturity model to understand the effort required to move to the next maturity level. Again, we need to run a holistic approach to identify the current state. The main goal of the discovery step is to understand the functional as well as non-functional requirements. We also need all essential *functional* and *non-functional* requirements for the target state. *Figure 11.1* shows the target platform for a cloud modernization project. Here, the Java applications are moved from on-premises to the IBM cloud. At the end of the modernization taking place, some applications are chosen for retirement as shown in *Figure 11.1*:

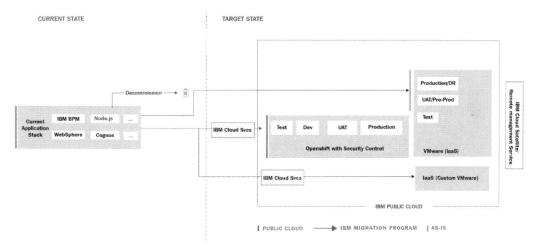

Figure 11.1 – A sample target state for application modernization and migration

Discovery and learning steps are often designed using the *co-create phase* in the **IBM Garage** practice. The goal here is to answer the following questions in the form of functional as well as non-functional requirements:

- What is the business' strategic imperative?
- What are the crucial business and operational challenges?
- What part of the business do we need to focus on for modernization?

Extensive automation and tool-based analysis are essential at this stage to discover all essential requirements. At the end of these steps, we will know the potential scope for modernization and migration with a high-level view of how the target state will look. The next step is to evaluate the scope for modernization and migration using KPIs.

Determining the KPIs

This step is the second part of the IBM Garage co-create phase where we evaluate each opportunity in the overall modernization and migration. We will also identify the most valuable options based on the business value, which is the crucial driver for the evaluation process. Here are some critical KPIs that need to be defined for the modernization program:

Area	KPIs
Cloud services	**Service-Level Agreement (SLA)** **Service-Level Objective (SLO)**
Application	The **Site Reliability Engineering (SRE)** golden signal includes latency, throughput, error rates, CPU utilization, migration factors for each application, and workload.
User experience	User experience is essential as, in the end, if the system is not user-friendly, it will drive away business value. There are different KPIs for measuring user experience for any system, such as a complexity degree based on the number of clicks for each functionality, page loading time, and interactivity.
Infrastructure	Network segmentation and security, and CPU utilization and usage
Automation	A degree of automation for each operational activity drives faster execution and efficient service management.
Business	The business value for each item in the overall scope is the key driver to prioritize different scopes and activities.

Table 11.1 – Important KPIs for a modernization roadmap

These KPIs help define the roadmap by aligning and prioritizing different items found in the discovery step based on the business value. In addition, we need to optimize performance during the operations of the new target state.

Prioritization and a planning roadmap

This step aims to establish the vision and get ready to execute modernization. First, we need to design a firm hypothesis of the business challenges identified in the discovery phase and their priorities, based on the business value and other KPIs. Each hypothesis is targeted to solve one business challenge with the help of collected data and an automated process around it to manage the business. Hypotheses are designed over multiple sessions to perform data-driven research, a persona-driven user experience, and a root cause analysis to understand the impact on the underlying business. Once all the hypotheses are generated, the next step is to design the roadmap to tackle them sequentially. For the roadmap design, we need to know the answer to the following questions for each hypothesis:

1. Which one is the most essential hypothesis for a business and its users?

2. Which one is the most feasible hypothesis to deliver quickly and grow sustainably over the long term?

3. Which one is the most available hypothesis based on business value?

Once we discover the answers to the aforementioned questions, they are sorted in descending order, based on the business value and feasibility score. Finally, the hypotheses are divided into multiple **Minimum Viable Products** (**MVPs**) and implemented in order.

Designing and building MVPs or Waves

This step starts with iterative experimental-based approaches over multiple waves, and each wave will enhance the MVP developed in the first wave. The first challenge is to identify the problem, with the highest business value as the most feasible MVP. The goal is to take the minimum chunk of applications and workload for modernization and migration to evaluate the hypothesis defined in the roadmap. The MVP is not built to be the best architecture or design but to make the right impact on user experience and business. Each MVP will require the execution of the following set of actions:

- Design a *high-level* and *low-level* architecture for the MVP around data, storage, scalability, backup, and other functional and non-functional requirements.

- Choose the cloud delivery model – either private, public, single, or multi-cloud.

- Design an infrastructure-as-a-code based blueprint for the landing zone.

- Build an automated process to deploy the landing zone.

- Define a set of metrics to measure success in terms of KPIs.

- Establish a governance team for organization and progress tracking.

- Apply the selected migration and modernization pattern for the applications.

- Build an automated process to monitor and govern the MVP to learn whether it is working in the way we expect it to and follows the required regulations.

- Build a pipeline to migrate data and enable secure communication.

- Identify a user demography to validate the MVP to determine success or failure.

- Measure user value delivered by the MVP using measurable metrics, insight, and user feedback.

- Validate the corresponding hypothesis quickly.

Once the MVP is completed, the selected applications for the MVP will be modernized and migrated to the *target state* and be ready for a *steady state*. The first MVP is completed and validated at the end of this stage. The next MVP in the pipeline will begin with *designing the architecture*.

Speed modernization with tools and an industry accelerator

Agility and **standard** are the most important KPIs for success in the case of **speed modernization**. Therefore, it is essential to adopt best practices and use efficient tools, automation, and an industry-specific accelerator. IBM and Red Hat are organizations that focus on offering a suitable technology suite powered by AI and hybrid multi-cloud technologies. IBM also has a broad set of accelerators for application modernization with AI, which helps to reduce modernization efforts and costs dramatically. Here is a list of industry-specific accelerators for application modernization that IBM provides at the time of writing:

- **Modernization Workflow Orchestrator** (**MWO**): This accelerator helps design the best transformation path or roadmap for any application using automation and tool-assisted orchestration, and it reacts to changing business values.

- **Application Containerization Advisor** (**ACA**): This recommends the right and most efficient path for any application to be transformed into a containerized cloud-ready application. Therefore, this accelerator helps to reduce the time and effort of containerization.

- **Candidate Microservices Advisor** (**CMA**): This accelerator identifies potential microservices from legacy applications. Traditionally, identifying a potential monolithic application for microservice transformation is a very lengthy process due to the complex dependencies of the application. However, CMA can automatically recommend a set of microservices with just some simple scanning and reduce the lifespan of a modernization project from more than a year to less than a month.

- **IBM Managed Red Hat OpenShift** (**IMRO**): This provides a ready-to-use environment by just clicking a simple button with very few parameters, enabling applications' modernization and running them at production scale.

Operation at scale

Once the MVP is deployed on a production or stage environment, the next goal is to satisfy the performance, resilience, security, and scalability of the applications migrated as part of the MVP or wave. The preparation for operations starts in the previous *Designing and building MVPs or Waves* section by setting up the following items:

- A blueprint
- A CI/CD pipeline
- A test framework
- Governance and a regulatory framework
- An automated process for operations

A continuous evaluation and learning process is established to understand the MVP and ensure that each MVP is better than the last one. **Operation at scale** leverages different practices such as **SRE**, **Development and Security Operations (DevSecOps)**, **policy as code**, **identity and access control**, and **infrastructure as code**. The success depends on the level of automation, and the extensive monitoring of the operation depends on the level of automation and the extensive monitoring of the application log, the application health check API, the golden signal, the activity on resources of the platform, security events, and vulnerabilities. The continuous operation should also maintain a framework to revisit the business value regularly to refine the existing MVPs in the roadmap or add new and advanced hypotheses. This regular validation should seek answers to the following questions:

1. What are the current business objectives?

2. What skills are missing from the current operation team?

3. What are the future skills required for the future MVP?

4. Which functional and non-functional requirements need to be added, removed, or modified?

5. How can the working environment be more exciting for the people who work with IBM Garage?

6. How are the current practices, tools, and cultures working for the operation? Do we need any modifications to the current practices, tools, and culture?

Modernization in the cloud will continue with a consistent and feedback-based operation, using an iterative approach.

Summary

Application modernization demands a faster time to market, but it is expensive and very complex. However, proper planning, tool-assisted automation, and best practices can expedite the development of a successful digital transformation. This appendix provided an overview of the different steps taken by industries for a fast and efficient application modernization project.

Further reading

- *Create a minimum viable product*: https://www.ibm.com/garage/method/practices/think/practice_minimum_viable_product/

- *Accelerate innovation with AI for app modernization*: https://www.ibm.com/blogs/journey-to-ai/2020/05/accelerate-innovation-with-ai-for-app-modernization/

- *Implement Site Reliability Engineering*: https://www.ibm.com/garage/method/practices/manage/site-reliability-engineering/

- *DevSecOps Reference Implementation for Audit-Ready Compliance Across Development Teams*: `https://www.ibm.com/cloud/blog/announcements/devsecops-reference-implementation-for-audit-ready-compliance-across-development-teams`

- *DevSecOps*: `https://www.ibm.com/cloud/learn/devsecops`

- *Infrastructure as Code*: `https://www.ibm.com/cloud/learn/infrastructure-as-code`

Index

I

Packt.com

Subscribe to our online digital library for full access to over 7,000 books and videos, as well as industry leading tools to help you plan your personal development and advance your career. For more information, please visit our website.

Why subscribe?

- Spend less time learning and more time coding with practical eBooks and Videos from over 4,000 industry professionals

- Improve your learning with Skill Plans built especially for you

- Get a free eBook or video every month

- Fully searchable for easy access to vital information

- Copy and paste, print, and bookmark content

Did you know that Packt offers eBook versions of every book published, with PDF and ePub files available? You can upgrade to the eBook version at packt.com and as a print book customer, you are entitled to a discount on the eBook copy. Get in touch with us at customercare@packtpub.com for more details.

At www.packt.com, you can also read a collection of free technical articles, sign up for a range of free newsletters, and receive exclusive discounts and offers on Packt books and eBooks.

Other Books You May Enjoy

If you enjoyed this book, you may be interested in these other books by Packt:

Go for DevOps

John Doak, David Justice

ISBN: 9781801818896

- Understand the basic structure of the Go language to begin your DevOps journey
- Interact with filesystems to read or stream data
- Communicate with remote services via REST and gRPC
- Explore writing tools that can be used in the DevOps environment
- Develop command-line operational software in Go
- Work with popular frameworks to deploy production software
- Create GitHub actions that streamline your CI/CD process
- Write a ChatOps application with Slack to simplify production visibility

Podman for DevOps

Alessandro Arrichiello, Gianni Salinetti

ISBN: 9781803248233

- Understand Podman's daemonless approach as a container engine

- Run, manage, and secure containers with Podman

- Discover the strategies, concepts, and command-line options for using Buildah to build containers from scratch

- Manage OCI images with Skopeo

- Troubleshoot runtime, build, and isolation issues

- Integrate Podman containers with existing networking and system services

Packt is searching for authors like you

If you're interested in becoming an author for Packt, please visit `authors.packtpub.com` and apply today. We have worked with thousands of developers and tech professionals, just like you, to help them share their insight with the global tech community. You can make a general application, apply for a specific hot topic that we are recruiting an author for, or submit your own idea.

Share Your Thoughts

Now you've finished *Hybrid Cloud Infrastructure and Operations Explained*, we'd love to hear your thoughts! Scan the QR code below to go straight to the Amazon review page for this book and share your feedback or leave a review on the site that you purchased it from.

`https://packt.link/r/1803248319`

Your review is important to us and the tech community and will help us make sure we're delivering excellent quality content.

Made in United States
Orlando, FL
06 April 2024

45535717R00189